KINGS & QUEENS

THE CONCISE GUIDE

KINGS &
QUEENS

THE CONCISE GUIDE

RICHARD
CAVENDISH
& PIP LEAHY

David and Charles

A DAVID & CHARLES BOOK
Copyright © David & Charles Limited 2007

David & Charles is an F+W Publications Inc. company
4700 East Galbraith Road
Cincinnati, OH 45236

First published in the UK in 2007

A catalogue record for this book is available from the British Library.

ISBN-13: 978-0-7153-2376-2 hardback
ISBN-10: 0-7153-2376-8 hardback

Printed in China by R. R. Donnelley
for David & Charles
Brunel House, Newton Abbot, Devon

Commissioning Editor: Neil Baber
Editor: Emily Pitcher
Project Editor: Ame Verso
Assistant Editor: Demelza Hookway
Senior Designer: Sarah Clark
Picture Researcher: Tehmina Boman
Maps: Ethan Danielson
Borders: Neil Bromley
Production: Beverley Richardson

Additional text by Tim and Anne Locke

Visit our website at www.davidandcharles.co.uk

David & Charles books are available from all good bookshops;
alternatively you can contact our Orderline on 0870 9908222
or write to us at FREEPOST EX2 110, D&C Direct, Newton
Abbot, TQ12 4ZZ (no stamp required UK only); US customers
call 800-289-0963 and Canadian customers call 800-840-5220.

Contents

This map shows some key locations in the story of the kings and queens of England, Scotland, Wales and Ireland. The Republic of Ireland left the Commonwealth in 1948. Northern Ireland is a constitutional part of the United Kingdom.

The first English Prince of Wales was created in 1301, but resistance against English rule continued for centuries. The thrones of Scotland and England were united when James I (James VI of Scotland) became King of England and Ireland in 1603.

Winchester was the capital of England under the kings of Wessex in the 9th and 10th centuries. London only became the centre of English royal and political powers in the 12th and 13th centuries.

Introduction

Monarchy is the oldest institution in Britain. It is older than Parliament, the Church, the army and navy, the law courts, the police force and even the civil service. The monarchy is older than the nation itself and there is no telling or understanding British history without the story of Britain's kings and queens. In particular, the monarchy played a major role in five key developments: the emergence of a sense of national identity; the unification of England, Wales, Scotland and Ireland under a single royal regime; the creation of the Church of England; the development of parliamentary democracy; and the evolution of limited constitutional monarchy.

Parliamentary democracy is perhaps Britain's greatest gift to the world. The House of Commons was first given a permanent existence in the 13th century by Edward I, one of the most authoritarian and dominating of all English kings, not with the idea of encouraging freedom, but as a way of ruling his realm more efficiently by communicating directly with the people who ran the country on the ground, in the countryside and the towns. From this beginning, democracy developed slowly over the centuries and when Charles I challenged Parliament, he lost his crown and his head. In time the royal role became to advise and warn, rather than to rule. The process was encouraged by monarchs including George III and Queen Victoria who still contrived to exercise more political influence than was evident to most people at the time.

Monarchy and Order

There have been rulers and chieftains of tribal groups in Britain for 5,000 years or more, but they are legendary figures until Roman times. The first Briton whose name is known to history was a king, Cassivellaunus, who led the

Edward the Confessor ruled over a unified and prosperous England. His death led to disputes about the throne and invasion by William the Conqueror in 1066.

opposition to Julius Caesar in 54 BC. There were powerful queens, too. Queen Cartimandua of the Brigantes was ruling in the north when Boudicca of the Iceni sacked the new Roman settlement of London in AD 61. After the Roman withdrawal, Celtic rulers returned to power. The Old King Cole of the nursery rhyme was a real king, Coel Hen, who fought the Picts and the Irish after the Romans left.

It is likely that the tribal chieftains of early times had an important religious role to play that ultimately matured into the theory of the divine right of kings. Chieftains and later kings were, or were meant to be, personifications and guarantors of the right, traditional order of things. Good

Design for Charles II's Great Seal. After the Interregnum, Charles II was welcomed to the throne by his subjects, who had had enough of the Puritanical rule of Oliver Cromwell.

kings were the ones who kept peace and order in the realm, with however savage a hand, to the benefit of most of their subjects. Harsh rule was preferable to anarchy and medieval chroniclers would say approvingly of a satisfactory king that 'he kept a good peace'.

A fundamental factor in keeping the monarchy in being for so many centuries, despite the shortcomings of individual rulers, was the widespread feeling that the whole edifice of society would be threatened if its capstone was removed. It was a conviction that experience of the republican experiment after Charles I's execution endorsed, and Charles II was welcomed back in 1660 with general rejoicing.

Subjects needed a king to keep the proper, accepted order in place. At the same time, if subjects needed a king, the king needed his subjects. Kings have always had to govern by personality and persuasion as well as by force, and successful monarchs have been keenly aware of the importance of public relations. Henry VII, Henry VIII and Elizabeth I were all masters at it. Part of effective public relations was the whole panoply of ceremonial majesty with which royalty took care to surround itself, from the coronation in Westminster Abbey to the crown, sceptre and orb of state, glamorous royal portraits and the pomp of royal pageantry.

Lines of Descent

The words 'king' and 'queen' are Anglo-Saxon, from Old English *cyning* and *cwen* respectively, and today's monarchy stems from the arrival of the English on Britain's shores in the 5th century AD. Queen Elizabeth II's lineage can be traced back through her Hanoverian, Stuart and Tudor predecessors to the Plantagenet rulers, then back through the Norman kings and William the Conqueror to the Anglo-Saxon rulers, beyond them to King Alfred and the kings of Wessex, and ultimately to Cerdic, chief of the West Saxons, who invaded what is now England some 1,500 years ago. He would have claimed descent from the great Germanic deity Woden, king of the gods themselves.

The present Queen's ancestry can also be traced back through James VI of Scots and I of England to the Stewart kings of Scots in the Middle Ages and beyond them to Robert the Bruce, Shakespeare's Macbeth and the early rulers of the Scots and Picts. Another enticing line runs back through the Tudors to medieval Welsh princes and, according to tradition, to the legendary King Arthur.

Some of the component pieces of such a long chain of descent are inevitably weaker than others, but the weaker links have produced some of the most competent and successful monarchs. William I was illegitimate and his dubious claim to England, which he enforced by conquest, lay through his great-aunt, who was the mother of Edward the Confessor. Henry II claimed the throne in right of his mother. Henry VII's slender claim, again enforced by conquest, also lay through his mother. The same was true of James I and Edward VII, while William III was king in right of his wife. Three successive dynasties – the Tudors, the Stuarts and the Hanoverians – came to the throne through the female line.

A Gallery of Characters

With all their historical importance, the British monarchs were human beings and their story is full of fascinating characters, whose lives knew laughter and tears, triumph and defeat. Most British monarchs died in their royal beds, but two were executed (Mary, Queen of Scots and Charles I), several were murdered and others were killed in battle. In Scotland, of the five kings from James I to James V, four died by violence. James II of England fled the country and Edward VIII abdicated. The youngest person ever to succeed to a British throne was Mary, Queen of Scots, when she was less than a week old, while the longest-lived British royal on record was Queen Elizabeth the Queen Mother, who died in 2002 at 101.

King Alfred, Cnut, William the Conqueror, Edward I, Robert the Bruce, Edward III and Henry V were all formidable war leaders. Henry III, Charles I and George IV were notable patrons of the arts; George III collected one of the finest libraries ever assembled; George V put together one of the world's best stamp collections, and Elizabeth I, Charles II and Queen Victoria presided over brilliant periods in literature, the arts and science. Stories about them, true or legendary, have been treasured in the national memory for generations.

By one of history's ironies, England, the dominant power in the British Isles, has been ruled since 1066 by dynasties that originally hailed not from England, but successively from France, Wales, Scotland and Germany. By another, while the power of the Crown steadily declined in Britain itself, the British monarchs found themselves the titular sovereigns of a quarter of the population of the globe in the largest empire the world has ever seen. The Queen still plays a valued role in the British Empire's successor, the Commonwealth.

European monarchies tumbled like skittles in the 19th and 20th centuries. The British monarchy survived because it accepted democracy and largely adopted middle-class ethical standards, including approval of hard work. The royal role had changed and the monarch had become a symbol of the country and its people at home and abroad, presiding with dignity over historic ceremonials, helping charitable work and generally encouraging British morale. When the present Queen celebrated her 80th birthday in 2006 after 54 years on the throne, she was calculated to have made 256 official visits overseas, opened 15 bridges, launched 23 ships, presided over 91 state banquets, endorsed 620 charities and organizations, received 3 million items of correspondence, entertained 1.1 million guests at garden parties and posed for 139 official portraits. It was a job that needed doing, and whatever republicans might say, to most Britons it seemed unlikely that anyone but a royal would do it better.

Early Kingdoms
& Territories

The seeds of British kingship were sown long before the Romans or the Anglo-Saxons arrived on England's east coast. When the Romans invaded in the 1st century AD, they found the inhabitants of the British Isles to be predominantly Celtic tribespeople, who had migrated from Europe in the preceding few centuries. The Celts had carved out their own numerous kingdoms, and they lived in organized, pagan societies ruled by a tribal king (or sometimes a queen). Rome imposed its own brand of civilization on some territories and left others (the greater part of Scotland, the wild uplands of Wales and all of Ireland) untouched. It was in these more remote territories, untamed by Rome and then left to their own devices when the Romans left, that the Celtic Christian heritage was kept alive during the dark, troubled centuries that followed the Romans' departure – centuries of invasion and settlement, internecine warring and expansionism, culture clash and assimilation. Kingdoms were formed, extended, divided and dismantled, Anglo-Saxon paganism and Celtic Christianity gave way to the Roman Church, and the concept of nationhood began to emerge.

Celtic and Roman Britain

500 BC – AD 410

The English Channel and Irish Sea were formed by ice melt around 6,500 BC when the British Isles were cleft from the Eurasian landmass. The islands were already populated by nomadic hunter-gathers who, a couple of millennia later, evolved into farmers: they cleared and ploughed the land, grew crops and kept livestock. Settlements were established, and hilltop enclosures and ring-forts provided shelter and protection. In the third millennium BC, the astonishing monument Stonehenge was erected on Salisbury Plain in Wiltshire. Much later, the arrival of Celtic influence from the continent from about 500 or 600 BC heralded the Iron Age. With the Celts came horse-drawn chariots, the organization of tribal kingdoms headed by dynastic rulers and chieftains, and increased trading links with mainland Europe, which would eventually facilitate the Roman conquest.

The Celtic tribes were highly territorial and often expansionist, their warriors fearsome, but they were also sophisticated: mining and manufacture, artistry and trade flourished, particularly among the more advanced southern cultures, which were influenced by their dealings with the Gauls and the ever-expanding Roman Empire.

The Romans first attempted an invasion of Britain in 55 BC under Julius Caesar, who claimed that the British tribes were collaborating with the Gauls who were by then under Roman rule. However, the Britons' abilities to fight tactically, and the mayhem that their war chariots caused in battle, were seriously underestimated by the Romans, and, when the weather prevented reinforcements arriving, the invaders were forced to withdraw. Caesar's second campaign, the following year, was more successful, although it was by no means an unqualified triumph for, once again, the Britons proved a force to be reckoned with. The Romans withdrew once more and went to deal with the troublesome Gauls across the Channel.

Nine decades later in AD 43, under the aegis of the Emperor Claudius, Rome launched another assault on the Kentish coast. Trade between Britain and the Roman Empire had vastly increased during the years since Caesar's expeditions, and so the invading Roman army met with assorted levels of resistance: while some tribal leaders fiercely resisted the Roman invaders, others took a more pragmatic view and quickly became client-kings, acquiring both wealth and status as a result. One such king was Prasutagus, chieftain of the eastern Iceni tribe. He died in AD 60 leaving his two daughters and the Emperor Nero as his heirs. Shortly after his death, the Romans moved into the territory with significant brutality and force, inciting a deep hatred among the Iceni and leading not only to the worst rebellion that the Romans faced during

Stonehenge is the most sophisticated prehistoric stone circle in the world. It was built 4,000 years ago by a society whose structure we can now only guess at.

their occupation, but also to the emergence of one of Britain's most enigmatic historical figures, the warrior queen Boudicca.

Boudicca was Prasutagus's widow. Enraged and deeply humiliated by the Romans she joined forces with a disaffected neighbouring tribe, the Trinovantes, and led a coalition force which marched south, savagely destroying almost everything in its path. When the terrifying army reached the Roman town of Camulodunum (Colchester), it was razed to the ground, its citizens and the Roman soldiers sent to defend it annihilated. Worse was to come. Boudicca's force, its numbers swelled by warriors joining her along the way, went on to destroy Londinium with merciless ferocity before turning its attention to Verulamium (St Albans). The warriors' rampage was halted in a final battle when triumph turned to disaster and the Roman forces, although heavily outnumbered, tactically outwitted the woad-painted Britons. A bloody massacre was the result. Boudicca is said to have survived the battle and later

poisoned herself. Terrible revenge was exacted upon the remaining Iceni and any other tribe that had even tacitly supported the rebellion.

After this, the Romans continued to consolidate their position in the province, putting down resistance wherever it arose, but now there was a shift in attitude. Britons and Romans worked alongside one another and, by the end of the 1st century AD, the conquest was mostly complete. By the 4th century, Britannia had become entirely Romanized, with highly organized systems of administration; Christianity had spread to the land, and bishops were appointed by Rome. When Rome finally and totally withdrew its support from the territory in the early 5th century AD, it left behind a largely assimilated culture: a standard language (Latin), the Christian religion, magnificent buildings and palaces, urbanized settlements, a vast network of well-engineered roads, sanitary and drainage systems, government institutions, and an educated Romano-Briton elite.

Maiden Castle near Dorchester is the largest Iron Age hillfort in Britain. Maiden is derived from the Celtic mai dun, meaning 'great hill'. The immense proportions of the fort – about the area of 50 football pitches – would have given a livelihood and protection to around 200 families from the region's Durotriges tribe.

Saxon England

AD 430–800

Pax Britannica, the relative peace that Britain enjoyed under Roman rule, was looking unsteady even before the last legions departed in AD 407: major raids on northern and south-east Britain by barbarians had already begun in 367. Now, without support from Rome, Britain struggled to defend itself. From the north there were incursions by the Picts and Caledonians; from across the Irish Sea came the Gaelic Scotti tribe; and from the east, on the other side of the North Sea, the Germanic races of the Angles, Saxons and Jutes were threatening.

A powerful figure surfaced in the first decades after the Roman departure, the overlord or high king Vortigern ('Wurtgern, king of the Britons' in the *Anglo-Saxon Chronicle*). His exact provenance is shrouded in conjecture, and the title may refer to more than one person, but it is known that Vortigern invited Saxon mercenaries (*foederati*) to Britain, promising them land in return for help in repelling the Picts and Caledonians. The legendary figures of the Jutish mercenaries Hengest and Horsa were major protagonists in establishing England's first Anglo-Saxon kingdom. They successfully fought the Picts but then rebelled against Vortigern, and Hengest established himself as King of Ceint (Kent). Vortigern organized a peace conference, but the treacherous Saxons used it to cause further mayhem, which resulted in the killing of hundreds of the British representatives.

Many stories surround the Dark Ages folk hero King Arthur but it is not certain that he existed. As proof of his royal blood Arthur is said to have drawn the sword Excaliber from a stone, where all others had failed.

Roman influence endured at least for a while, and for a long time in some places, but the economic repercussions of the split with Rome saw many of the country's systems failing (for example, it appears that by around AD 430 coinage was no longer used). By the middle of the 5th century, Britain was dealing with famine, weak government, civil war, and tension between pro-Celtic Christians (whose religious faith had assimilated aspects of Celtic culture and spiritualism and had been influenced by the ideas expounded by the monk Pelagius, condemned by Rome as a heretic), and pro-Roman Christian traditionalists.

Angles, Saxons and Jutes (collectively the 'English') began to invade and settle on Britain's eastern seaboard, eventually pushing west and northwards while the indigenous pro-Celtic people were ultimately driven into Cornwall, Wales and parts of the north. British aristocrats and urbanites migrated in great numbers to Armorica (now Brittany) in north-western Gaul.

Some time between 460 and 470, Vortigern's arch-rival, the pro-Roman Ambrosius Aurelianus, became high king and led the resistance against the Saxons. Years of warring ensued during which time many of the ancient hillforts that had been abandoned or weakened during the Romanization of Britain – such as Cadbury Hill in Somerset – were re-fortified. It is likely that it was during this period that the Wansdyke, one of Britain's largest linear earthworks, was begun.

Britain was in the midst of the Dark Ages, a murky period when written records were scarce or non-existent. But it was also the time that spawned one of Britain's greatest folk heroes, King Arthur. Claimed by most of the ancient Celtic kingdoms as their own, Arthur was thought to have been the son of the Cornish ruler Uther Pendragon and was supposedly the founder of the iconic kingdom of Camelot. His story – one of battles and miracles, chivalrous knights and round tables, the wizard Merlin, magical swords, beautiful queens and the Holy Grail – has been told, embellished, and taken out of historical context over many centuries. Geoffrey of Monmouth in his 12th-century *Historia Regum Britanniae* ('History of the Kings of Britain') greatly promoted Arthurian legend; a millennia and a half later Arthur's spectre still provokes debate. Certainly the Celtic and Romano-British kings took up the fight to keep the flame of Roman civilization alive against the pagan invaders, but there is no hard evidence that the Arthur of legend, if he existed at all, was a king.

Arthur's story though includes a tale of victory in 12 battles fought between *c.* 485 and 496, which endowed him with the reputation of invincible warlord. If Arthur was a figment of a fertile imagination then Aurelianus seems a likely candidate for the inspiration behind it. Apparently possessing many 'Arthurian' qualities, Aurelianus purportedly led the Britons to a victory at the Battle of Bladon Hill, where the Saxons were severely defeated and quietened for a generation. The exact date and location of the battle are unknown, but it was fought around the end of the 5th century (or early in the 6th), possibly in the vicinity

Celtic Christianity

A bond among the pagan Celtic tribes was their Druid priests who had authority over tribal chiefs and roamed freely throughout the land. These priests were at the pinnacle of Celtic society: when the Romans invaded they fled to Anglesey in Wales where they were eventually routed. Christianity spread throughout the British Isles, but where Celtic influence remained strong – in Wales, Scotland and Ireland – there was a fusion of traditions and beliefs, which was often at odds with the Roman Church. These territories kept scholarship and learning alive when Europe descended into the Dark Ages.

Yeavering, or Ad Gefrin as it was also known, was a stronghold of the Dark Age Northumbrian kings, who visited the palace several times each year. This painting shows Ad Gefrin as it may have looked during the reign of King Edwin in the 7th century. In the centre is the Great Hall, which would have been used for feasts and ceremonies. The palace was destroyed after Edwin was killed by the Mercian ruler Penda in 633.

of the re-fortified stronghold of Little Solsbury Hill near Bath. However, given that by this time Aurelianus was probably elderly – or even dead – perhaps it was Arthur who routed the Saxons at Bladon Hill (as the Welsh chronicler Nennius suggests in his 9th-century work, *History of the Britons*).

Anglo-Saxon Kingdoms

As the Saxons migrated in ever-greater numbers to aid in the conquest of Britain, they established territories led by tribal warlords who styled themselves as kings. These kings appointed or tacitly acknowledged one of their number as overking, known as the Bretwalda; the first of these was Aelle, King of the South Saxons (Sussex) from AD 477. Aelle has been credited with successfully, and uniquely, besieging and taking the Roman shore fort of Anderida (Pevensey); it may also have been Aelle who led the Saxon forces in the Battle of Bladon Hill.

Around the same time as the battle at Bladon Hill, the Germanic king Cerdic and his son Cynric landed on the south coast and established what would, in time, become the greatest of the Anglo-Saxon kingdoms, West Saxon (Wessex). Cerdic's grandson Ceawlin, ruling in the second half of the 6th century, was the second Bretwalda. The third, descended from Hengest's lineage, was King Ethelbert I of Kent. The first of the Christian Anglo-Saxon kings, Ethelbert was converted to the faith by St Augustine and then issued a code of laws, which was possibly the first document written in English.

By the end of the 6th century the Germanic invaders held huge swathes of territory: the Saxons settled in the south and west, the Jutes on the Isle of Wight and nearby mainland, and the Angles in the east and north. The different tribes shared a common language and customs, and came to be regarded as one people, the Anglo-Saxons. The southern Celtic Britons had been driven into the west

Sutton Hoo

One of the greatest of all British archaeological finds was made
at Sutton Hoo in 1939. Within a group of mounds comprising an
Anglo-Saxon cemetery was a 7th-century ship burial, complete
with a warrior's helmet, a shield, stupendous gold artefacts and
remains of an 89ft (27m) ship. This was a royal burial, possibly of
King Raedwald of East Anglia (died *c.* 624). He had converted to
Christianity, probably for political reasons, and the objects placed
around him showed a blend of Christian and pagan symbolism. The
body was surrounded by treasures, including this gold belt buckle,
as well as food and musical instruments, needed for the afterlife.

country (where there was the large Celtic kingdom of Dumnonia) and into
what is now Wales. Over the following 25 years, Saxon Northumbria expanded
to cover most of northern England. Seven of the Saxon kingdoms formed a
confederacy known as the Heptarchy, of which the dominant kingdoms of East
Anglia, Mercia, Northumbria and Wessex jostled for supremacy.

Raedwald, King of the East Angles and associated with the burial ship
discovered at Sutton Hoo, was the fourth Bretwalda. He had helped King
Edwin of Deira conquer Northumbria, after which Edwin went on to take the
kingdom of Elmet and to establish the kingdom of Northumbria as a major

player in the Heptarchy. Edwin, the first of the northern Bretwaldas, had his royal residence at Yeavering, known as Ad Gefrin, which was mentioned by the Venerable Bede and excavated in the 20th century. Edwin's victories secured Northumbria's domination of the North and ensured the succession of two more Northumbrian Bretwaldas: St Oswald, a pious man who grew up at the monastery on Iona and is associated with having a miraculous incorruptible arm, and King Oswiu, who had both Northumbria and Mercia under his control. Oswiu called the Synod at Whitby (AD 664) and ruled that his kingdom should follow the Roman Church (rather than the Christian Celtic Church, which had been predominant in the north). This was followed by Northumbria's 'Golden Age', when the kingdom flowered as a cultural and intellectual powerhouse; it lasted until early in the 9th century, although political domination and control shifted south to the central kingdom of Mercia, culminating in the reign of King Offa from AD 757.

Christianity and King Offa

The unstoppable influence of Anglo-Saxon rule caused the dismantling of centuries of Romanization, and Britain's culture began to echo what it had been in pre-Roman times. The Germanic tribes were rural, illiterate pagans, and their buildings were made of wood not stone; unless they were lords or kings, their tools of battle were iron-tipped wooden spears and leather-covered shields. Towns disappeared. While systems of administration, justice and commerce existed to an extent they weren't organized into the cohesive entities that they had been under the Romans. Their kings were peripatetic tribal warlords whose power was reliant on their prowess in battle and on their plundering riches for their followers, the thanes (or thegns) and ceorls, who took their title according to the number of hides of land they owned.

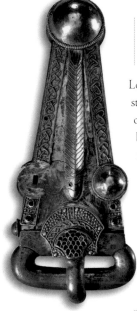

A mid-7th-century Anglo-Saxon silver and gold buckle decorated with a fish (an early Christian symbol) – grave-goods discovered in 1861 in Crundale Down, Kent. The grave also contained a highly decorated iron sword.

Lowest in the Saxon pecking order were slaves. A steady supply of slaves was assured as a consequence of the constant warring that took place not just between Saxons and native Britons but between rival Saxon tribes; so while many slaves were the conquered Britons, there were Saxon slaves, too.

At first the Anglo-Saxon communities were relatively egalitarian, but during the middle of the 6th century the appearance of burial mounds containing lavish booty known as grave-goods suggest that society was becoming more complex and divisive. Ancient pagan Anglo-Saxon beliefs resonate down the centuries through the English language (Woden, the chief Saxon deity, is represented by Wednesday for example), but when the Roman Benedictine monk St Augustine was sent by Pope Gregory the Great to convert England's pagan elite at the end of the 6th century, he launched a sea-change in Anglo-Saxon society, turning it towards Rome. Augustine's mission was politically well-timed, for it had not gone unnoticed by the English rulers that the Germanic Frankish tribe that had similarly conquered Gaul, now Francia, was reaping not inconsiderable benefits by embracing sub-Roman culture and Christianity. Augustine pinpointed a likely target for conversion in Kent's Ethelbert I, who was married to Bertha, a Christian Frankish princess. Ethelbert allowed Augustine to preach to the Kentish people and converted to the Roman religion himself. Augustine founded a monastery in Kent at Canterbury, which became the seat of Roman Christianity in Britain. A contemporary of Augustine took the religion to Northumbria whose king, Edwin, was married to Ethelbert's daughter Ethelberga. By the end of the 7th century, around the time when the monks at the centre of the Celtic Christianity movement on Lindisfarne completed their famous illuminated gospels, all the kingdoms of the Heptarchy had converted. Celtic Christianity held sway in the northern kingdoms while the south was aligned to the Roman Church (which

Written Records

In the Dark Ages, monasteries were the only centres of education and learning, so it is in the writings of monks that we find the few contemporary accounts of the period. Gildas (*c.* 493–570) was an opinionated Celtic monk whose *De Excidio Britanniae* ('Concerning the Ruin of Britain') gives the British version of events from the Roman invasion to the 6th century. Later, the Venerable Bede (*c.* 673–735), a Northumbrian monk and the greatest of all the Anglo-Saxon scholars, completed his comprehensive, *Historia Ecclesiastica Gentis Anglorum* (Ecclesiastical History of the English People) at the monastery in Jarrow. One of the most important medieval documents, the *Anglo-Saxon Chronicle*, first compiled by various monks under Alfred the Great in the 9th century, describes English history from the Roman invasion to the 11th century. English literature's oldest surviving epic poem, *Beowulf*, also provides a historical resource for this period: this tale of a heroic adventurous Scandanavian war leader and king in 6th-century England was written in Old English around the 10th century AD. Descriptions of Beowulf's burial echo the finds at Sutton Hoo.

had been careful to incorporate pagan rituals into their calendar to make their thinking more acceptable to the Saxon people). It was King Oswiu's Synod of Whitby in AD 664 that united the two factions in England.

Pope Adrian I referred to King Offa, the ninth Bretwalda, as 'King of the English'. Offa's kingdom, Mercia, dominated the English heartland, its territory intersected by two great Roman roads, Watling Street and the Fosse Way. Then Offa took control of Kent, Sussex and East Anglia. His power and influence were recognized even by the Frankish Emperor Charlemagne. Offa's reign was often brutal, but it was also remarkable. He was the first Saxon ruler to re-establish coinage, using it to trade with the Frankish empire. Offa's silver penny, embellished with his name and image, was the prototype for modern coins. He established an effective administration and a burgeoning economy, and he felt himself equal to negotiating with Charlemagne and the Roman Church. What Oswiu had engendered for Northumbria's culture, Offa achieved for the country's politics and economics. The construction of Offa's Dyke, the great linear earthwork that runs north from Chepstow to Prestatyn and marked the boundary between Wales and England, was the greatest testament to the organization that was being wrought in 8th-century Anglo-Saxon society.

To ensure the succession, King Offa had his son Egfrith anointed in AD 787, but Egfrith survived his father by only six months. Both kings died in AD 796. Shortly afterwards, Mercian supremacy withered and passed to Wessex, but another threat was on the horizon. Three years before Offa's death the Vikings had launched a surprise attack on the holy island of Lindisfarne and invaded Britain for the first time.

A carpet – or decorative – page from the Lindisfarne Gospels, c. 698–c. 700. The Gospels are thought to have been written and illuminated by a monk named Eadfrith, who was Bishop of Lindisfarne from 698 to 721.

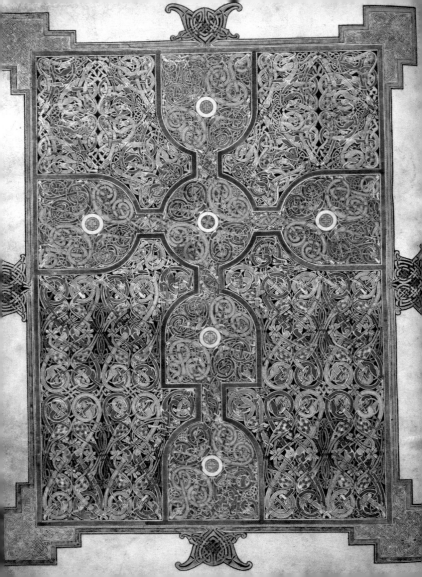

Wales

AD 440–1301

Roman occupation never truly conquered Wales: the territory was subdued and under military rule, but the Romans allowed the native tribes a degree of self-government. Once Wales was entirely free from Roman domination, the strong tribal tendencies of its Celtic people re-established themselves. Infighting, immigration, and the threat of Saxon and then Norman occupation meant that territorial fortunes shifted continuously in the centuries that followed the Roman withdrawal. Wales's fate would finally be sealed with the investiture of an English Prince of Wales in 1301.

A s Scottish tribes invaded northern Britain and Saxons came from the east, the Gaelic tribes from Ireland and the north of England moved to settle in Wales. The Saxon invasion stopped at the Welsh border (probably because of the country's inhospitable terrain), and many native Britons were hounded into Wales. By the mid-10th century the numerous tribal territories that formed in Wales during the early years of Anglo-Saxon rule in England had coalesced into four main kingdoms: Gwynedd and Powys in the north, and Deheubarth and Gwent in the south. Gwynedd, the land of the ancient Celtic tribes of the Deceangli and Ordovices, was to become the most powerful of the Dark Age kingdoms in Wales. At its heart was the 'Dark Isle' (Anglesey), seat of the Druid priests during the early years of Roman occupation.

The reign of Hywel Dda (the Good) was a golden age for Wales. Hywel was an admirer of English organization so he issued his own code of laws. The stability of Hywel's rule did not last after his death in 950.

St David

While Christianity in England had diminished under the influence of the pagan Saxon invaders, the Christian Church in Wales was free to remain vibrant and unremittingly Celtic. The kingdom's patron, St David (c. 520–601), was born in Pembrokeshire and was a descendant of Cunedda (legend has it that he was also was the uncle of King Arthur). He was active as a bishop long before St Augustine's arrival in England and the emergence of Roman Christianity in the Anglo-Saxon kingdoms. He is said to have founded 12 monasteries in Wales, including the one at Menevia of which he was bishop when he died; after his death it was called St David's. Once England was converted, the differences between the Roman and Celtic forms of Christianity became more obvious and, despite considerable pressure on the Welsh clergy to conform to the Roman Church, it was not until a century after the Synod of Whitby (AD 664) that they finally adopted the Roman ecclesiastical calendar.

It was possibly Vortigern (known as Gwrtheyrn by the Welsh), who, in the middle of the 5th century, called on Cunedda of the Gododdin tribe to settle in north-west Wales in order to repel the Irish. Gododdin is the Welsh word for the Votadini, a tribe that inhabited the north (at one point their capital was Edinburgh's Castle Rock). Cunedda (possibly the grandson of a high-ranking Roman official) and his nine sons successfully eliminated the Irish Scotti tribes in Wales and established the Royal House of Gwynedd, a dynasty that would, more or less, hold supremacy in Wales until the 13th century when Wales finally came under English rule.

The first of Gwynedd's great leaders emerged in the 9th century when Viking raids were wreaking havoc all around the British coast. The Norsemen were targeting wealthy ecclesiastical houses, so they had an interest in Anglesey where there were two important monasteries; they also threatened Gwynedd's royal court at Aberffraw. Rhodri Mawr (ruled 844–78) won his accolade of 'Great' by successfully repelling both the Anglo-Saxons, who were coming into the east of his kingdom, and the Vikings, who were launching attacks on its western coastline. In 856 he killed the Danish leader Gorm (Horm) and so gained a reputation as a mighty warrior, not only in Wales but also in England and France. Rhodri succeeded – mainly through inheritance rather than war – in becoming the leader of both northern and south-western territories of Wales, although this partial unification didn't last long beyond his death.

Rhodri's grandson, Hywel Dda (the Good), brought together the kingdoms of Dyfed and Seisyllwg to create the southern territory of Deheubarth in 920. By the time he died he was ruler of most of Wales, and his reign is remembered as a golden age. He codified the country's laws around 940 and was the only Welsh king to issue his own coinage. Recognizing the benefits of a close relationship with England, he acknowledged the King of Wessex as his feudal master; he admired English organization and was influenced by a pilgrimage he made to Rome. Despite his legacy of reforms, Hywel's death in 950 heralded another period of turmoil for Wales in which Deheubarth was split and Gwynedd and Powys were reclaimed as separate kingdoms. It wasn't until nearly a century later that a single ruler would be able to claim dominion over the greater part of Wales.

Brutal and bloodthirsty as it was, Gruffydd ap Llywelyn's reign, which began in the first half of the 11th century, concluded with his having a power that was recognized by the English king, Edward the Confessor, and control over all of Wales. Gruffydd, a descendant of Rhodri Mawr and distant cousin of Hywel Dda, was politically astute and a fearsome warrior. He defeated his enemies both at home and across the border in Saxon England, and he made

This illustration comes from the Topographia Hibernica *(The Topography of Ireland) by the 12th to 13th-century scholar Giraldus Cambrensis. The cleric was a prolific writer and also completed two important works about his Welsh homeland.*

considerable inroads into the territory east of Offa's Dyke. His nemesis was Harold Godwinson (later Harold II, the last of the Saxon kings), who tired of Gruffydd's expansionism and launched a surprise attack on his royal seat at Rhuddlan. Gruffydd escaped but Harold defeated the Welsh troops and demanded that they desert their leader. The last 'High King of Wales' was slain by one of his own men who sent his head to Harold as a sign of submission. Wales was a divided territory once again. Three years after Gruffydd ap Llywelyn's death, England's Saxon rulers were swept aside by the army of the Norman king, William I.

Norman Invasion

William the Conqueror's policy on Wales was one of isolation and containment. Dividing the lands on the Anglo-Welsh border between a few of his faithful nobles, he established the Marcher lordships, which gave these nobles carte blanche to control and expand the territories as they saw fit. Still reeling from the defeat and death of Gruffydd ap Llywelyn, a fragmented Wales allowed substantial Norman advances and, by 1085, the conquest of much of the territory was complete.

Central to the consolidation of the Norman advances were their castles: hundreds of their formidable motte and bailey fortresses were erected over the occupied territories, many of them built by the potent Marcher earls and the more minor barons and lords who formed a second wave of Marcher settlement in 1093. One of the most powerful of these fortresses was at Chepstow, begun by the Marcher earl William FitzOsbern less than a year after William I was crowned King of England. It provided a focus for many Norman forays into Wales, while the formidable castle at Pembroke served as a base for Norman expeditions into south-west Wales and Ireland.

Welsh resistance to the Normans strengthened and was dominated at first by Owain Gwynedd ap Gruffydd (ruled 1137–70), who was the son of Gruffydd ap Cynan (ruled 1081–1137, the longest reign of all the Welsh rulers). Together with his brother Cadwallon, Owain established control of northern Wales: the civil war in England during King Stephen's reign had given the Welsh princes an opportunity to reassert their authority and regain some of the territory under English occupation. When England's stability was restored under the fiery and mighty Henry II, Owain was forced to negotiate, although he asserted the Welsh cause and succeeded in becoming accepted by Henry as the premier ruler in Wales. On Owain's death his kingdom was split up among his sons – in keeping with the Celtic Law of Partible Succession (whereby territories were divided equally between all the children of the deceased) – and an insurrection ensued. This was not entirely surprising, for partible succession was the primary cause of the endless dismantling and rebuilding of Welsh territories, and it was this that prevented Wales consolidating into a unified, well-structured society – the achievement of which might otherwise have been within its grasp at several points in history.

Rhys ap Gruffydd (ruled 1155–97) came to rule over the southern Welsh kingdom of Deheubarth at roughly the same time as Henry II came to the throne of England. Rhys submitted to Henry II's show of force in Wales to the extent that he handed back much of the territory that had been reclaimed from

Edward III's eldest son was known as the 'Black Prince', and was Prince of Wales from 1343–76. His emblem, the three ostrich feathers, was adopted as part of the royal heraldry and became synonymous with the Wales title.

Gerald of Wales

Giraldus Cambrensis (Gerald of Wales) was born at Manorbier Castle in Pembrokeshire around the middle of the 12th century. He was of mixed Norman and Welsh blood and a nephew of the Bishop of St David's; his family also claimed a connection with Rhys ap Gruffydd. Giraldus, a prolific writer and scholar, completed two important and contemporary historical works on Wales, the *Itinerarium Cambriae* in 1191 and the *Descriptio Cambriae* in 1194. He wrote these after a tour around his native land with the Archbishop of Canterbury in 1188. Despite repeated appeals, Giraldus never achieved his ambition of taking up the bishopric of St David's (his nomination was rejected by Henry II on the grounds that he was Welsh); nor did he succeed with his plea to elevate St David's to the status of an archbishopric. Giraldus Cambrensis wrote of the Welsh, 'If they would be inseparable, they would be insuperable.'

the Normans in the previous 20 years and agreed to give up his kingly title. Since then he has always been known as the Lord Rhys. Nevertheless, in 1162 Rhys began a series of raids on Norman-held territory and, despite a period of imprisonment and further capitulation to Henry II, managed to regain much of his lost territory. He was able to rebuild and hold on to Deheubarth, and he emerged as one of the leaders of Welsh resistance. Eventually he was given the title of justiciar of his kingdom and became known as Prince of South Wales.

Reconciliation and Retribution

The meteoric rise of Llywelyn ap Iorwerth – also called Llywelyn Fawr and Llywelyn the Great (ruled 1195–1240) – presented Wales with probably its finest opportunity for independence. As son-in-law to King John, Llywelyn's relationship with the English Crown was cordial at first, and the king gave this Welsh prince more power over Wales than had been granted to any previous ruler. However, relations with King John soured: John, growing wary of Llywelyn's increasing dominance, invaded Wales, probably in 1211. Llywelyn stood his ground, and John retreated to deal with domestic strife among his barons in England.

By 1216, Llywelyn, using the tactics of statesmanship, brinkmanship and war, had expanded his dominion to the extent that he was able to declare himself Prince of all Wales. Llywelyn's power remained undiminished and reached such a height that he was able to order the death of one of the leading Marcher lords for committing adultery with his wife. It was during Llywelyn's reign that the Welsh began to match the complex designs of the strongholds of the Marcher lords and to construct their castles in stone.

Keen to prevent his legacy from breaking up, Llywelyn succeeded in introducing the rule of primogeniture so that he could pass his lands and title to his eldest legitimate son Dafydd, to whom in 1226 all the senior Welsh lords and princes swore fealty. Dafydd (ruled 1240–46) was also recognized as Llywelyn's sole heir by the Pope and by Henry III.

Dafydd's reign was one of mixed fortunes and skirmishes with his uncle Henry III. He died without an heir in 1246, so his nephew Llywelyn (II) ap Gruffydd – Llywelyn the Last – came to rule Wales until his death in 1282. Henry III, taking advantage of this change in leadership, launched a campaign that reclaimed vast areas of Welsh territory for the English Crown. The Treaty of Woodstock in 1247 reduced Llywelyn and his brother Owain to the status of vassal kings of Gwynedd, a much diminished kingdom that had lost all its lands east of the River Conwy. Determined to reverse his fortunes, Llywelyn diverted his energy into securing the support of his neighbours, and between 1255 and 1258 he managed to reclaim all the territory lost to Henry. The 1267 Treaty of Montgomery recognized Llywelyn ap Gruffydd as sovereign of Wales.

During Simon de Montfort's campaign against Henry III and his son Edward, Llywelyn ap Gruffydd aligned himself with the rebellious baron, eventually marrying his daughter Eleanor and gaining considerable territories in the Welsh Marches in the process. Henry's royal authority was reasserted after the Battle of Evesham in 1265 when de Montfort was killed. Llywelyn was beginning to lose support in his homeland: he was increasingly overreaching his power, he had no heir, and the Welsh Marchland was becoming anarchic. When Edward I came to the throne in 1272, Llywelyn's refusal to attend the coronation or to pay homage to the new king gave rise to a swift campaign by Edward. In 1277 Edward invaded Wales with the largest army seen in Britain since 1066: within a year Llywelyn was forced to submit to the English king, who began his first programme of castle building in northern Wales (the beginning of his 'Ring of Iron', which helped achieve the subjugation of the Welsh).

Llywelyn was still Prince of Wales but in name only. The Welsh leader then tried to improve his position diplomatically but his hothead brother, Daffyd ap Gruffydd (1233–83), started the chain of events that would lead to the undoing of Wales. He led an uprising in the Welsh Marches, which Llywelyn felt obliged to support. The continuous trouble-making proved too much for Edward and sparked his relentless campaign for the annexation of Wales. For the first time, Edward's army included paid troops with superior armour and weaponry. Llywelyn was killed in December 1282, possibly at the hands of a traitor. Dafydd assumed the mantle of Prince of Wales and continued fighting the English forces for four months. He surrendered at Castell-y-Bere and was executed as a traitor in October 1283.

In 1284 The Statute of Rhuddlan (Statute of Wales) declared Edward I the conqueror of Wales. The prospect of Welsh independence withered and died: Wales was now an English colony, subject to English law and a county system that replaced the Welsh kingdoms. Local princes were dispossessed and a governor-general was appointed. Edward embarked on his second programme of castle building and strengthened his 'Ring of Iron' with his monumental castles and bastide towns at Caernarfon, (the seat of English monarchy in Wales), Conwy and Harlech; later he built the extraordinary and perfectly concentric Beaumaris. Edward's son, the first of the English princes of Wales, was born at Caernarfon Castle in 1284 and invested at Lincoln in 1301.

Two Gwenllians

Llywelyn ap Gruffydd and his wife, Eleanor de Montfort, had one child – a daughter, Gwenllian, Princess of Wales. When Edward took the Wales title for the English Crown, Gwenllian, aged just one at the time of her father's death (her mother had died in child-birth), was taken to a convent at Sempringham in Lincolnshire where she lived for the rest of her life, dying at the age of 54 in 1337. Maes Gwenllian (Gwenllian's Field) north of Kidwelly is named for an earlier 12th-century heroine, the wife of Gruffydd ap Rhys, Prince of Deheubarth. While Gwenllian's husband was in north Wales, garnering support for resistance against the Normans, the Norman Lord of Kidwelly launched an attack against Deheubarth. Gwenllian led an army against the aggressors and a ferocious battle ensued. Gwenllian was killed but she is remembered for her bravery. Her son, the Lord Rhys, was to succeed in banishing the Normans from the kingdom.

Scotland

TO 1034

The Romans never truly succeeded in subjugating the tribal kingdoms of Scotland. But by the 10th century, pagan religions had been largely replaced by Christianity, and settlers and invaders from other parts of Britain, Eire and Scandanavia had helped to bring about the growth of relatively large kingdoms that would gradually subsume the smaller tribal territories of the past. By the 11th century, most of these kingdoms had combined to rule an area that loosely mirrors that of Scotland today.

L ike other tribal cultures of the British Isles, the early tribes of Scotland evolved from prehistoric rural farming settlements such as that of Skara Brae in the Orkney Islands. This ancient settlement, only uncovered at the end of the 19th century, paints a vivid picture of the communities that existed before 2,500 BC. While this is the best-preserved example of a Neolithic village in northern Europe, there is other evidence throughout Scotland of fortified dwellings (crannogs) constructed in marshes, stone towers (brochs), and hillforts, all built to provide shelter and protection for these early peoples.

It was the Roman chronicler Eumenius who first named the Picts in 297 when he described the 'painted' (or tattooed) people of the northern British Isles as Picti. At this time, the Picts were the largest tribal group in the north of the British Isles. Irish legend tells us that King Cruithne was the founder of the

Picts. His seven sons gave their names to the seven provinces of Pictland, and it was from Cat, the ruler of the kingdom known as Caithness, that the line of the Pictish kings descended. The Picts were one of the only races to select kings by matrilinear succession (that is, on the basis of their kinship to their mother); Pictish princesses were therefore greatly revered.

The Romans made occasional attempts to push into the inhospitable territories and subdue the barbarians over their border: Agricola and his army inflicted a crushing defeat on the northern Caledonii tribe at the battle of Mons Graupius in the summer of AD 84, but then Roman attention was diverted elsewhere and the impetus to occupy the difficult territory north of Britannia was lost. In AD 122, the Emperor Hadrian built his immense defensive wall to contain the barbarians in the north and to keep them from aligning with the tribes that lived in Roman territory. Around 20 years after the construction of Hadrian's Wall the Romans drove north again in order to subdue and conquer the fertile lands of lowland Scotland. A new frontier was established with the Antonine

The Orkney Islands' Ring of Brodgar megaliths mark the high point of prehistoric tribes in the northernmost territories of the British Isles. Built around 4,000 years ago, the circular monument was used for purposes that are not properly understood.

Wall, which stretched between the Clyde and the Forth. This was abandoned shortly after the death, in AD 161, of Antoninus Pius, the Roman emperor who had ordered its construction; the Romans retreated south again.

Pictish tribes were frequently menacing the Roman occupation force and, by AD 367, when the entire Roman Empire was under threat from various quarters, they managed to overwhelm Hadrian's Wall. Taking advantage of Roman preoccupations and the consequently weakened defence on the northern border, the Picts formed an alliance with the Irish Gaels, who had settled in the west of Scotland and formed a colony known as Dalriada. The Dalriadans gave their territory the name Oirer Ghaideal (Ar-Gael or Argyll, meaning 'coastland of the Gael'). The Romans called them the Scotti (the Latin name for the Irish). Picts and Dalriadans began a series of attacks on northern Britannia and, within a few years, they were penetrating deep into Roman-occupied territory. By the start of the 5th century, the Romans had left Britannia to its own devices, and the northern tribes were free to raid the Romano-Britons.

It was to combat the menace of the Pictish raiders that the overlord Vortigern first invited the Germanic mercenaries, the *foederati*, to England, setting in motion the conquest of England by the Anglo-Saxons. As Anglo-Saxon dominance grew, the native Britons were driven north (as well as to the west and south-west); those that went north established a kingdom called Strathclyde. By the 6th century there were three main peoples inhabiting the north: the Dalriadans (Scotti), the Picts and the Britons. Like the Roman occupation force before them, the Anglo-Saxons never truly wielded their influence in these northern territories: they were roundly defeated by the Picts at the battle of Dunnichen (Nechtansmere) in 685, and the Saxon king Egfrith of Northumbria was killed – a victory that was to pave the way for the emergence of a Scottish kingdom.

Around the beginning of the 6th century, Fergus Mor came from Ireland and created a new dynasty of Irish rulers in Dalriada. The fortress of Dunnadd was established as the capital. It was supposedly Fergus Mor who brought the renowned Scottish symbol of sovereignty, the Stone of Destiny, over from Ireland to the island of Iona. All that remains of Dunnadd today is a rocky outcrop on the banks of the River Add, but from the 6th century to around 900 the fortress was one of the most important places in Scotland.

In *c.* AD 563, another member of the Irish royal family, Columba, travelled to Dalriada. He was a monk on a mission to convert the tribes of northern Pictland, then ruled by King Brude. Dalriada was currently under the rule of King Conall I (Brude had killed the previous Dalriadan ruler, Gauran). Conall welcomed Columba as an ally against the Picts and gave him the island of Iona to establish a monastery.

Aedan Mac Gabhran, ordained by Columba as king

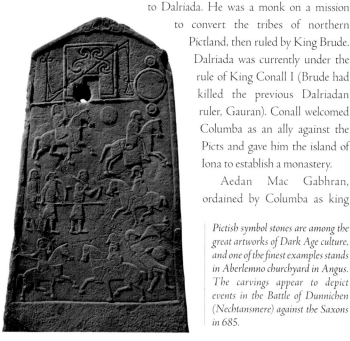

Pictish symbol stones are among the great artworks of Dark Age culture, and one of the finest examples stands in Aberlemno churchyard in Angus. The carvings appear to depict events in the Battle of Dunnichen (Nechtansmere) against the Saxons in 685.

In uigilia sanctum andree apli
leo prima. Sedm iohanne..
N illo tempz. Stabat ioha
nes et ex disapulis eius
duo. Et respiacens ihm a
bulantem dicit. Ecce ag
nus dei. Et audierunt eu

dno disapulii loquentem
et secuti sunt ihm. Et rel.
Omelia uenerabili bede pbri.
Stabat iohannes et
ex disapulis eius
duo. Stabat iohanes qui
ardebat in domino et dno

St Andrew (on the left of the painting) has been Scotland's patron saint since the Declaration of Arbroath in 1320; St Andrew's Cross, the Saltire, became Scotland's national emblem in 1385. St Andrew the Apostle came to be associated with Scotland when St Rule was instructed by an angel to remove some of the apostle's relics to the 'ends of the earth'. St Rule landed in Scotland and founded the settlement of St Andrew's.

in c. 574, was the first significant leader of the Dalriadan Scots: a powerful warlord, he established the kingdom as a major force in northern Britain. His son, Eochaid Buide (the Yellow-Haired), who ruled the Scots' territory from 608 to 629, gave shelter to the children of Ethelfrith, ruler of Northumbria, after their father was killed by Edwin of Deira. Under Eochaid's protection the children converted to Christianity, as did later Northumbrian overlords (Bretwaldas), Oswald and Oswiu. It was Oswald who, when he became ruler of Northumbria in 633, invited the Ionian monk St Aiden to establish a monastery at Lindisfarne. The first ruler to have dominion over both the Picts and the Dalriadans was Angus I, a Pictish king whose reign began in 729. Not unusually, a civil war was raging in Pictland and he emerged as victor. Conflict was also the theme in the Gaelic Dalriadan territories, and Angus embarked on a series of attacks against the Dalriadans and took the fortress of Dunnadd. Angus then reigned over both territories for 14 years, although dynastic infighting, Pictish rebellions and his ill-advised attempts to dominate Strathclyde meant that his hold on power was at best precarious: the kingdoms were by no means united when he died in 761.

It was not until the 9th century that the territories would once again come under one ruler. Constantine Mac Fergus, the son of a Dalriadan king, first made a challenge for the Pictish throne (it is probable that his mother was Pictish, for he was accepted as King of the Picts in 789); then, in 811, he successfully claimed the throne of Dalriada. It was during Constantine's reign that the Vikings first began to invade and sack the western coastline: the first recorded Viking attack on Scotland was an assault on Iona in 795. Consequently Constantine sought to strengthen his kingdom: he built a new fortress at the Pictish capital of Fortrenn in Perthshire and a church at Dunkeld, which provided refuge for the Ionian monks who were suffering a series of increasingly brutal incursions by the Vikings. Large-scale settlements of Norwegian Vikings on the Northern Isles (Shetland and Orkney) began around 800; the Western Isles and the northern Scottish mainland had Viking settlements around 50 years later. Constantine's reign ended in 820, and he was succeeded by his brother Angus Mac Fergus, Angus II, the first ruler to inherit the kingship of both the Picts and the Scots (Dalriadans). After Angus died various claimants to the thrones ruled the kingdoms separately. But a necessary unity against the growing Viking threat meant that Angus's son Eogan (Owen) reigned over both territories from 837 until a monumental battle at Forteviot with the Vikings in 839 virtually eliminated the Pictish and Dalriadan elite.

After Forteviot, Kenneth McAlpin (Kenneth I) claimed dominion over Dalriada and then looked to become ruler of Pictland (he was one of several nobles who had a claim to the throne of both the Picts and the Scots). Kenneth's early background is obscure, and there has always been the suspicion that his success in part owed to his having formed some kind of alliance with the Norsemen. However, he is said to have defeated his Pictish rivals by cunning rather than outright war. Giraldus Cambrensis in his *De Instructione Principus* tells of Kenneth's treachery when he invited the Pictish ruling nobles to a banquet at Scone and trapped and killed them once they were drunk. Kenneth was crowned at Scone in 843 and is remembered as the first King of the Scots (although the first to use the title was his grandson, Donald II) and the man who began to create a united Scotland: he joined the territories of Dalriada and Pictland to create one kingdom, Alba, and strengthened his alliances through his daughters' marriages. He moved the spiritual centre of Celtic Christianity in Scotland from Iona to Dunkeld, and he was the first king of the McAlpin dynasty, which would last until Macbeth. Kenneth's rule ended in 858, and he was succeeded by his brother Donald and then his son Constantine I, whose reign was dominated by battles and then deals with the Vikings.

In 866 the Viking Norse king Olaf launched a major campaign in Scotland with the aim of gaining access for his ships to be transported from coast to coast across the land. Olaf defeated Constantine I and established

Columba's Monastery

Columba's monastery became the seat of Celtic Christianity in Scotland and the revered burial place of the Scottish kings. Columba, who died in 597, can be credited with the Christian conversion of the northern Picts in the face of virulent opposition from the Druids, but he was also an asset to the Gaelic warrior kings: in return for their protection, Columba served as an advisor and ambassador to the kingdom, and his monastery provided education for their sons. Columba's story was written down by Adomnán, the ninth abbot of Iona, in his *Vita Colum Cille* ('Life of Columba'). Although he is described as Scotland's most spectacular saint, he was not Scotland's first Christian missionary (that was St Ninian, who built the church at Whithorn late in the 4th century). Nor did he become the country's patron saint; instead the Scots would eventually adopt the apostle St Andrew, whose X-shaped cross graces the Scottish flag.

himself as overlord. His victory was to facilitate the Danish conquest of York and East Anglia. In 870 Constantine, Olaf and the Viking leader Ivar the Boneless, attacked the stronghold of Dumbarton, and their victory meant that the territory of Strathclyde (which had been established by Britons fleeing the Saxons) would be absorbed into the expanding Alban kingdom. Eochaid map Rhun, the last native ruler of Strathclyde, also reigned over the kingdom of Alba jointly with his cousin Giric until Donald II deposed them both. It was Donald II, coming to power at the very end of the 9th century, who first took the title King of Scots (or Ri Alban) and established Strathclyde as a sub-kingdom under Scottish rule.

The long-lived Constantine II came to the Alban throne as the 9th century turned into the 10th. He ruled for 43 years and then abdicated to enter the church. Constantine fought two major battles against the Vikings in 914 and 918, both at Corbridge on the River Tyne. The Norse and the Scots then formed an alliance against the Saxons of Wessex who were moving north-wards. The Saxon king Athelstan was incensed when Constantine married his daughter to the Norse Olaf Gothfrithson, breaking an agreement between the Scottish and English monarchs. Constantine doggedly remained supportive to the Vikings and Athelstan led a campaign into Alba, which resulted in a coalition force of Scots, Britons and Vikings facing the Saxons at the 937 Battle of Brunanburh. The battle resulted in the carnage of the coalition force and is regarded as one of the greatest of all Saxon victories; a poem about it appears in the *Anglo-Saxon Chronicle*. On Constantine's abdication in 943, his cousin Malcolm succeeded to the throne of the Scots.

St Columba was a renowned scholar who came from Ireland to Dalriada in the 6th century, founded an influential monastery on the Hebridean island of Iona, and converted the northern Picts to Christianity.

To ensure his support against the Vikings, Edmund of Wessex gave Malcolm I the kingdom of Cumbria (although at the very end of Malcolm's reign the territory was once again taken by the English). Malcolm's rule was mainly punctuated by skirmishes with the nobility in Moray, who believed they had an equal claim to the throne of Scotland. Moray was one of the seven Pictish kingdoms and had remained almost autonomous throughout the unification of Alba; it didn't become a part of Scotland until after 1130, although the Moray dynasty came to the Scottish throne with Macbeth. Malcolm I was killed in a battle near Dunnottar in 954.

Malcolm's son Kenneth II ruled Scotland for just four years, from 971–5. He is listed in Roger of Wendover's *Flores Historiarum* as one of the sub-kings who swore fealty to the Anglo-Saxon king Edgar in 973; the Scottish ownership of Lothian (the land between the Tweed and Forth rivers) was confirmed by Edgar around this time. Kenneth also attempted to introduce patrilinear succession to the monarchy, a move that was only partially successful as it was not until a decade after his death that Kenneth's son Malcolm II, the last male McAlpin heir, became King of Scotland.

At the beginning of the 11th century the Vikings still held territory in the far north of Scotland. The earls of Moray remained steadfast and ultimately threatening in their separate kingdom, but Malcolm II (who had killed his cousins Kenneth III and Giric II in order to secure the Alban throne), was the first king to reign over a Scotland whose borders would be familiar today. His victory at the Battle of Carham in 1018 regained the territory of Lothian (which had been annexed by the Northumbrians in 1006), and ensured the consolidation of Alba. When he died in 1034 he had used all his powers to eliminate the enemies of his grandson Duncan (Malcolm only had daughters). His reign ended murderously, as it had begun.

Although it seems unlikely now, this rocky outcrop was once one of the most important places in Scotland. The fortress of Dunnadd was the capital of the kingdom of Dalriada founded by incoming Irish tribespeople known as Scotti.

Ireland

AD 400–1183

Although Agricola, the Roman Governor of Britannia, planned an invasion of neighbouring Hibernia in AD 82, the land across the Irish Sea was never subjected to even minimal Roman occupation. Roman influence, of a kind, was to come in the form of St Patrick, but, while Britain was undergoing the major changes wrought by the Roman Empire, Irish society continued in much the same way as it had for centuries. When the Romans abandoned Britannia and left it languishing in the Dark Ages, along with much of continental Europe, an undisturbed and stable Ireland was able to flourish.

The Celts, or Gaels, arrived in Ireland about a century before Christ's birth. They imprinted their identity indelibly on the country and, by the beginning of the 5th century, there were about 150 kingdoms of various sizes. Although separate, they were united by language, culture and what was possibly the most advanced code of law in the ancient world, The Brehon Laws. Passed down orally in ancient times (St Patrick was instrumental in codifying and Christianizing some of these statutes in the work *Senchus Mor*), the laws were the basis of the Irish judicial system until the 17th century when they were eradicated by the English.

In Celtic Ireland there were three grades of king: a king of a local tribal kingdom or 'tuath', an overlord of a group of tuaths, and the king of a province; the Ard Ri was the king of all the provinces and therefore High King of Ireland, a title conveying recognized status rather than overall dominion in practice. The Hill of Tara, north-west of Dublin, was the Ard Rí's traditional seat of power. In the late 5th century, Ireland's high king was Niall of the Nine Hostages (Niall Noígiallach) – founder of the Uí Néills, a dynasty that would provide most of the Irish high kings for centuries. (St Columba was one of his descendants, and several Scottish clans are connected with him.) A powerful warrior, Niall spent his time raiding the coastlines of Britannia and Gaul and, legend has it, was ultimately responsible for bringing St Patrick to Ireland as a slave.

Whatever the circumstances of his enslavement, St Patrick, the son of a Romano Briton, escaped and travelled to Europe, where he became a priest. He returned to Ireland in *c.* AD 432 to convert the Gaels to Christianity. His years of slavery paid off: he could speak Gaelic and understood Celtic rituals and, although he wasn't the first Christian missionary to visit Ireland, it was Patrick's message that had most impact. Beneath all the myth and legend that surrounds Ireland's patron saint, there is no doubt that Patrick oversaw the start of the fusion between Gaelic ritual and Christianity. What followed was a golden age for Irish scholarship, artistry and literature, and Irish civilization shone like a beacon in Dark Ages' Europe. For around three centuries, powerful monastic communities were established, the finest works of art and literature were produced, and the Irish monastic tradition extended across Europe.

It was 795 when the first Viking raiders appeared in Irish waters, and by the early 840s the Viking settlement of Dublin was established. While Viking control was firm in some places it was by no means countrywide: total dominion was made impossible by the political instability caused by feuding between the various Irish kings and the Vikings' shifting alliances with them. However, it was the legendary figure of Brian Boru who finally halted Viking ambitions to create a Norse kingdom in Ireland. When Boru was crowned High King of

Ireland in 1002 at the Rock of Cashel, his aim was to rule as Ard Ri over a united Ireland; by 1011 all the provincial rulers deferred to him. At Clontarf in April 1014 he secured a decisive victory over a combined force of Norse and Leinster armies, although he was killed in the battle. Clontarf was a turning point: the Viking spirit was broken, but the victorious Irish were left leaderless. Although many laid claim to the Irish high kingship, Boru's O'Brien descendants managed to retain the title for most of the 11th and 12th centuries until they were ousted by the kings of Connacht, who gave Ireland its last Ard Ri, Rory O'Connor. When Dermot Macmurrough, who had been deposed by O'Connor as King of Leinster, sought support from the English king, Anglo-Norman barons arrived in Ireland. The loss of Ireland's independence followed swiftly, the country's fate sealed by Rory's enforced submission as vassal to Henry II in 1175.

White Island, close to Lower Lough Erne in County Fermanagh, is the site of an early monastery and famous for its enigmatic statues. The 8th-century Celtic Christian figures are a perfect example of the fusion of Gaelic culture and Christianity.

Pre-Conquest England

From the end of the 8th century the British Isles came increasingly under the influence of the Vikings. By the 870s, Wessex was the only independent territory, and it was the Wessex king Alfred the Great who ensured a Saxon foothold remained in England. Alfred and his successors then set about expanding their kingdom and subduing the Vikings. As administration, law-making and organization became increasingly sophisticated, and monastic traditions were revived, a great national identity began to emerge. Commercial and cultural life burgeoned, marriage alliances were forged with mainland Europe. Anglo-Saxon England was an important kingdom, one whose wealth and resources made it irresistible to new invaders – such as the Danish King Cnut. Under Cnut and his successors England became part of a vast Danish maritime empire, but much of the Saxon aristocracy and system of government remained. When English sovereignty was re-established under Edward the Confessor it seemed that the Saxon hold on the country was secure. In January 1066 Edward's successor, Harold Godwinson, was crowned king. Little more than nine months later he was killed by William of Normandy's army. The last of the Saxon kings had succumbed to England's last conqueror.

The Vikings

By the end of the 8th century, Anglo-Saxon England was beginning to emerge as a cohesive, outward-looking society. Although it was far from stable, its growing economy and organizational skills were evident in the great monastic settlements that were being established and the scholarly works that were produced, as well as in the renewed use of coinage and flourishing trade with the Continent. But then came a new invasion, one that would make the carnage associated with the early Anglo-Saxon occupation pale in comparison. The pagan and piratical Vikings – the collective name for the raiders from Norway, Sweden and Denmark – would change parts of the British Isles as significantly as the Normans would do in their Conquest of 1066.

The first Viking raids on Britain took place in 787 when an isolated party landed on the south coast at Portland and killed the king's reeve (chief magistrate) at Dorchester. Then, in 793, the monastery on the island of Lindisfarne was attacked and, two years later, Norwegian Vikings raided the Scottish island of Iona and three islands off the northern and western Irish coast. By targeting the monasteries, the Norse were striking at the fabric of Christian Britain and its cultural and political powerhouses. They totally sacked and desecrated these wealthy enclaves

The Lewis Chessmen were probably made in Scandinavia in the 12th century. They are dressed and armed in the typical Viking style of their time and earlier. They are now in the British Museum.

– sometimes time and time again (Iona was attacked five times) – carried off their fabulous artefacts and sacred objects as booty, and murdered or enslaved their occupants.

The Vikings were not an organized force. These primary raids were almost always isolated incidents, with marauding bands of Norsemen taking opportunities where they presented themselves. For the most part, they were farmers and traders who returned home with their slaves and loot and either got on with daily life or went on a raid elsewhere. However, they were also highly skilled warriors and expert shipbuilders, navigators and seafarers. Their efficient and lethal longships, designed with a shallow draught, allowed them to reach far inland by river. Equipped with both sail and oar they were more than able to make intrepid journeys and stealthy landings.

Where the Vikings encountered resistance they were completely ruthless. Their legendary battle prowess stemmed partly from their belief that to die a brave warrior's death in combat was the way to please their heathen gods (the infamous 'beserkers' in particular believed they were under the protection of Odin, the god of war, and therefore superhuman). They were further motivated by the need to expand their own overcrowded and under-resourced territories. It was not only Britain that came under attack. These fearsome plunderers also raided what was to become Russia (the word Russia is based on the Slavic name for Viking, *Rus*) and throughout the Frankish empire; they went east to central Asia, south into North Africa, and west to Iceland, Greenland and Newfoundland.

During the 830s, the raids on Ireland and Anglo-Saxon England escalated, and the Norsemen's aims began to extend beyond mere plundering: increasingly, they were endeavouring to settle. By this time, Viking settlements were already established on the islands of Orkney and Shetland and the Isle of Man (giving the Scandinavians effective control of the Irish Sea), and they were poised to settle on the Western Isles and the northern Scottish mainland. In 841–2, Norwegian Vikings overwintered for the first time in Dublin. Once established there, many were assimilated into local society and became known as Hiberno-Norse (Irish-Norwegians), who would spread their influence into England over the remaining centuries of the Viking era. From their bases in Ireland and Scotland the Vikings set out on further raids on British territories. In the meantime, Danish Vikings had taken to overwintering in Kent. Ethelwulf, King of Wessex, defeated the Danes at the Battle of Acleah in 851 but, increasingly menaced, the Anglo-Saxons' answer to the invaders' sacking and pillaging was to try to buy them off. Later, under Ethelred II, this strategy became extremely costly.

Earldom of Orkney

The most enduring Viking kingdom in the British Isles was established on the islands off the northernmost tip of Scotland. Renegade warrior leaders on the islands raided not only the coasts of Ireland and Britain but also of Norway, prompting Norway's first king, Harald Fairhair, to bring Orkney and Shetland under his control in around 875. Harald appointed jarls (earls) to rule the territory on his behalf, and this line of earls, starting with Sigurd the Mighty, retained power until 1231. The territory remained under Norwegian/Danish control until the 15th century; at its height it embraced the Hebridean islands and land in Caithness and Sutherland on the Scottish mainland, as well as the Isle of Man (which still has a Norse system of government, the Tynwald).

In 865 a huge Viking force known as the Great Army arrived. The kingdom of Northumbria, which was already weakened by internal strife, fell first in 867, East Anglia two years later. (East Anglia's King Edmund, killed by the Vikings in 870, later became the region's patron saint.) Another great wave of Danes, known as the Summer Army, arrived in 871. Mercia was invaded and eventually conquered in 875, and the Danelaw – the territory defined as subject to Danish rule – was established throughout most of former Anglo-Saxon England. The Saxon rulers who managed to hold on to their lives were installed as puppet kings. Wessex, under Alfred the Great, was the only Saxon kingdom to retain its independence.

Gains and Losses

From around 866 through to the second half of the 10th century, one of the most important Danish kingdoms in England was Jorvik, a large area that included present-day York and started out as essentially the same territory as the Saxon kingdom of Deira. Jorvik was first sacked by the enigmatic Viking ruler Ivarr the Boneless, son of Ragnarr Lodbrok (Leather or Hairy Breeches), who had been killed by King Aelle of Northumbria. Ivarr's 'bonelessness' derived from his being unable to use his legs, which meant he had to be carried everywhere on a shield. According to the Scandinavian sagas, the affliction was the result of a curse, but it is more likely that he was suffering from a genetic disease. Ivarr is described as being clever and wise, which is perhaps how he hung on to power despite his disability. He attacked Dublin in 853 and ruled with the Norwegian Olaf the White. With his brothers Halfdan and

This 7th- to 8th-century Viking helmet with its spectacle-like visor comes from a grave site at Vendelin Sweden. Helmets were probably only worn by Viking leaders and contrary to popular myth, Norse helmets were not horned.

The Lindisfarne Stone, a carving showing seven Viking warriors, is displayed at the Yorkshire Museum in York, once the Viking capital Jorvik. The Holy Island of Lindisfarne, the centre of Christian scholarship and art, was the scene of the first Viking raid on England.

Ubbe, Ivarr led the Great Army into Britain in 865 and exacted revenge for his father's death upon King Aelle – allegedly by cutting his ribs and ripping out his lungs. Ivarr and Olaf went on to sack Dumbarton Rock, the capital of the kingdom of Strathclyde, an onslaught that would bring about Strathclyde's eventual assimilation into Scotland. Ivarr died in Ireland in 873 as 'King of the Northmen of All Ireland and Britain'. Halfdan, known as the first Viking king of Jorvik, divided the Jorvik territory into three ridings (thrithings or thirds). Like Dublin, York became a thriving trading centre, which continued to flourish even after the Vikings were driven out following the death of the last Viking king of Jorvik, Eric Bloodaxe, in 954; by then, their trade routes had connected with the Byzantine Empire and beyond.

Under Alfred the Great's son and successor Edward the Elder, the military strength of Wessex was increased and the Danish territory of East Anglia retaken. West Saxon expansion continued under Edward's descendants. Large areas of the Danelaw were brought under Saxon control, and in the ongoing battle for Jorvik – in which rival Danish and Norwegian Vikings as well as the Saxons struggled for supremacy – the Danes suffered a crushing defeat by the Saxons at Brunanburh in 937. Nevertheless, the Vikings as a whole were by no means vanquished. By 940, the Norwegian Viking Olaf Gothfrithson had retaken Jorvik and was ruling an area that included Viking Ireland, the Isle of Man, and the hitherto Danish territory known as the Five Boroughs (Derby, Leicester, Lincoln, Nottingham and Stamford). After Olaf's death in 941, Viking infighting and the continued expansion of Wessex combined to undermine and destabilize his kingdom, Jorvik was incorporated into Wessex, and it seemed that the Viking era in England was finally coming to an end. Towards the end of the 10th century, however, there were renewed invasions led by Harold Bluetooth and his son, Sweyn Forkbeard. This time, there was no Alfred the Great to repel the onslaught. Instead, there was Ethelred II, whose inability to defend his kingdom would eventually lead to England's subjugation to the Scandinavian empire of the formidable King Cnut.

Alfred the Great
871–899

BORN	*c.* 849 in Wantage
PARENTS	Ethelwulf, King of Wessex and Kent, and Osburh
CROWNED	Acceded 871
MARRIED	Elswyth of Mercia
CHILDREN	Four or five, including Athelfleda 'Lady of the Mercians' and Edward the Elder
DIED	26 October 899, aged *c.* 52

The most outstanding of the Anglo-Saxon rulers, Alfred not only contained the Danish Vikings and kept Wessex independent, but he also laid the foundations for a unified English kingdom. He built fortified towns, reorganized the army, created a new navy, and established new and more efficient systems of administration, defence and justice. His reign also saw a great revival in the arts. Despite suffering frequent bouts of ill-health, this deeply religious man ruled with intelligence, compassion and political foresight. He was the first ruler to be acknowledged as King of all the English Folk and – alone of all the English monarchs – has been given the epithet 'the Great'.

Hamo Thornycroft's bronze statue of Alfred the Great at Winchester. The site of Alfred's royal palace, Winchester remained the capital of Wessex, and later of England, until after the Norman conquest.

Mercian supremacy of the Anglo-Saxon Heptarchy gave way to the dominance of Wessex under King Egbert at the beginning of the 9th century. Greatly expanding the Wessex territories to include the kingdoms of Essex, Kent, Sussex and Surrey, as well as the hitherto unconquered West Wales (modern Cornwall), Egbert established the strong Anglo-Saxon powerbase upon which Alfred and Alfred's successors would build so successfully. Egbert had become king in about 802, just as the impetus of Viking raids was gathering strength. By the time Alfred's elder brother Ethelred I was on the Wessex throne (866–71), Scandanavian occupation of most of England had been brutally consolidated. Christian Anglo-Saxon England, reeling from the Viking's 'scorched earth' tactics, was in imminent danger of being obliterated.

Now Ethelred's Wessex came under determined attack from the Danes. With Alfred at his side he defended his realm in a series of battles in which Alfred distinguished himself as a capable war-leader, most notably at the Battle of Ashdown in Berkshire in 871 in which the West Saxons secured an important victory. However, the kingdom remained in grave danger of a takeover and, within a few months, Ethelred had died and Alfred had succeeded him; soon afterwards, Alfred was defeated by a Viking force at Wilton. The Danes were moving freely through the territory, sacking and pillaging, and it became clear to Alfred that he would have to buy peace. Temporarily appeased, the Danes set their sights on Mercia, which was entirely under their control by 875.

In January 878, a new Viking force led by Guthrum, leader of the East Anglian Danes, attacked the Anglo-Saxon stronghold at Chippenham while Alfred was in residence. Taken by surprise, the king and a band of followers fled to Athelney in the Somerset fens. It was here that the enduring story of Alfred and the burnt cakes originated: incognito, the king took shelter in a swineherd's hovel, where he was asked by the swineherd's wife to keep watch over some cakes as they were baking; he was so preoccupied with devising his strategy against the Vikings that he let the cakes burn. It is a tale that illustrates a monarch's closeness to his people – the keynote of Alfred's reign.

The Vikings set up camp in Wessex and Danish fleets waited off the

The Witenagemot

Moots were Anglo-Saxon meetings, and The Witenagemot was a gathering of the most important officials in the king's court, including senior members of the aristocracy and clergy. These gatherings could take place at more or less any time and in any part of the kingdom, depending on where the king was holding court at the time. Anglo-Saxon kings moved their court from place to place on a regular basis, and those called to The Witenagemot would be those who happened to be where the king was. Each of the early Anglo-Saxon kingdoms had its own Witenagemot, and it was only with King Alfred and his heirs – who fashioned what we now call England – that The Witenagemot came to represent the wider country. The Witenagemot discussed high affairs of state, foreign affairs and so forth, and advised the king on such things. In theory, it also selected new kings, as it was not a foregone conclusion that a king's son or immediate heir would ascend to the throne at his death. In reality, and with very few exceptions, The Witenagemot did 'elect' the king's immediate heir. Famously, Ethelred the Unready was badly served by his advisors. Ethelred's Saxon nickname (Unraed) actually means ill-advised, and his reign became a byword for calamitous, wrong-headed and ill-considered decisions.

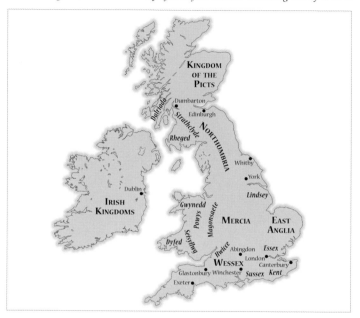

Anglo-Saxon England. This map shows the islands of Britain before the Viking onslaught. In the end, only Wessex withstood the Viking attacks on what eventually became England, and that was only after Alfred achieved a stunning victory in 878.

kingdom's coasts. Alfred built up and rallied his troops, then came out of hiding and, playing for the highest stakes, defeated Guthrum and the Viking forces in a decisive battle at Edington in May 878. Realizing that it would be impossible to defeat the entire Danish force – even if he destroyed the army that was within his grasp – Alfred negotiated peace with Guthrum. But he had the upper hand and was in a position to impose terms: the Viking leader was forced to accept baptism as a Christian and to withdraw his forces to East Anglia.

Sensing that the truce with the Vikings would not hold indefinitely, Alfred pressed his advantage. He recaptured London and liberated the south-western part of Mercia from Viking control, bringing it under the overlordship of Wessex during the early 880s. Saxon Mercia would now be ruled by an ealdorman, whose authority was subject to the king. In 886, a treaty with Guthrum finally agreed and formalized the Danelaw (the Viking territories), which were established as the land east of a line between London and Chester. In effect, the country was divided between the English south and west and the Viking east and north. As King of Wessex, the only independent Saxon kingdom, Alfred was now recognized as supreme monarch of all the English.

Building a Kingdom

In the periods of relative peace that followed the battle of Edington, Alfred began the various reforms that would consolidate his position. He organized the kingdom's defences by establishing a naval force (Alfred is acknowledged as the father of the English navy), pioneering warships that more than matched Danish sea-power. He offered thegnship (knighthood) to larger landowners in return for one month out of three in military service and put his regular army (the *fyrd*) on a similar rotational system, so there were always rested troops ready for deployment as well as manpower available for running daily life. Both the economy and the defence of the kingdom benefited under this scheme.

Most importantly, Alfred established a series of fortified settlements whose prime purpose was defence. These *burhs* were sited so that none was more than a day's march away from the next. They were carefully organized with appropriately sized garrisons, and each was granted enough land to support it on a full-time basis. Many of these communities would later develop into flourishing commercial centres and townships with their own mints, creating urbanization on a scale not seen since the Roman occupation. Winchester, already one of the kingdom's important religious centres, was one of the *burhs* established on Roman foundations. Rebuilt and revived by Alfred, who set up his royal palace there, Winchester was to remain the capital of Wessex – and later of England – until after the Norman Conquest.

Alfred also arranged politically advantageous marriages. He himself married Elswyth of Mercia. He married one of his daughters to the Count of Flanders, which was of strategic importance in resisting the Vikings. Another daughter, Athelfleda – destined to become a great warrior queen – was married off to Ethelred, Ealdorman of Anglo-Saxon Mercia, and together they extended the establishment of *burhs* into their land. Plans and statistics for these settlements were recorded in the document known as the Burghal Hidage. All of these reforms meant that when the Vikings beset Wessex again between 892 and 896 they came up against a highly effective set of defences.

Alfred believed that to rule well required knowledge. His belief in the benefits of a literate administration were in part shaped by his travels to Rome as a young boy, when he also spent time at the Charlemagne-influenced Frankish court of Charles the Bald, an atmosphere that nurtured his passion for scholarship. When Alfred succeeded to the Wessex throne, Saxon cultural life was in a dire state after decades of Viking destruction. The king lamented the decay of learning and came to believe that scholarship should not be confined to the clergy. With this in mind he established a school for the young nobles at his court, obliged his administrators to learn to read, and instigated the translation of Latin texts into the vernacular Anglo-Saxon, adapting the language to appeal to the general population (and to put a personal 'spin' on them). He studied the laws of Ethelbert of Kent, Ine of Wessex and Offa of Mercia and, in consultation with his councillors, codified laws of his own.

With the help of the Welsh cleric Asser and other scholars, Alfred received Latin tutelage and then undertook the translation of four works himself, including Pope Gregory the Great's *Pastoral Care*, which was made available for public consumption. It was Alfred's quest to 'bring it to pass ... if we have the peace, that all the youth now in England ... may be devoted to learning'. Alfred is renowned for his association with the most famous of all the Dark Age documents, the *Anglo-Saxon Chronicle*, which was begun at his behest.

Certainly Alfred was a great war-leader; but he also had a breadth of vision that extended the hallmark of earlier Saxon rulers and created conditions in which literature and scholarship could flourish. His achievements were phenomenal, his thinking unique for the time. Against the odds he managed to expand his kingdom in every way, constructing an embryonic nation poised to shake off the mantle of Dark Age disorder and creating a benchmark that would survive far beyond England's Saxon era.

The Anglo-Saxon Chronicle

This set of historical accounts comprises eight surviving manuscripts written by monks in various parts of England. These were compiled over several centuries and arranged mostly year by year. The earliest part of the Chronicle – the Winchester Manuscript – is thought to have been commissioned by King Alfred around AD 890, and they were copied and added to by scribes in monasteries throughout the land for some 250 years. The Chronicle gives an unrivalled insight into events and life before the Norman Conquest, beginning with the birth of Christ: there are descriptions of battles with the Vikings, the power struggles of kings and religious leaders, and poetry. This is the very first history of any country in Europe in its own language.

The Heirs
of Alfred
899–1016

For almost a century after his death, Alfred's successors continued the expansion of Wessex and consolidated England's nationhood. Rivalling the great continental dynasties, the house of Wessex reached its apogee with the magnificent coronation of Alfred's great grandson Edgar in 973, who ruled a nation that was growing in prosperity and stature. It was culturally and politically sophisticated, organized and well administered; the Danes had been subdued, and the kings of Scotland, Wales and Ireland swore fealty. But the weaknesses of Edgar's son Ethelred turned triumph to disaster when the Vikings began a renewed campaign of aggression from the 980s. In 1013 a bloodied, battered England finally capitulated and a Danish king ascended to the English throne.

E
dward the Elder was born at around the time that Alfred came to the throne of Wessex. As was customary, he began to share royal duties with his father at an early age and was a familiar figure when he was crowned King of Wessex in the early summer of 900. Edward's tactic in dealing with the Danes was to go on the offensive. With the assistance of his formidable sister, Athelfleda of Mercia, he cut a swathe through the territories of the Danelaw and defeated the Danes of Jorvik at the Battle of Tettenhall in 910.

Athelstan's tomb at Malmesbury Abbey. The king was the abbey's most important benefactor and he requested that he should be buried there. A contemporary church charter described Athelstan as 'King of the English, elevated by the right hand of the Almighty to the Throne of the whole Kingdom of Britain'.

However, Ivarr the Boneless's grandson, Ragnall, took advantage of Edward's routing of his rivals and immediately claimed Jorvik for himself. Ragnall expanded his territory into Bernicia, devastated Strathclyde and proclaimed himself King of Man and of the southern Hebrides. But his support dwindled and by 920 he was forced to submit to the increasingly powerful Edward.

As the Normans would later build motte and bailey castles to consolidate their victories, Saxon Edward built fortified towns or *burhs*. Edward and his sister continued to fortify the Wessex/Mercian territories, building a chain of *burhs* along the border with the Danelaw. These proved essential when the Danes

attempted another invasion of Mercia and Wales. They were stopped when Edward confronted and conquered them at Tempsford in 917 and their king, Guthrum II, was killed. Shortly after, the East Anglian Danes, and those in the Danish territory of the Five Boroughs, capitulated and accepted Edward as their king. By then, Athelfleda had died and Edward had taken direct control of Mercia; by

Athelstan presented a 9th-century psalter to the Old Minster in Winchester where this illustration of Christ in Majesty was added.

922 Edward directly ruled over most of England and was overlord of much of Britain. The Welsh princes under their high king Hywel Dda (the Good) had sworn fealty to him, and both Constantine II of Scotland and the kingdom of Strathclyde thought it prudent to accept Edward's protection and acknowledge his supremacy. For the first time since the end of the Roman occupation, England was essentially under the control of a single ruler. When Edward died in 924 he had been married at least three times and had a family of 18 or 19 children. His eldest son Athelstan was crowned King of the English: a nation had emerged.

Athelstan was possibly illegitimate, which might explain why the West Saxon Witan (council) elected his brother Elfweard to inherit Edward's throne. Elfweard was supposedly a hermit, perhaps not the best candidate for the kingship of a newly born nation. In any case he died, uncrowned, 16 days after his accession. His more glamorous brother Athelstan, who had been brought up at the Mercian court of his aunt Athelfleda, had already been declared king by the Mercians. After Elfweard's death, the Witan followed suit, although their reluctance to do so was apparent as they left Athelstan uncrowned for over a year after his accession.

An Arthurian Figure

Athelstan was tall and thin with flowing golden hair. He had a strong and generous personality and, it is said, more regard for his subjects than for the courtiers and nobles that surrounded him (which may account for the Witan's circumspection). Like Alfred, he became a patron of the arts, an instigator, collector and dispenser of medieval *objets*, and renowned as a religious benefactor; moreover he was a highly effective administrator and an active lawmaker (it was during Athelstan's reign that Sunday trading was first outlawed). He also introduced a single currency throughout the kingdom. As a major player on the international political scene (helped by numerous marriage alliances forged by his many female relatives) he became friendly with the Norwegian king Harald Fairhair – so friendly that Harald's son was sent to the English court. Commercial and cultural life in England burgeoned, and Athelstan's court became the most splendid of all that had gone before. Presiding over an increasingly united realm it was the envy even of the great continental dynasties.

Athelstan consolidated the gains of his father and grandfather and added to them. In 927 he conquered Jorvik and then set about securing his primacy over the Scottish and Strathclyde rulers, as well as those of Northumbria, Wales and Cornwall. For a period he was truly the overlord of a united, flourishing and relatively untroubled kingdom. Then, in 934, after Scotland's Constantine II broke his agreement not to support a Norse claim to Jorvik, Athelstan launched a mighty campaign in Scotland, which ended with the famous Saxon victory against a combined Scottish/Strathclyde/Danish force at Brunanburh in 937. England was confirmed as Anglo-Saxon. Shortly before his death in 939, Athelstan instigated England's first military involvement in Europe when he sent help to his Carolingian nephew Louis IV, who was trying to regain the French throne. Athelstan died unmarried and childless, and was buried in the abbey he had supported at Malmesbury.

Struggle for Unity

The next King of the English was Athelstan's half-brother Edmund, the first child of Edward the Elder's third marriage. Edmund was around 25 years Athelstan's junior but had fought alongside him at the Battle of Brunanburh two years previously. One of the first things to happen in

Edmund's reign was the seizure of Jorvik by the Norwegian Olaf Gothfrithson, King of Dublin, and the subsequent Norse sacking of the Mercian territories. Edmund had to negotiate with Olaf, and awarded him rule over the territories of Jorvik, East Anglia and the Five Boroughs. It was an inauspicious start. Still, Edmund lived up to his appellation of 'the Magnificent' when he recovered the territories in 942 and replaced Gothfrithson's distinctly unfriendly successor in

York, Olaf Sitricson, with someone more amenable. Sitricson fled to Strathclyde, where he continued to make trouble. Edmund led an army into northern Britain, brought Jorvik back under Saxon control and drove Sitricson to Ireland. Edmund handed his conquered Cumbrian Norse lands to Malcolm (I) of Scotland in return for his allegiance. A reign that started badly had been turned around.

In May 946, at the age of just 24, Edmund was murdered by an outlaw,

Edgar the Peaceable oversaw a significant revival of English monasticism. The king is represented here with St Dunstan and Ethelwold in the Regularis Concordia or 'Rule of Agreement', a document binding the Benedictine monasteries together. From the 10th to 16th centuries Benedictine monks played a significant role in every aspect of English life.

and since his heirs were still infants he was succeeded by his brother Eadred. Almost immediately, Eadred had to contend with the treacherous Witan in the kingdom of Jorvik who, despite professing loyalty to the new Saxon king, allowed the terrifying Erik Bloodaxe to become their ruler. A man with a weak constitution but an iron will, Eadred hit back. Finally, in 954, he ousted Erik Bloodaxe (who was killed shortly afterwards), and the English, Norse and Danes of Jorvik accepted Eadred's direct rule. In effect, Eadred was King of all England when he died the following year in 955.

Given the glorious reigns of Alfred's descendants thus far, Edwy – Edmund's son and Alfred's great-grandson – was a dangerous disappointment. Only 14 when he ascended to the throne of Wessex, he ruled with the help of Oda, the Archbishop of Canterbury, and Dunstan, the Abbot of Glastonbury, both of whom became openly hostile to him – so much so that Edwy's death in 959 after a short four-year tenure, can only be regarded as suspicious. Edwy's fractious incumbency threatened the new Anglo-Saxon stability: Mercia and Northumbria had rebelled at his leadership and elected his younger brother Edgar to be their king. Edwy's early death averted civil war and left Edgar to become King of the English.

During Edgar's reign, the Wessex dynasty reached its zenith and there was an unprecedented period of national peace and stability. Edgar and his council (which included Dunstan, newly appointed as the Archbishop of Canterbury) cemented the relationship between Church and State. Together they introduced a great revival of monasticism in England, rebuilding the monastic infrastructure (which had been battered almost to oblivion by the Vikings), and greatly increasing the number, wealth and power of English monasteries. Edgar also reformed the currency and reorganized the division of land by implementing the county and shire system, which remained more or less unchanged until late in the 20th century. Although the monastic revival had opponents, Edgar's reforms brought growing national prosperity and stability, and better, more manageable local administration and law enforcement. By 973, England's king (and his kingdom) was among the most respected in Christendom and he had earned his appellation 'the Peaceable'. To mark this flowering of the English monarchy, Edgar arranged a spectacular ceremony at the abbey church of St Peter in Bath in May 973, where he was the first monarch to be solemnly crowned and anointed as King of England. His wife, Elfrida, was crowned Queen. After the coronation Edgar went to Chester where he received the homage of his vassal kings from Wales, Scotland, Ireland and the north: it is said that eight or more kings rowed Edgar along the River Dee. The coronation rite devised for Edgar endures in essentially the same form to the present day.

A Rich Prize

When Edgar died, the years of tranquillity ended and a period of dissension and confusion followed the succession of Edward, Edgar's eldest son (by his first wife Athelfleda). Edward's reign was to last only three years: he was murdered at Corfe Castle in Dorset where he was visiting his stepmother, Elfrida, and her son (Edward's half-brother). Elfrida was implicated in Edward's death because as a result, her young son Ethelred came to the throne. Edward, although apparently prone to violence, was later declared a saint and a martyr.

Ethelred II's appellation 'the Unready' derives not from a word meaning unprepared but from the Saxon *unraed*, meaning badly advised or unwise (an ironic addendum to his birth name, which actually means noble counsel). This king was never going to be remembered fondly, or gloriously, as it was during his reign that many of the achievements and attainments of King Alfred and his successors were lost, along with a great deal of the national wealth. During his early years as ruler, Ethelred was firmly under the thumb of his mother and the Mercian ealdorman Alfhere; but when Alfhere died he began a not wholly unsuccessful attempt to stamp his own mark on his kingship. Ethelred was an able administrator, whose most memorable achievements included the creation of the Wantage Code (which gave credence to local law and forms the basis of contemporary Common Law), the introduction of shire-reeves (sheriffs) to represent the king's authority in the shires, and a greatly improved fiscal system. Such reforms were important in maintaining royal power in what had become a large kingdom. But Ethelred was not a natural leader, he was not decisive, and he was certainly not a warrior. Such weaknesses would come to prove disastrous when the kingdom faced renewed Viking attacks from the 980s.

The Vikings of this period were not the bands of freebooting raiders that had harassed the kingdom's coastline two centuries previously. Led by the formidable Danish kings, Harold Bluetooth and his son Sweyn, they were a well-organized fighting force with an alarming military machine, and they had their eye on the rich pickings of a very prosperous nation. In 991 the Vikings inflicted a major defeat on the Anglo-Saxons at Maldon in Essex. Ethelred's response was to offer money (Danegeld) and hope they would go away. They didn't. Instead, over a period of 20 years, the riches of England slid into Danish hands as Viking demands for silver became ever more excessive. England's morale, and its newly found identity, was dwindling, and Ethelred was losing support. In 1001 he attempted to strengthen his position by marrying Emma, the daughter of the Duke of Normandy (an alliance that would allow an even greater disaster to take place in 1066). Increasingly paranoid, in 1002 he ordered the co-ordinated massacre of every Dane living in England. It was the beginning of the end. England became a miserable, famine-ridden, bloody battlefield, and by the summer of 1013 resistance had collapsed and the kingdom had started to surrender. By Christmas Sweyn was recognized as King of England and Ethelred had fled to exile in Normandy. He was recalled when Sweyn died only three months later and Sweyn's son Cnut returned to Denmark, but his rule was conditional, on terms that were set out and recorded. It was the first constitutional settlement in English history. He died in 1016 as the longest reigning but most unfortunate of the Anglo-Saxon kings of the English.

Ethelred's reputation as one of England's most disastrous kings is not wholly deserved. The king, depicted here in a 19th-century stained-glass window at Winchester Cathedral, lacked leadership skills but he was an able administrator and introduced some of the kingdom's existing judicial systems.

Pre-Conquest England Succession

King	Born	Parents	Crowned
EDWARD THE ELDER (899–924)	c. 871/872	Alfred the Great and Ealswith of Mercia	900 at Kingston upon Thames, aged c. 29
ATHELSTAN (924–939)	c. 895	Edward the Elder and Egwina	925 at Kingston upon Thames, aged c. 30
EDMUND THE MAGNIFICENT (939–946)	c. 921	Edward the Elder and Edgiva	939 at Kingston upon Thames, aged c. 18
EADRED (946–955)	c. 923	Edward the Elder and Edgiva	946 at Kingston upon Thames, aged c. 23
EDWY (955–959)	c. 941	Edmund the Magnificent and Elgiva	956 at Kingston upon Thames, aged c. 15
EDGAR THE PEACEABLE (959–975)	c. 943	Edmund I and Elgiva	973 at Bath Abbey, aged 30
EDWARD THE MARTYR (975–978)	c. 962	Edgar and Athelfleda	975 at Kingston upon Thames, aged c. 13
ETHELRED II (THE UNREADY) (978–1013; 1014–1016)	c. 968	Edgar and Elfrida	978 at Kingston upon Thames, aged c. ten
EDMUND IRONSIDE (1016)	c. 989	Ethelred II and Elgiva	April 1016 at Old St Paul's Cathedral, aged c. 27

MARRIED	CHILDREN	DIED
(1) Egwina; (2) Elfleda; (3) Edgiva	18, possibly 19	924 at Farndon-on-Dee, aged *c.* 53
Unmarried	None	939, aged *c.* 44
(1) Elgiva; (2) Ethelfled	Three, including two sons: Edwy and Edgar	May 946 (murdered at Pucklechurch), aged *c.* 25
Unmarried	None	November 955, aged *c.* 32
Elgiva (annulled)	None	October 959, aged *c.* 18
(1) Athelfleda; (2) Elfrida	Three legitimate, including Edward and Ethelred	July 975, aged *c.* 32
Unmarried	None	March 978 (murdered), aged *c.* 16
(1) Elgiva; (2) Emma of Normandy	16 including Edmund Ironside and Edward the Confessor	April 1016, aged *c.* 48
Edith	Two, including Edward the Atheling	November 1016, aged *c.* 27

Cnut and his Successors
1016–1042

England's era as a part of the vast Scandinavian empire ruled by the Danish King Cnut was peaceful and stable. Though he started out as a ruthless Viking conqueror he became a wise, efficient, respected and almost English king of England who adhered to many Anglo-Saxon customs. Like Alfred, he was a deeply pious man with good communication skills and a firm grasp of his administration, and his choice of Winchester for his burial place illustrates the high value he placed on his new kingdom. His sons and successors, however, failed to fulfil the promise of his reign and Danish rule in England ended with them.

W hen Cnut arrived in England in September 1015 to declare his claim to the throne, his principal rival was Ethelred's son Edmund Ironside, who in defiance of his father had taken control of the Danelaw. When Ethelred died in April 1016 Edmund was swiftly crowned king. Unlike his father, Edmund was a fierce warrior and he had numerous clashes with Cnut's forces. Eventually, the battle-weary leaders reached an agreement that gave Edmund rule of Wessex and Cnut control of the territories north of the Thames. However, Edmund died a few weeks later, paving the way for the coronation of England's first Danish king. Within two years, Cnut had succeeded his brother as King of Denmark and, by 1030, he had conquered Norway and was

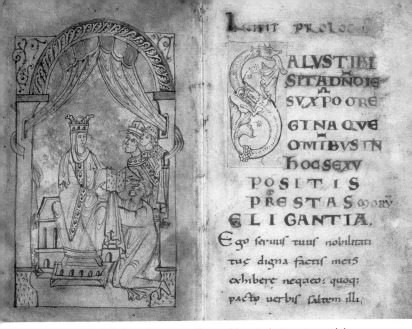

Cnut married Ethelred's widow Emma, illustrated here in the Enconium with her sons Edward the Confessor and Harthacnut. Emma was wife or mother to four kings of England and operated as a significant political figure in her own right. Eventually Edward tired of his mother's allegiance to the Danes and stripped her of her powers.

recognized as the most powerful leader in northern Europe. His empire was vast, and England was the jewel in its crown.

Cnut began his kingship by banishing or executing his Saxon rivals, including Edmund Ironside's brother, but he realized that to consolidate his empire he needed to rule over a stable, prosperous, well-administered England, and to achieve this he needed the English onside. He aligned himself with the bishops and issued his own code of laws based on those drawn up by the Saxon King Edgar. To set the seal on his kingship, he married Ethelred's widow, Emma, and it was agreed that their son, Harthacnut, would take precedence over Emma's children by Ethelred as well as over Cnut's children by his first wife, Elgiva (who was still living as his queen in Denmark).

As Cnut's position was secured he took on the qualities of the great Anglo-Saxon kings, becoming deeply pious, generous to the Church and well respected by Rome (he attended the coronation of the Holy Roman Emperor Conrad II, and his daughter Gunhilda married Conrad's son). The famous tale of Cnut sitting on his throne at the edge of the sea and demonstrating his powerlessness by vainly ordering the tide to halt its advance, highlights his impatience with fawning courtiers who proclaimed him to be so powerful that he could truly rule the waves. If the story is based on fact, proving his impotence in this way was an affirmation of his deeply held Christian belief; it was also an act of pure showmanship.

When Cnut died at a relatively young age, Harthacnut was busy fighting battles elsewhere in his empire, so Cnut's son by Elgiva, Harold Harefoot, was appointed as regent to rule jointly with Emma and the gangster-like Earl Godwin of Wessex. Harthacnut's absence allowed Harold, with Godwin's support, to make a bid for the throne, and he was crowned king in 1037. When Harthacnut finally arrived in 1040 to overthrow Harold, he found that the usurper had just died. He claimed the crown unopposed, exhumed Harold's body and threw it into a ditch. Like Harold, but worse, Harthacnut was a harsh and unpopular king, chiefly remembered for his punishing taxes. Since he was also unmarried and childless, he was without an heir. He recalled his half-brother Edward (son of Ethelred and Emma) from exile in Normandy and installed him at court as his co-ruler and successor. Edward did not have to wait long for sole occupation of the throne: in June 1042 Harthacnut was struck down with a seizure and died. Cnut's dynasty was finished and Wessex rule was restored in England.

Pre-Conquest England Succession

	CNUT (1016–1035)	HAROLD I (1037–1040)	HARTHACNUT (1035–1037; 1040–1042)
BORN	c. 995, in Denmark	c. 1012	c. 1018
PARENTS	Sweyn I (Forkbeard) and Gunhilda	Cnut and Elgiva	Cnut and Emma of Normandy
CROWNED	January 1017, at Old St Paul's Cathedral, London, aged c. 22	1037 at Oxford, aged 25	June 1040 at Canterbury Cathedral, aged c. 22
MARRIED	(1) Elgiva; (2) Emma (d. 1052)	Unmarried	Unmarried
CHILDREN	Five, including Harold I (Harefoot) and Harthacnut	None	None
DIED	November 1035 at Shaftesbury, Dorset, aged c. 40	1040 at Oxford, aged c. 28	June 1042 at Lambeth, aged c. 24

Edward the Confessor

1042–1066

BORN	c. 1003 at Islip, Oxfordshire
PARENTS	Ethelred (the Unready) and Emma of Normandy
CROWNED	April 1043 at Winchester, aged c. 39
MARRIED	Edith Godwin (d. 1075)
CHILDREN	None
DIED	January 1066 at Westminster, aged c. 62

Edward – the last in the line of Wessex kings descended from Alfred the Great – was neither a skilled warrior nor a statesman. His kingship was dominated by the immensely powerful Godwin family under whose influence he ruled over a peaceful and prosperous England that increased its hegemony over the Scottish and Welsh territories. Canonized in the 12th century in recognition of his piety, he was assigned the sobriquet 'the Confessor' and became a cult figure who for a time was regarded as the patron saint of England.

This depiction of Edward with Earl Godwin is taken from an early section of the Bayeux Tapestry, which illustrates the story of the Norman Conquest.

Though Edward had been recalled from Normandy and nominated Harthacnut's heir, there were other legitimate, Scandinavian, contenders for the English crown. The fact that Edward prevailed was largely due to the efforts of Earl Godwin who, with an eye on being the power behind the throne, backed Edward. The son of a Saxon thegn, Godwin had risen to the earldom of Wessex during Cnut's reign and had consolidated his increasingly powerful position during the tenures of Cnut's sons, switching allegiance as circumstances dictated. Edward must have mistrusted his mentor, who was implicated in the murder of Alfred, Edward's brother, a few years previously, but he needed the support of the English magnates – support that could be rallied through Godwin's bullying tactics.

Edward had not expected to be crowned a king. His passions were hunting and the Church, and he appeared more suited to the priesthood than to the throne. Though he was Anglo-Saxon by birth, his life in exile had made him essentially a Norman, and he promoted Normans to key positions at court, antagonizing Godwin who for his own ambitious reasons favoured Saxons and Danes. To manoeuvre his family closer to the throne, Godwin arranged for the king to marry his daughter Edith. Whether or not the marriage was consummated, they never had children, and while this added chastity to Edward's aura of piety it left an immense question mark over the succession.

Edward was perhaps not as feeble as Godwin might have thought. The king had already punished his Machiavellian mother for her past lack of support by stripping her of much of her wealth and importance. (Emma's riches were later restored; her potency was not.) And six years after his marriage – when the friction between Edward and the Godwins, fuelled by Edward's pro-Norman attitudes, came to a head – Edward banished the entire Godwin family and sent Edith to a convent. In their absence, the king entertained his cousin William of Normandy, and it is not inconceivable that during this time he made him his heir (as William would later claim). The Godwins, though, returned in force to demand the restoration of their earldoms. They were successful, not least because the Witan did not want Edward to instigate a civil war by fighting them. England's first family were back, and more powerful than ever.

Godwin died in 1053 and his son Harold Godwinson inherited the earldom of Wessex; by 1055, his other two sons were the earls of Northumbria and East Anglia respectively. The seniority of the Wessex earldom afforded Harold the post of supreme royal advisor, a position he filled with skill, determination, and – in all likelihood – a long-term strategy to take the very top job. Either his style suited the king, or the king knew when he was outflanked, for Edward appeared, more or less, to hand him the reins of governance while he concentrated on his pet project: building a palace and England's largest and most magnificent abbey church at Thorney Island near London. West Minster, dedicated to St Peter (to pair with the East Minster of St Paul), would become the place of coronation for all the future monarchs of the realm; the palace would become the hub of the nation's politics.

The succession remained uncertain, even as King Edward lay on his deathbed after a reign that had been long, peaceful, pious and, against the odds, successful. He was buried on 6 January 1066 in the newly consecrated West Minster. On the same day and in the same place, Harold Godwinson was crowned King of England.

Westminster Abbey

In 1066, the coronation of William I started a tradition: ever since, all the nation's monarchs have been crowned here, at the very heart of London. Edward the Confessor founded the abbey, consecrating it in 1065. For 600 years it was an abbey for Benedictine monks until dissolution in 1540. What exists today is largely a legacy of the rebuilding by Henry III in the 13th century and completed in the early 16th century, but many monastic buildings survived, due to the abbey's royal connections. Henry VII honoured the Virgin Mary by building an exquisitely fan-vaulted chapel, one of the finest examples of the peculiarly British Perpendicular style. Famed for its monuments of the great and the good, it is the resting place for monarchs, statesmen, scientists, actors and writers; Geoffrey Chaucer was the first of many poets honoured with burial in Poets' Corner.

Harold II
1066

BORN	c. 1022
PARENTS	Godwin, Earl of Wessex, and Gytha of Denmark
CROWNED	6 January 1066 at Westminster Abbey, aged c. 44
MARRIED	(1) Edith Swan-neck; (2) Edith of Mercia
CHILDREN	Seven
DIED	14 October 1066 at Hastings, aged c. 44

Having inherited his father's wealth and position in 1053, Harold Godwinson established himself first as indispensable to Edward the Confessor and then, finally, as heir. His short nine-month reign as Harold II was beset by rival challenges, but he was tenacious and highly organized, and his destruction of the Norse army at Stamford Bridge in September 1066 was the most magnificent of all English victories over the Vikings. Had it not been for William of Normandy, he may have gone on to prove himself one of the greatest Saxon kings, rather than the last.

T he swiftness with which Harold was crowned after Edward the Confessor's death reflects the Witan's imperative to act quickly: there were others who might lay claim to the throne, such as Edmund Ironside's grandson, Edgar the Atheling (who had the most obvious hereditary claim but was very young), Norway's King Harald Hardrada, and Edward

Harold's victory at Stamford Bridge, depicted in this 19th-century painting by P. N. Arbo, marked the end of England's Viking era.

the Confessor's cousin William of Normandy (who maintained that in 1064 Harold had sworn to defend William's right to the kingship of England). Of all the contenders, the half-Saxon, half-Danish Harold was the Witan's obvious choice. Although his claim was extremely tenuous, and he was purportedly a vicious man – he had almost certainly murdered his rival Edward (Edmund Ironside's son) – Harold had proved himself as a leader and military general. He knew the workings of the realm, had a massive powerbase, had popular support in the country and, most importantly, he was ready to take control.

With so many rivals Harold knew his accession was unlikely to go unchallenged. He also had another problem in his brother Tostig, whose mismanagement had led to him being ejected from his Northumbrian earldom. Far from supporting him, Harold arranged to have him replaced with someone whose efficiency could be depended upon, and Tostig was now plotting revenge. Aware of the multiple threats, the new king increased the country's defensive

capabilities. He also moved to strengthen his personal defences: although he was already married to Edith Swan-neck, he entered into a strategic second marriage to Edith, Gruffydd ap Llywellyn's widow and daughter of the Earl of Mercia, in order to secure the allegiance of the northern earls.

On 24 April 1066 Halley's comet appeared in the skies; to many it was a disastrous omen. In May, with the comet still in evidence, Tostig launched an unsuccessful attack on England's south coast. After trying and failing again in Northumbria, he formed an alliance with Harald Hardrada. William of Normandy meanwhile was building an enormous fleet at the mouth of the River Dives in northern France and garnering the support of Rome to turn his planned invasion into a Holy Crusade against the 'ungodly' Godwin dynasty. William received his blessing from the Pope along with the papal banner and ring.

By the summer, Harold's own vast army was stationed on the south coast awaiting the offensive. In the first week of September, unable to keep his men

The Bayeux Tapestry records that Harold was warned of the arrival of Halley's comet in April 1066. The Saxons saw the comet as an inauspicious omen.

lingering for an enemy that hadn't appeared, Harold stood his army down and returned to London. On 19 September Tostig and Hardrada sailed up the Ouse with a fleet of 300 ships. On 25 September Harold and his army surprised Tostig and Hardrada at Stamford Bridge and, much to Harold's credit, routed the Norsemen. Both Hardrada and Tostig were killed, and less than three dozen of the Scandinavian fleet returned home.

Three days later, William of Normandy landed on the east coast with the greatest invasion force that England had seen since AD 43. Harold marched south to meet it. He died at the hands of the Normans on 14 October 1066 and was buried at Battle Abbey, Sussex (his remains were later moved to Waltham Abbey in Essex). Anglo-Saxon England was finally at an end.

The Battle of Hastings

On 28 September 1066, William disembarked from a fleet of about 500 ships at Pevensey Bay on the Sussex coast. Harold was still in the north, and although his fleet was waiting for an attack it was stationed to the west on the Isle of Wight. The Normans therefore landed unopposed and moved on to Hastings. From Hastings, William marched north to confront Harold on 14 October at the place now known as Battle. Vastly outnumbered, and at the bottom of Senlac Hill, the Normans had the odds stacked against them. However, Harold's men were exhausted from the march south following their victory at Stamford Bridge. The Normans emerged victorious after a full day of fighting in which Harold was killed when he was pierced through the eye with an arrow. This, the last successful invasion of Britain by a foreign power, was immortalized in the Bayeux Tapestry.

Meanwhile...

789   Charlemagne, King of the Franks, issues a declaration encouraging learning, scholarship and the arts.

800   Alcuin, the head of York cathedral school, compiles *The Lives of the Saints* and works on a version of the Bible.

801   Emperor Charlemagne wrests Barcelona from Islamic occupation.

826   After baptism at Mainz, Harold of Norway returns home with Ansgar who spreads Christianity in Scandinavia.

843   The Carolingian empire is divided into three by the Treaty of Verdun, as civil war ends in Frankish lands.

861   The Vikings continue their raids, now attacking Worms, Aix-la-Chapelle, Paris, Toulouse and Cologne.

876   The Viking kingdom of Jorvik (York) is founded and lasts until 954.

789   861   876   899   911

877   Danish soldiers settle the 'five boroughs' – Derby, Leicester, Lincoln, Nottingham and Stamford.

890   Alfred instigates fairs and markets, and a militia and navy, and enlarges the powers of the king's courts.

c. 891   Alfred creates laws against acts of treason to the king; these are punishable by loss of property and execution.

892   Viking raiders arrive in Kent in some 250 ships and attack a scarcely defended burh before setting up camp at Appledore.

899   Swedish Viking descendants known as Varangians, or Rus, establish a trading route from the Baltic to the Black Sea.

911   Viking chief Rollo founds the Norman dynasty, settling his people in Normandy and swearing allegiance to the French king.

926   Athelstan marries his sister to Sihtric, the Norse king of Jorvik, to cement his ties to the north.

943	Abbot (later Saint) Dunstan introduces the strict Benedictine monastic rule to Glastonbury Abbey.
948	King Eadred destroys the monastery at Ripon.
964	Athelwold, Bishop of Winchester, clamps down on bad behaviour in monasteries and expels drunken and lecherous clerics.
1000	Ethelred II ravages Norse settlers in Cumbria and on the Isle of Man.
1019	Following the death of his brother, Cnut travels to Denmark to claim the Danish throne.
1027	Cnut attends the coronation of Emperor Conrad II in Rome. This indicates his status within Europe.
1028	Cnut defeats Olaf Haraldsson and takes control of Norway.
1030	At Canterbury mapmakers produce the most accurate representation yet of Britain, Europe and the known world.
1031	Cnut travels to Scotland and subdues the Scottish kings.

948   1000   1019   **1031**   1043

1043	Earl Leofric founds Coventry Abbey. His wife Lady Godiva rides naked through the city to spare the townspeople taxes.
1053	William Duke of Normandy marries Matilda, daughter of the Count of Flanders.
1056	A band of Welsh and Irish attackers led by Gruffydd, a Welsh prince, burn down Hereford Cathedral.
1057	Edward 'the Exile', son of Edmund Ironside and potential heir to the throne, returns to England, but dies mysteriously.
1063	Harold Godwinson and his brother Earl Tostig of Northumbria launch a two-pronged attack on Wales.
1064	Accounts report Harold and William meeting in France and agreeing that William should succeed Edward.

Scotland
1034-1329
Modernizing a Kingdom

The 12 kings from Duncan I to Alexander III were descended from the Celtic line founded by Kenneth McAlpin. They were kings 'of Scots', the people, not of Scotland the country (which was at that time a vague concept), but they slowly took at least nominal control over almost all of the area that is recognized today as Scotland. The primogeniture principle of father-to-son succession replaced the Celtic system, which had given various male relatives a claim and been the cause of much mayhem and bloodshed. Lowland Scotland became less Celtic and more English in many ways: the royal administration followed the English pattern, Anglo-Norman baronial families were lured to Scotland as supporters of the Crown, and Celtic Christianity gave way to the Roman Catholic variety. These Anglicizing developments, which brought Scotland closer to mainstream Europe, were pushed forward by the Scots monarchs themselves. Many of them had English wives and English estates and owed their thrones to English backing. At the same time, they resisted the efforts of the kings of England to establish themselves as overlords of the Scots. Alexander III's death in 1286 gave the formidable Edward I of England an ideal opportunity to make this claim to overlordship good, at least for a time, until the coming of Robert the Bruce in 1306.

Duncan I
to David I
1034–1153

The Scottish Succession 1034–1153

KING	BORN	REIGN	RELATIONSHIP TO PREDECESSOR
DUNCAN I	c. 1010	1034–40	Grandson
MACBETH	c. 1005	1040–57	Cousin
LULACH	c. 1032	1057–8	Stepson
MALCOLM III	c. 1031	1058–93	Cousin to Macbeth
DONALD III	c. 1033	1093–7	Brother
DUNCAN II	c. 1060	1094	Nephew
EDGAR	c. 1074	1097–1107	Nephew
ALEXANDER I	c. 1077	1107–24	Brother
DAVID I	c. 1084	1124–53	Brother

Little but the name links the real Duncan I with the Duncan of Shakespeare's *Macbeth*. The real king was a young man, not the greybeard depicted in the play, and he was killed in battle rather than murdered. He inherited the throne through his mother – a daughter of Malcolm II – which was unusual, and was overthrown by Macbeth Macfinlay, ruler of the Moray area, who was also descended from the royal line. Macbeth's

ALCOLO
ſalutem
quand.
pro ſa
S3 poſt
uenerab
locuſ ille

ſita eſt ſup ripam fluminis tvede. in loco qui dr̄ l
pali ſubiectione libam ē̄ conceſſit. Ita ſcilicet ut ab
& oleum. & ordinationem ipſi abbatis & monacho
rate dn̄i mei regis ƀƀ. patruſ mei comitaſ henrici.
elemoſinam confirmo. Videlicet uillam de kelcho c
dam terram quam gerolduſ dedit iuxta diuiſas
in ſollennitatibʒ. uel in aliiſ diebʒ ſeruitium d̄ſ au
molendino. ru....dnel de braſio uneguel d

*David I and his grandson and successor Malcolm IV are shown in an
illuminated initial letter from the 1159 charter of Kelso Abbey.*

wife, Gruoch, was the original Lady Macbeth (who may or may not have been given to sleepwalking, as in the play). Shakespeare made Macbeth the best-known villain in Scottish history, but in fact he was a much more efficient king than Duncan had been. He kept such good order that in 1050 he was able to take a holiday and make a pilgrimage to Rome, where he flung cash about like a man sowing corn. His nemesis was Duncan's son Malcolm Canmore ('Bighead'), Malcolm III. Malcolm, who was only a boy when his father was killed, had been spirited away to Northumbria, where he bided his time. In 1054 he invaded Scotland with an English army, which marched north killing and plundering to defeat Macbeth in battle at Dunsinane. Three years later, Macbeth was killed in a skirmish at Lumphanan and his head was brought to Malcolm on a pole.

St Margaret

Most Scots at this time spoke Gaelic and the Celtic Church was flourishing, but things were about to change. An Anglo-Saxon princess called Margaret fled to Malcolm III's court after the Norman conquest of England in 1066, and Malcolm took her as his second wife. Deeply pious – she was canonized as a saint in 1250 – Margaret was self-righteously determined to bring the benefits of English civilization and Roman Catholic Christianity to her husband's benighted realm. Malcolm, a fierce illiterate warrior and rough diamond, 20 years older than his cultivated wife, adored and stood in awe of her. He allowed her to give their children English names, make the court at Dunfermline speak English (she never learned Gaelic) and import English priests and monks. She was not able to persuade him to stop his raids into England, however, and in 1093 a foray into Northumberland proved one too many when he and their eldest son Edward were ambushed and killed.

There was just time to tell Margaret the news of Malcolm's death before she herself died in Edinburgh Castle. Once she was out of the way, a fierce reaction against the Anglicizing policies drove her remaining sons Edgar, Alexander and David to safety in England and sent the numerous English at the royal court packing. Malcolm's younger brother, Donald III Bane ('the Fair'), took over, briefly interrupted the next year by his nephew Duncan II (a son from Malcolm III's first marriage), who was soon murdered. Donald Bane's restoration was not to last, however: he was overthrown – caught, blinded and imprisoned – by his nephew Edgar when he returned to Scotland in 1097 with an army provided by William II of England. Edgar admired England and started transforming the Scottish kingdom on the Anglo-Norman model. He and his brothers and successors, Alexander and David, founded new monasteries and bishoprics through which they could exert greater control of their realm while resisting the earnest efforts of the archbishops of York to gain authority over the Church in Scotland.

Since Edgar did not marry he was succeeded by his brother Alexander I, who left no legitimate children. The next in line was the youngest, longest-lived and most effective of Edgar's brothers, David I, who had spent his teenage years at the court of Henry I of England, where he was raised in Anglo-Norman high society. He lured Anglo-Norman families, such as the Bruces, the Balliols and the Stewarts to the Lowlands from England with grants of land and fostered the feudal system. He also encouraged Flemish immigration principally for wool and textile trading. David founded Cistercian and Augustinian monasteries, including Melrose and Holyrood, created an efficient civil service, issued Scotland's first royal coinage, and encouraged the growth of trade and towns. He spent his later years happily gardening at Edinburgh Castle and experimenting with the grafting of apple trees before his death in his late sixties.

Malcolm IV to Alexander III
1153–1286

The Scottish Succession 1153–1286

KING	BORN	REIGN	RELATIONSHIP TO PREDECESSOR	AGE AT DEATH
MALCOLM IV	1141	1153–65	Grandson	24
WILLIAM I	c. 1142	1165–1214	Brother	early 70s
ALEXANDER II	1198	1214–49	Son	50
ALEXANDER III	1241	1249–86	Son	44

Malcolm IV ('the Maiden') was 12 years old when he succeeded his grandfather David I. Warlords who saw the new king's minority as an opportunity to take greater power for themselves included Somerled of Argyll and the Western Isles, who was said to have invented the hinged rudder, which improved the performance of his warships. Somerled was defeated as he advanced up the Clyde, and he lost his head, literally. As it turned out, Malcolm, who had a delicate constitution, died young and unmarried at age 24, to be succeeded by his vigorous, red-headed brother William, a bonny fighter in tournaments.

King for almost 50 years, William I was later called 'the Lion', possibly because he adopted the rampant lion badge that became the heraldic emblem

Alexander II is depicted on horseback in the then fashionable style of armour, on the reverse of his great seal of around 1214. The inscription hails him as King of Scots under the guidance of God.

of Scots royalty. When invading Northumberland, his horse fell on him and he was trapped and then captured by the English. Henry II of England forced him to accept English overlordship of Scotland before letting him go, although William later bought cancellation of the concession from Richard I, who needed money for crusading. He put down risings in the south-west (in

Galloway) and in the north, where he was tightening the royal grip. The royal grip fastened on women as well, and William sired a brood of illegitimate children before, in 1186, marrying Ermengarde de Beaumont, who was descended on the wrong side of the blanket from Henry I of England. In the 1190s there was trouble with the Earl of Orkney. William took the earl's son hostage, had him blinded and castrated, and reasserted himself in the north-east.

Alexander II was the first surviving legitimate son born to a king of Scots for some 70 years. He was 16 when he succeeded his father, who had trained him for the task, and he proved equally forceful and ruthless. He reduced Argyll and Galloway to obedience, and when one of his northern bishops was murdered, he had 80 men's hands and feet cut off because they had been present at the crime. He showed off the severed heads of unsuccessful opponents in the north and had Galloway rebels torn to pieces by horses as a public spectacle in Edinburgh. On the other hand, he inaugurated a period of peace with England. Alexander married Henry III of England's sister, Joan, and at last formally dropped the Scottish claim to Northumberland and other areas of northern England. In 1237 the border with England was fixed at the point where it has generally remained ever since. Joan died childless in 1238 and Alexander married a French woman, Marie de Coucy. He died on an expedition to wrest the Western Isles from the Norwegians.

Alexander's son, Alexander III, who was only seven when he acceded to the throne, survived his minority in which rival factions struggled for control of him, and of Scotland. In 1263 he defeated a Norwegian attack, and in 1266 he bought the Western Isles and the Isle of Man from the king of Norway. The Norwegians kept Orkney and Shetland, but the young king's realm now covered all the rest of modern Scotland. When he was only ten, Alexander formally married Henry III's 11-year-old daughter Margaret. She died in 1275, and Alexander's sons also died early. In need of an heir, he married Yolande of

Dreux in 1285. Within a few months, on his way to his new wife at Kinghorn in Fife, he rode too close to the cliff and his horse stumbled, throwing him to his death on the beach below.

By the time of Alexander's death, Gaelic had been driven out of much of Lowland Scotland by a form of northern English, which would develop into the distinctive Scots brogue. His reign was looked back on as a golden time of prosperity and peace that was shattered by his sudden death. His heir was his baby granddaughter Margaret ('the Maid of Norway'), daughter of King Eric of Norway. Two bishops accompanied the little girl to Scotland in 1290, but she died on the way, in Orkney. A crisis over the succession followed, with Robert Bruce and John Balliol being the principal competitors for the throne. As supposed overlord of Scotland, Edward I of England decided between them and chose John Balliol, who was crowned at Scone in 1292. The matter, however, was far from settled.

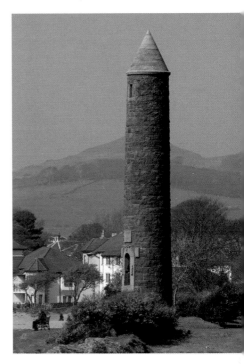

The 'Pencil' monument at Largs in Ayrshire today commemorates Alexander III's crucial defeat of a Norwegian invasion force in 1263.

Robert
the Bruce
1306–1329

BORN   11 July 1274 at Turnberry Castle, Ayrshire

PARENTS   Robert Bruce and Marjorie, Earl and Countess of Carrick

CROWNED   1306 at Scone, aged 31

MARRIED   (1) Isabel of Mar (d. 1296) (2) Elizabeth de Burgh (d. 1327),
                daughter of the Earl of Ulster

CHILDREN   A daughter, Marjorie, by Isabel, three surviving children
                by Elizabeth and five recorded illegitimate children

DIED   7 June 1329 at Cardross, Dunbartonshire, aged 54

Two legendary Scottish heroes emerged from the opposition to
English rule – William Wallace and Robert Bruce. John Balliol,
who had been appointed king by Edward I, reigned as the
English king's puppet until, in 1296, his master demoted him
('ridding himself of a turd', as he put it) and installed an English
administration backed by an army of occupation. Many Scots
acquiesced, but a resistance movement was led by Wallace, who
waged a brutal guerrilla war against the English until his army
was decisively defeated in battle at Falkirk in 1298. Wallace got
away, but was captured in 1305 and taken to London to suffer a
horrible death at Smithfield.

This statue of Robert the Bruce at Stirling Castle looks towards the national monument to William Wallace, the other great hero of Scottish resistance to the English under Edward I.

The Bruces were lords of Annandale in the Borders from the 1120s. The Robert Bruce who had lost to John Balliol in the scrabble for the throne in 1290 claimed descent from a younger brother of William the Lion. His son, also called Robert, was carried off to Turnberry Castle by the widowed Countess of Carrick, who was passionately in love with him, and they married. Their eldest son was the celebrated Robert the Bruce, who inherited his grandfather's claim to the throne and veered uneasily between supporting Wallace (who was pro-Balliol) and the English. In 1306 he came out against Edward I and got himself crowned at Scone. Defeated by the English in battle, Robert escaped to Rathlin Island off the Irish coast while three of his brothers were executed and his sister Mary was hung in a cage like an animal on the wall of Roxburgh Castle for four years. At this nadir of his fortunes, the story goes, utterly depressed and ready to give up, Robert sheltered for the night in a cave. There he watched a spider's attempts to spin its web, persisting over and over again in spite of repeated setbacks. He took the lesson to heart and his courage and resolution were restored.

In 1307, the year Edward I died, Robert was back. With the aid of his surviving brother, Edward, he waged guerrilla war on the mainland against both the English and the Balliol supporters and by 1314 had been sufficiently successful to confiscate some of their land. Gradually, the English garrisons of castles were driven or starved out. The crunch came that year, when Robert confronted the might of the English under Edward II at Bannockburn, near Stirling. He crushed them, even though he was heavily outnumbered. Edward II got away, but many English leaders were killed or captured.

Berwick fell to the Scots in 1318, punishing raids were made into northern England, and the lands of those who did not support Robert were confiscated and given to those who did (strengthening the Douglases, among others).

The struggle cemented a sense of Scottish national unity. The Declaration of Arbroath, endorsed by eight Scottish earls in 1320, declared Scotland independent under Robert I and stated that if he failed them they would 'choose another king to defend our freedom; for so long as a hundred of us remain alive, we will yield in no least way to English dominion'. An English invasion in 1322 was forced to retreat by a scorched-earth policy of destroying all supplies of food. A peace treaty recognizing Scottish independence was signed in 1328, when Robert was already seriously ill. Leprosy was rumoured, although this seems unlikely. He died the following year, leaving a glowing reputation for courage, generosity and fairness.

Robert had long wanted to go on crusade, and after his death his heart was extracted from his body and Sir James Douglas and an escort of knights set out to carry it to the Holy Land. They got no further than Spain, where Robert's heart was borne defiantly into battle against the Moors. Sir James was killed, but it is said that the heart was brought back and buried at Melrose Abbey.

The Stone of Destiny

The Scots coronation ritual preserved the time-honoured Celtic forms. The new monarch was proclaimed King of Alba on the venerated Stone of Destiny, which was said to be the one on which Jacob pillowed his head when he saw angels descending and ascending a ladder to heaven. Edward I carried it off to England in 1296 as the symbol of Scots sovereignty and put it in Westminster Abbey. Or he thought he did. There is a belief that he was palmed off with a substitute and that the real stone was hidden on the Isle of Skye. The stolen stone was returned to Scotland on St Andrew's Day, 30 November 1996.

The Normans
1066–1154

The last foreign invasion of England until 1688 took place in September 1066 when William, Duke of Normandy, landed with the largest fighting force since the Roman occupation and defeated the Anglo-Saxon king, Harold II. By December, William I had been enthroned at Westminster Abbey, the first in the line of England's Norman monarchs. By the end of his reign Anglo-Saxon England had been irretrievably altered. Instead of burhs, built by the Saxons to protect the people, castles were erected to intimidate them. Monumental churches were built, French and Latin became the languages of the land, and the Anglo-Saxon nobility were replaced with a new ruling class of haughty foreign aristocracy.

Despite William's policy of ruthlessly and brutally extinguishing resistance to this new order, he was well respected as a leader and is remembered as the most potent of all the British kings. His sons and successors – the louche and unpopular William II, and the cunning and capable Henry I – managed to tighten the grip of Norman rule over both England and France. Things were looking good until rivalry between Henry's daughter Matilda and his nephew Stephen destabilized the realm. The resulting anarchy and chaos led to much more than the ravaging of England: it meant the end of the House of Normandy.

William I (the Conqueror)

1066–1087

BORN	1027 at Falaise, Normandy
PARENTS	Robert I, Duke of Normandy, and Herleva
CROWNED	25 December 1066 at Westminster Abbey, aged 38
MARRIED	Matilda of Flanders (d. 1083)
CHILDREN	Ten, including Robert II, Duke of Normandy, William II, Stephen, Count of Blois, and Henry I
DIED	9 September 1087 at Rouen, aged 59

William I was a tall, red-haired, charismatic but intemperate warrior leader whose victory over England was a catalyst that would alter Anglo-Saxon society irrevocably. Initially, resistance to the new Norman order was strong, and William applied ruthless tactics to staunch rebellion. A complicated man, William was terrifyingly harsh but also just, keen on worldly pleasures but pious and respectful of the Church. Once England had been subjugated, the king's attention turned back to his continental territories and he died in Normandy as he had lived, a fearless combatant.

William I, represented on a coin from his reign, was descended from the Scandinavian earls of Orkney. Vikings had taken the mantle of French aristocracy in Normandy, so his conquest meant that England was again essentially in the hands of the Norsemen.

William was illegitimate, but as his father's only living son he inherited the title of Duke of Normandy in 1035 at the age of seven. As a minor he was vulnerable and over the next dozen years there were plots to usurp him; several of his guardians were assassinated and attempts were made on his life. However, by the mid-1040s, when he came of age, William was able to assert his own authority and began a campaign of relentless warring and expansionism. At the age of 26 he married Matilda, the daughter of the Count of Flanders, to consolidate an alliance (it was a marriage of convenience but also a love match) and then, in 1062, he successfully invaded the French territory of Maine.

As a descendant of the Scandinavian earls of Orkney and the great-nephew of Emma of Normandy (wife of King Cnut), William believed he had a legitimate claim on the English throne. Further, he maintained that his distant cousin, the childless Edward the Confessor, had promised it to him and that Harold Godwinson, the most powerful man in England, had agreed to support him. When Harold reneged on this alleged agreement and took the crown for himself, William was said to be incandescent with rage. True to form, he decisively and swiftly organized an invasion of England in order to take what he believed was rightfully his.

William took a risk in attacking England, for Harold was a very capable, well-organized military leader and William would have to confront him on his own territory. Had it not been for the almost simultaneous onslaught by Harald Hardrada of Norway at the opposite end of the country, the kingdom might have remained in Saxon hands. As it was, the Norman victory at Hastings, in which Harold was killed, set in motion a cataclysmic change for the Anglo-Saxon ruling classes. William, now hailed as 'the Conqueror', lost no time in mercilessly applying his superiority, marching his army through

The Domesday Book

The Domesday Book – a survey of who owned what in William's kingdom – was completed in 1086. It was essentially intended to be used as a reference for tax purposes (although William himself would derive little benefit from it for he died the following year), but it was also a testament to the legacy of Anglo-Saxon organization and Norman efficiency. Royal officers were sent to collect information from every shire in the country and included details of the numbers of people who lived in each settlement. The detailed record shows the seismic changes in land ownership that had taken place since 1066 and the extent to which Norman rule had tightened its grip over England. The old English ruling class had dwindled to almost nothing, and the new barons, numbering just short of 200, were the new land-owning classes.

the countryside and employing slash and burn tactics to gain submission from the English. Steadily and strategically the Normans moved towards London, taking control of major towns as they went.

On Harold's death, the Witan had pinned a feeble hope on maintaining a Saxon monarchy by declaring Edmund Ironside's young grandson, Edgar the Atheling, as their king. However, Edgar's noblemen were unable to muster enough resistance to combat the largest invasion force since the Romans and Edgar was forced to submit to William at Berkhamsted, in Hertfordshire. By Christmas Day 1066 the Duke of Normandy was at Westminster Abbey in London being crowned William I, King of England. William had achieved his immediate goal, but he was not yet secure. Even the coronation was marred by panic when cries of adulation inside the abbey were interpreted by the Norman troops outside as an English rebellion. Chaos ensued when the Norman guard set fire to the Saxon dwellings surrounding Westminster Abbey; according to the 12th-century Anglo-Norman historian, Orderic Vitalis, William was left trembling with his terrified clergy and a very diminished congregation to continue with the coronation amid scenes of confusion and disarray.

Tides of Rebellion

To begin with, William's control of the country was limited to the south and a part of the midland kingdom of Mercia. Determined to assert his dominance throughout the rest of the kingdom, he swept away the Witan and set about consolidating his gains, gradually subjugating the remaining parts of the territory. By February 1067 William felt confident enough of his authority in England to make a triumphant nine-month visit to Normandy, leaving his half-brother Odo, Bishop of Bayeux, and the Norman magnate William FitzOsbern in control.

But William's problems were far from over. Shortly after he returned from France, and his wife Matilda had been brought to London and crowned Queen in May 1068, William started to face rebellion after rebellion. Resistance came from every direction: Harold's sons raided the south-west from their base in Ireland; Exeter (where Harold's mother, Gytha, was living) withstood a siege of more than two weeks before finally capitulating; and in 1069 the Danes, supported by Prince Edgar the Aetheling and other English nobles, invaded the north and took York. There were also uprisings in the midlands and, under the Saxon resistance leader Hereward the Wake, in East Anglia, while the Scots and the Welsh were causing trouble on England's borders. William acted decisively, paying off the Viking invaders with Danegeld and striking at the territories that were causing him so much grief. To contain the troublesome

Welsh, he created the Marcher lordships, which gave his most trusted nobles (including FitzOsbern) huge territories on the Anglo-Welsh border to rule as they saw fit. In 1069 he began his infamous campaign known as the Harrying of the North, which entailed unprecedented genocide across the country between York and Durham and subsequent decades of famine as food stores and agricultural tools were destroyed. In 1071 East Anglian resistance was finally crushed at the Siege of Ely, at which point William turned the pressure on Malcolm III, King of Scotland, who was invading the north of England. However, in 1072 Malcolm was forced to sign the Treaty of Abernethy, which marked a truce: the Norman subjection of England was complete.

William ruled his new kingdom by merging the existing Saxon administrative system with a political system that came to be known as feudalism. The country was divided up into large areas of land, which had been confiscated from the Saxons and handed by way of reward to the Norman barons who had

Royal Hunting Forests

Hunting forests, such as the New Forest, were first set up by William the Conqueror. These were reserved for the sole use of the king, his huntsmen and his nobles. In many cases their creation involved the destruction of Saxon villages and ancient woodland (the word 'forest' was applied to any land designated for hunting and as such included heath and farmland as well as wooded areas). Strict laws – the so-called Forest Laws – banned hunting by other people and stipulated extremely harsh punishments for transgressors. The laws also imposed a blanket prohibition on farming, felling trees and cutting peat. Under William's successors more than half of England was designated as royal hunting forest.

supported William's invasion. In return they had to swear an oath of loyalty to William, collect taxes from their land, which were paid to the monarchy, and provide men for military service when required. As these areas were too large to be governed effectively by one baron, each area was divided again between trusted knights, who in turn swore the same oaths to their ruling baron. For most of the 1070s and early 1080s, the reins of English government were left in the hands of these powerful barons as William's attention turned to his continental territories. The Conqueror returned in 1085 with an army against a threatened attack by the Danish king Cnut IV and it was during this visit that he commissioned the first great census of England, the Domesday Book.

William was fatally injured as the result of a riding accident in 1087 while besieging the French town of Mantes against a rebellion in which his own

son Robert had sided with the enemy. According to Orderic Vitalis, the king expressed sorrow for his treatment of the English before he died. He was buried at the Abbey of St Stephen in Caen, and was succeeded as king of England by his son William Rufus. It appears England was forgiving and recognized William's achievements and his rule as harsh but just: the Conqueror's obituary in the *Anglo-Saxon Chronicle* describes him as 'more splendid and powerful than any of his predecessors'.

The Bayeux Tapestry was commissioned by William's half-brother Bishop Odo and it may have been made in England. The embroidery, which is half a metre/yard wide and about 70m (230ft) long, tells the story of events leading up to the Norman Conquest and the Battle of Hastings. This section shows the invasion getting under way.

Castles

With the Norman invasion came a spate of castle building. The castle was not only a means of defence but also a dramatic representation of power and status, and the Normans stamped their authority in spectacular style soon after 1066 with castles at Cambridge, Warwick, Nottingham, Huntingdon, Lincoln, York and elsewhere. Hundreds of Norman castles survive to this day, although they are in various states of preservation.

The early Norman design was the motte and bailey – a central tower (or keep) on a mound (motte), within one or more enclosures (baileys). Up until Henry II's reign the majority were wooden structures (notable exceptions included Colchester and Rochester), but later stone was employed. The motte was created from earth dug out of the encircling ditch. The bailey had a timber tower and its own stockade that effectively constituted the outer wall. Together the motte and tower provided a home for the family and servants, and were sufficiently high above ground level to be the main points of defence. Many castles, such as Windsor, originated as timber and earth motte and bailey and were rebuilt in stone during the 11th and 12th centuries. Stone looked more impressive and had the practical advantages of being stronger and less susceptible to fire. During the time of Stephen and Matilda, when civil strife prevailed, many castles were erected hurriedly, some with a nearby siege castle for the attackers.

Cardiff Castle is a superb example of a timber motte and bailey castle that was converted to stone. The earliest castle was raised in about 1080 on the site of a Roman fort by the Norman Lord of Gloucester. Henry I chose Cardiff as a prison for his brother Robert, Duke of Normandy. Subsequent centuries saw additional buildings erected, including the Black Tower in the 13th century.

Castles gradually became more sophisticated and self-contained. Increasingly they were designed to provide comfortable living accommodation, with kitchens, store-houses, lavatories (called garderobes, and draining directly through the walls into the outside world), stables, workshops, a chapel, and a great hall. The last of these represented the hub of life in the castle, with a high table raised on a dais for the lord, his family and guests, and lower tables and benches for the rest (rather like a dining hall in an Oxbridge college). The earth floor would be strewn with rushes, and the tables, benches and walls perhaps hung with carpets. From the 13th century, window glass began to appear.

As castles were rebuilt, the shape often remained unaltered. Shell keeps were circular ones, built on the original motte, such as Cliffords Tower in York. Tower keeps were a formidably strong, square or rectangular design – such as the White Tower in the Tower of London. Keeps needed to be able to withstand a siege, so they had stores, a well (plus perhaps a method of collecting rainwater), kitchens and living quarters; windows were only on the upper floors. Windsor, successively added to in later centuries, is now Europe's largest inhabited medieval castle.

As the techniques of attack grew more sophisticated, castle design evolved further. The entrance was a particularly vulnerable point, and gatehouses were fortified with portcullises; battlements were crenellated to assist defence by archers, and moats were dug – as at the Tower of London. Towers on the curtain walls gave further points of security, and this became more important than defence from the inner keep or castle tower.

The Tower of London has a long, grim history of imprisonment and execution. Begun in 1067, and rebuilt in stone between *c.* 1077 and 1097, it is strategically placed at a vantage point on the Thames. Among this castle's famous towers are the White Tower – one of the most imposing fortifications of this date in Europe – which contains the virtually unchanged St John's Chapel. The Bloody Tower was supposedly the site of the murder of the princes in 1483.

William the Conqueror built the first motte and bailey fortress at Warwick in 1068. The original buildings have long since disappeared and Warwick Castle today is an impressive and imposing fortress. William's mound is all that remains of the earliest castle.

William II (Rufus)

1087–1100

BORN	c. 1057 in Normandy
PARENTS	William the Conqueror and Matilda of Flanders
CROWNED	26 September 1087 at Westminster Abbey, aged c. 30
MARRIED	Unmarried
CHILDREN	None
DIED	2 August 1100 in the New Forest, aged c. 43

William Rufus inherited the throne of England despite expectations that his elder brother's claim would succeed. As a result, there was great rivalry between them, which lasted for years and threatened not just William's tenure while he was alive but the stability of the realm after his death. He was an unpopular king, particularly with the Church, but like his father he was a great warrior and continued to consolidate Norman rule in England. His reign was cut short by what was judged to be a hunting accident but might have been murder: when he died there were few who mourned him.

Willimus ii

William I's eldest son was the treacherous Robert who had fought against his father at the siege of Mantes, and although Robert inherited the dukedom of Normandy it was William's third son, who had remained loyal to his father, who took England. William Rufus might have been the Conqueror's favourite child, but Robert's claim was a legitimate one, and William's journey to London from his father's sick bed in Rouen was therefore undertaken at high speed. He was crowned just over two weeks later.

Both contemporary and later historians paint William as an unpopular, unappealing king with red hair and an almost matching ruddy complexion, hence his nickname 'Rufus'. At times his dissolute court, lack of interest in all things religious, and coarse, arrogant manner threatened to undo the fledgling Norman rule in England. His licentious lifestyle angered churchmen and many of his magnates, and to make matters worse he evaded appointing bishops and abbots in order to appropriate the Church's considerable revenues for the Crown. (By the time of his death in August 1100, he had claimed the revenues of three bishoprics and a dozen abbeys.) Many considered his brother Robert a far more suitable king, giving rise to the constant threat of rebellion, and early on in his reign

A stone memorial to William II was erected where he was said to have been killed by an arrow fired by William Tirel while hunting in the New Forest; in 1865 it was replaced by a cast-iron monument, but is still known as The Rufus Stone.

William's uncle Odo led a serious, albeit unsuccessful, uprising in favour of Robert. The rivalry was assuaged when, in 1096, Robert made William regent of Normandy in exchange for funding his travels on the First Crusade.

William appeared to have a lucky streak. The monk Eadmer wrote that 'in war and in the acquisition of territory he enjoyed such success that you would think the whole world smiled upon him'. But his achievements cannot always be accredited to fate: he was an excellent soldier, a keen strategist and wily negotiator. His campaigns in Wales led to increasing control of the Marcher lordships and several Welsh princes recognized him as overlord. In Scotland, William engineered the overthrow of the anti-Norman king Donald in favour of Duncan II and his brother Edgar.

It was the Church that so vexed William, and the feeling was mutual. When Lanfranc, Archbishop of Canterbury, died in 1089 William refused to nominate a successor until 1092 when he appointed Anselm, Lanfranc's student and friend. At the time the Church had two rival popes, Urban II and Clement III. Anselm supported Urban; William sat on the fence and was angered that his archbishop should presume to support either papacy without his authority. In 1095 the Council of Rockingham was convened to discuss the issue: Anselm refused to budge. Eventually William decided to support Urban but he wanted the pope to depose Anselm. Urban refused and the relationship between Crown and Church deteriorated to such a degree that in 1097 the saintly Anselm chose to go abroad.

William's end has given rise to numerous conspiracy theories. At the time, rightly or not, it was judged that he was unwittingly shot with an arrow while out hunting in the New Forest. There was no grand state funeral for the king: his body was taken by farm cart to Winchester and buried under the tower of the cathedral in the early hours of the next morning.

Henry I
1100–1135

BORN	September 1068, Selby, Yorkshire
PARENTS	William the Conqueror and Matilda of Flanders
CROWNED	6 August 1100 at Westminster Abbey, aged 31
MARRIED	(1) Matilda (formerly Edith), daughter of Malcolm III of Scotland; (2) Adeliza, daughter of Geoffrey VII, Count of Louvain
CHILDREN	Four legitimate, of which only Matilda survived; at least 25 illegitimate
DIED	1 December 1135 at St Denis-le-Fermont, Rouen

The Conqueror's youngest son was the only one of the Norman kings who was literate: he had been groomed to enter the Church, so unlike his brothers he had been properly educated, and he was known as Henry Beauclerc ('good writer'). But he was also ambitious, and when William II was killed – either by accident or design – Henry seized the throne. His reign was long and successful. He could be harsh to the point of savagery, but he inspired loyalty among his followers and he was capable, clever and adept at diplomacy. During his firm rule England was peaceful and the kingdom was expanded into Normandy.

Despite having numerous children, Henry died without a male heir when his two legitimate sons, William and Richard, were drowned in the White Ship when it foundered outside Barfleur in the English Channel in 1120. Their deaths left Henry distraught and would eventually lead to civil war. It is said the king never smiled again.

Apres will le rous reg
na le primer henry

If William Rufus had been murdered, then the finger of suspicion would surely have pointed towards Henry, a member of the fateful hunting party. Almost as the king drew his last breath, Henry headed to Winchester to secure the Treasury and within a matter of days he was crowned. Speed was crucial: he had to act before his brother Robert's imminent return from the Crusades. Henry knew his position was vulnerable, so he recalled the exiled Archbishop Anselm – to ingratiate himself with the Church – and he married the daughter of Malcolm III of Scotland (who was also the niece of Edgar the Atheling), forming a bond with both the Scots and the Anglo-Saxons. To curry favour further, Henry included in his coronation oath all sorts of promises that would distance him from William Rufus' unpopular reign, and he filled the ecclesiastical posts that had been kept vacant by his brother.

Since William Rufus had nominated Robert as his heir (in part to prevent Henry from taking the throne), invasion from Normandy was inevitable. In June 1101 it came. Robert arrived with an army, but the incursion ended in negotiation rather than battle when Henry agreed to pay Robert an annual pension in return for the throne. Five years later the tables were turned when Henry invaded Normandy in order to put down rebel barons. He captured Robert at the Battle of Tinchebrai in September 1106 and had him imprisoned until his death. With this, Henry became Duke of Normandy as well as King of England – no small feat for one who had inherited no land and no titles, only silver.

In the meantime, relations between the king and Archbishop Anselm had soured over appointing and investing the clergy, which had always been in the gift of the king. The pope decreed that lay investiture of churchmen was unlawful, which meant that the king might have little say in who would wield a great deal of the nation's power. Henry took no notice of this edict, until the threat of excommunication forced him to reach a compromise: the king renounced lay investiture; but he retained authority over church lands, and prelates would continue to pay homage to their fiefs. This way, the Crown kept the revenues and the final say about who lived in church properties, and the churchmen recognized their masters on secular matters. This was a defining moment in the history of the English monarchy: for the first time the king was identified as human, not sacred.

Henry's reign was going well. He had succeeded in securing his territories in France with an expert mixture of diplomacy and force; his eldest son was married to the daughter of the Count of Anjou and Maine and his daughter to the Emperor of Germany; he had two legitimate male heirs and, despite high taxes, England was peaceful. But in November 1120 both his sons were drowned when their ship went down. Henry had other sons, but they were illegitimate, leaving Henry with only one option – to nominate his daughter Matilda as heir. It was a decision that would eventually lead to civil war, but not before Henry's reign ended, which it did in 1135 when he died, according to legend, from eating a surfeit of lampreys.

A 12th-century illustration of Henry I at his coronation in 1100. Henry's promises in his coronation oath, which distanced him from his brother William II, were put in a Charter of Liberties – which became a model for the 13th-century Magna Carta.

Stephen
1135–1154

Born	c. 1097 at Blois, France
Parents	Stephen, Count of Bois, and Adela (daughter of William the Conqueror)
Crowned	(1) 26 December 1135 at Westminster Abbey; (2) 25 December 1141 at Canterbury Cathedral
Deposed	April 1141
Restored	November 1141
Married	Matilda of Boulogne
Children	5, plus at least 5 illegitimate
Died	October 1154 at Dover, Kent, aged c. 57

Henry I's nominated heir Matilda was an unwelcome choice among the Anglo-Norman nobles, so when Stephen – a favourite nephew of Henry I – made a bid for the throne he was successful. Intelligent and extremely well-liked, Stephen was quite different from his ruthless Norman predecessors. But his reign was sabotaged by rivalry from Matilda, and England was plunged into civil war resulting in 15 years of chaos and anarchy during which the Normandy territories were lost. Stephen eventually gained the upper hand, but he proved to be the last of the Norman kings when Matilda's Angevin son Henry was accepted as his successor.

Henry had made Stephen extremely wealthy by granting him lands in both England and Normandy, but he had by no means made him his heir. Almost a decade before Henry died, he had insisted that the Anglo-Norman barons swear an oath of fealty to Matilda, but when the time came for her to succeed they expressed two main objections: she was female, and she was married to Geoffrey, Count of Anjou. (As long-standing enemies of the Angevins, the Anglo-Norman barons had no desire to see one become king to Matilda's queen.) It was therefore with the majority support of the Norman barons that Stephen manoeuvred himself on to the English throne within three weeks of his uncle's death.

Stephen's affable character was a welcome contrast to the harsh and sometimes brutal personalities of his Norman predecessors, but this lack of ruthlessness was also a disadvantage for it allowed his kingdom, on both sides of the Channel, to fall into anarchy and chaos. To begin with, there were skirmishes with David I of Scotland and with Matilda's husband, Geoffrey of Anjou (who had his sights on Normandy), but the real threat to his throne came when one of Henry I's numerous illegitimate children, Robert Fitzroy of Gloucester, switched allegiance from Stephen to Matilda. At around this time Stephen started to make enemies, including his brother Henry of Blois, whose desire for the see of Canterbury was thwarted, and Ranulf, Earl of Chester, who was enraged when the castle at Carlisle was given to the Scots. Most catastrophically, in 1139 an increasingly panicky Stephen had three leading bishops, including the powerful Roger of Salisbury, arrested for plotting against him. In the same year, Matilda came over from France.

The king took Matilda captive at Arundel Castle, but then lost this early chance to gain control when she was freed. She set up a rival court in the west country, a threat that Stephen managed to contain until support for the imprisoned Bishop of Ely caused an uprising in East Anglia and then Ranulf of Chester seized Lincoln. In the ensuing battle for Lincoln (February 1141), Stephen was captured and thrown into prison at Bristol. Matilda took control, moved to London and began to rule as queen. She was high-handed, unpleasant and greedy, and support for the uncrowned queen dwindled. Stephen's queen rallied the Londoners and the usurper was driven out before her coronation.

Soon afterwards Matilda's ally Robert of Gloucester was captured, and she was forced to trade prisoners – Stephen for Robert. Although Stephen was restored to the throne (and given a second coronation in December), the civil war raged on for another six years, the constant conflicts and sieges continuing to ravage large areas of the English countryside. Opportunist barons took advantage of the mayhem to exercise their increasingly untrammelled power, building hundreds of unauthorized castles, which, according to the *Anglo-Saxon Chronicle*, were filled 'with devils and wicked men ... never

did a country endure greater misery'. In 1147 Robert of Gloucester died and Matilda gave up the fight and returned to Normandy, which had been taken by her husband in 1144. But she harboured ambitions that her son Henry might ascend to the throne of England, and in the event Matilda got her wish. Stephen's son Eustace died in the summer of 1153 and Henry was recognized as Stephen's successor. A new French dynasty had come to rule England.

This illuminated manuscript showing King Stephen on his throne is from the early 14th-century Chronicle of England *by Peter of Langtoft.*

Meanwhile...

1068	Edgar the Atheling flees to the court of Malcolm III in Scotland, where Malcolm marries Edgar's sister Margaret.
1070	Rebel leader Hereward the Wake sacks Peterborough Abbey and later seizes the Isle of Ely.
1071	Norman Archbishop Lanfranc rebuilds Canterbury Cathedral, to a design based on his abbey in Caen.
1075	Amid a major castle-building programme, William I starts the construction of Windsor Castle.
1077	The Bayeux Tapestry, showing scenes from William's conquest, is displayed for the first time in Bayeux Cathedral.
1085	William I orders the Domesday survey of the condition, population, value and ownership of his kingdom.

1066   1085   **1088**   1093   1095

1088	In a dispute with his brother Robert over the succession, William II besieges Pevensey Castle in Sussex.
1089	Archbishop Lanfranc dies and William II keeps the post open for four years, annexing the revenues for himself.
1093	Construction starts at Durham Cathedral, one of the earliest churches in Europe to use ribbed stone vaulting.
1094	William II reconsecrates Battle Abbey, the site of the Battle of Hastings and Harold II's death, after building works.
1095	Pope Urban II urges action against Muslim conquests in the Middle East, giving impetus to the Crusade movement.
1096	Building work begins at Alnwick Castle and Norwich Cathedral.

1107	Winchester Cathedral Tower collapses: superstition attributes this to the wicked bones of William Rufus, buried beneath.
1124	Henry I and his son-in-law plan to attack France; Louis VI of France mobilizes huge forces to deter them.
1127	Henry I requires the barons to swear allegiance to his daughter Matilda as his heir.
1130	As Henry I attends the consecration of Rochester Cathedral, a fire breaks out in the city, damaging the new building.
1134	Cistercian monks set up Fountains Abbey in Yorkshire. Their sheep-rearing paves the way for the area's wool industry.
1134	Henry I's brother Robert dies at Cardiff Castle, after 28 years' captivity.

1127   1134   1141   **1153**   1184

1138	David I's Scottish army attacks Northumbria, Lancashire and Yorkshire. The English defeat him in August.
1141	In June, Matilda enters London for her coronation. It never takes place: Stephen is re-crowned in December.
1146	The Welsh have a series of victories over the Normans – brothers Cadell and Maredudd regain parts of western Wales.
1147	Matilda's son Henry of Anjou invades but runs out of money: Stephen pays for Henry's return to Normandy.
1149	Henry of Anjou is knighted at Carlisle by David I of Scotland.
1153	Henry invades England again: Stephen eventually recognizes him as his heir in the Treaty of Wallingford.

Angevins & Plantagenets
1154–1399

In 1154 Norman rule gave way to the Angevin dynasty (rulers from Anjou in France) with the mighty Henry II at its head. He was the first in a long line of the fiery, good-looking Plantagenet kings whose rule over England would last for more than three centuries. Henry's phenomenal accomplishment in holding together the largest empire in western Europe heralded a fundamental reformation in Anglo-Norman culture and society.

When Henry II reigned over England its ruling class was essentially French in instinct, culture and language. Two and a half centuries later, as Richard II abdicated in favour of his cousin Henry IV, a unique English nationhood could be fully acknowledged. By then most of the French lands had been lost and the Anglo-French conflict known as the Hundred Years War had begun. Wales and Ireland had been subjugated and brought under English dominion. Governance and administration, which had proved astoundingly stable, had grown increasingly sophisticated. Above all, royal authority, which had been immeasurably strengthened by the adoption of patrilinear succession and courtly medieval ethics, was nevertheless subject to the ideals of the Magna Carta and to a fledgling parliament that had begun to represent all levels of English society.

Henry II
1154–1189

BORN	5 March 1133 at Le Mans, France
PARENTS	Geoffrey, Count of Anjou, and Empress Matilda
CROWNED	19 December 1154 at Westminster Abbey, aged 22
MARRIED	Eleanor of Aquitaine
CHILDREN	Eight, including Henry 'the Young King', Richard I, and John, plus at least 12 illegitimate
DIED	July 1189 at Chinon Castle, Anjou, aged 56

Henry II was one of the most extraordinary and charismatic characters in the history of the English monarchy. At the height of his powers he had dominion over most of the British Isles and much of France, holding together his empire by sheer force of personality and endless energy. For bringing order to an England that had been ravaged by civil war, Henry has been described, with good reason, as the greatest king that England ever knew. The only shadows on his reign were the grisly murder of his chancellor and friend Thomas Becket and the rebellion and the treachery of his own family. Henry died, at the end of a magnificent reign, the enemy of his wife and sons.

Despite his fiery temperament Henry was attractive to know. He was highly intelligent, literate, and an excellent linguist who could understand the many languages of the territories under his rule.

By the time Henry succeeded to the English throne in 1154 he was already ruling over a formidable empire. He had inherited dominion over Normandy, Anjou, Touraine and Maine when his father Geoffrey of Anjou died in 1151; and his marriage to the former wife of Louis VII, Eleanor of Aquitaine, in May 1152, had expanded the empire further until Henry held more territory than his overlord, the King of France.

In his youth, Henry had attempted to continue his mother Matilda's war against Stephen after she abandoned the conflict and returned to France in 1148; but he was unable to make any real impact and finally followed her home. In 1153, bolstered by greater resources, Henry returned to England and tussled inconclusively with Stephen and his son Eustace. However, Eustace's sudden death gave Henry the chance to secure baronial support for his appointment as Stephen's heir, so when the king died in October 1154 Henry came unopposed to the throne of England, the first monarch to do so since 1066. For the next half a century England would be a part of the largest empire in western Europe: Henry's dominion stretched from the Scottish border south to the Pyrenees.

Only a forceful personality could control such a vast and disparate territory and Henry certainly owned that, along with boundless energy and many other kingly attributes. Stocky and swarthy with piercing grey eyes, he also had a temperament that matched his red hair: his rage could be immense and on more than one occasion he is said to have been frothing at the mouth in an apoplectic fit of anger. Despite this, an informal, approachable style of kingship was his

The Angevin Empire towards the end of the 12th century. Henry II made England part of the empire when he took the throne in 1154, at the same time bringing peace after years of anarchy. Ireland, Scotland, Wales and what became southern France all paid tribute to the empire at its height. The empire began to crumble during the reign of King John, who was no match for his enemy Philip II of France. In 1259, at the Treaty of Paris, Henry III surrendered his claim to Normandy, Anjou and Poitou.

Legend

Territory taken by Henry II from his brother in 1156

Territory acquired through his sons marriage treaty in 1158/1160

Area secured by military campaign by 1171

Welsh Marches, around 1180

Vassal or paid homage territory

Territory remaining French Royal domain

trademark, reflected sartorially in the simple riding attire that he habitually wore. With such a large empire under his command Henry spent a great deal of time in the saddle, hawking and hunting as he progressed, frequently changing his schedule and happily sending numerous households and his own courtiers into panic and confusion.

If his attitude to royal life was one of studied informality, his zeal to restore his ancestral heritage and reinstate the laws and customs prevailing during the reign of his grandfather, Henry I, was intense and serious. In order to restore stability to a kingdom that had known only anarchy for the best part of two decades Henry set out to re-establish royal authority and bring the over-confident Anglo-Norman magnates (many of whom had created their own mini-kingdoms during the anarchy of Stephen's rule) to heel. The monarch destroyed so many of their unlicensed castles that he became known as 'castle-breaker'. Then he negotiated the return of Northumbria and Cumbria with the young Malcolm IV of Scotland and launched a campaign in Wales to secure the fealty of the Welsh princes. Henry was unbeatable, particularly with the backing of Pope Adrian IV who formally recognized the king's authority over all of Britain and Ireland. Four years after his accession England was secure enough for Henry to return to France. Henry would spend more than 20 years of his three-and-a-half decade reign abroad and he was renowned for riding tirelessly from one corner of his empire to the other, seeming to appear everywhere at once. It is to his credit that England not only survived his long absences in good order but flourished and expanded.

To reclaim royal authority over the judicial system (which was then regionally variable and overseen by powerful local barons) Henry set out the Assizes of Clarendon in 1166, which established the principles of Common Law – law that was consistent and accessible throughout the realm to all free men. Trial by a jury of 12 was formalized, and later circuit judges in the employ of the Crown were introduced. Then Henry tried to curb the Church's dominance and clashed head on with his confidant and chancellor, Thomas Becket, the Archbishop of Canterbury. Thomas's murder in 1170 threatened to destroy, and then later define, Henry's kingship, and it is a testament to his strength of character that though his personal remorse was great his rule remained firm.

Security of the succession was uppermost in Henry's mind. His eldest son, Henry, was confirmed as the nominated heir and, following in the tradition of French monarchs, he was crowned king-designate in 1170. (A second coronation took place in 1173 after a dispute over the legality of the first ceremony.) Henry 'the Young King' also inherited Anjou and Normandy and the second and third surviving sons Richard and Geoffrey were to be given dominion over Aquitaine and Brittany respectively. Later, in 1177, John, the youngest of Henry's four sons, was given the lordship of Ireland as his inheritance. Henry always acted decisively if he sensed a threat, and in 1171 he had launched the first of a series of invasions of Ireland to check the increasingly potent Norman baron Strongbow (Richard

Thomas Becket (c. 1118–1170)

In 1162 Henry II made his chancellor and then favourite, Thomas Becket, Archbishop of Canterbury. Thomas became a champion of the independence of the Church from royal power, thus beginning a feud with the king, and he countered Henry's attempts to collect taxes from Church lands. Four knights took Henry's remark, 'Will no one rid me of this turbulent priest' at face value and murdered Thomas while he was praying. Pope Alexander III canonized him three years later, and Canterbury became a centre of pilgrimage.

Henry's queen, the formidable Eleanor of Aquitaine, was cultured, educated and one of the most powerful women in Europe. Her first husband was Louis VII of France, but the marriage was dissolved in 1152 and shortly afterwards she married Henry. Initially devoted to one another, Henry and Eleanor became increasingly estranged until eventually the queen plotted her husband's overthrow. Eleanor outlived her husband and her son Richard I and died well into the reign of her youngest son, King John. Here, Henry is leading Eleanor into captivity after her part in the rebellion by her sons against their father in 1173.

FitzGilbert). The Irish campaign forced the submission of the last Ard Ri (High King) of Ireland and John was sent to rule in his place.

Keeping close control of his empire was one of Henry's greatest strengths but his wife and sons grew increasingly impatient with his reluctance to relinquish any real authority. This dissatisfaction was exacerbated by the fact that the passionate union between Henry and Eleanor had soured. The queen had become resentful of Henry's promiscuity – particularly with his public liaison with royal concubine Rosamund Clifford – and she retired to her court at Poitiers to plot her husband's downfall and the advancement of her favourite son, Richard. When, in 1173, the self-important Henry the Young King, Richard and Geoffrey rebelled, Queen Eleanor actively encouraged them. She was not alone: the King of France, William the Lion of Scotland and some of Henry's barons who were appalled by Becket's murder also backed the insurgency. Henry crushed the mutiny, forced the submission of the Scottish king and placed Eleanor under house arrest. John appeared to be the monarch's only loyal son.

In June 1183 Henry the Young King died of fever, and two years later Geoffrey was killed in an accident at a tournament. Henry's empire would now be divided between Richard and John, but the dynastic rivalry continued unabated. In the summer of 1189 Richard joined forces with the antagonistic Philip II (who had replaced King Louis VII on the French throne) to challenge the worn out and prematurely aged English monarch. Henry was forced to negotiate a humiliating peace and, worse still, discovered that his favourite and hitherto loyal son John had fought alongside his enemies. It was alleged that it was this heartbreak that caused Henry's death just two days later from a massive haemorrhage. Henry's heirs, for whom he had tirelessly defended and expanded his empire, were absent from his bedside. He was buried in France at Fontevrault Abbey, as was his wife.

Richard I (Lionheart)

1189–1199

BORN	September 1157 at Oxford
PARENTS	Henry II and Eleanor of Aquitaine
CROWNED	2 September 1189 at Westminster Abbey, aged 31
MARRIED	Berengaria of Navarre
CHILDREN	None legitimate; possibly two illegitimate
DIED	6 April 1199 at Chalus, France, aged 41

Richard the Lionheart spent nearly all of his reign abroad, viewing England as a source of funding for the defence of his territories in France and for his Crusade. Despite this, he is remembered as a national hero. The king was a brilliant, highly trained warrior and knight, he was tall and handsome, probably homosexual, and also arrogant, petulant and vicious. During his absences, his able Chief Justiciar, Hubert Walter, continued to expand the realm administratively, and Richard died with his father's empire still intact and a reputation celebrated in both France and England.

Miniature from Flores Historiarum, *by Matthew Paris.*

As the second (and favourite) son of Eleanor, Richard had already inherited his mother's realm, Aquitaine, in 1172. With the death of his elder brother in 1183, he also became heir to the English throne and beneficiary of Henry the Young King's titles and lands. Despite his improved fortunes, he refused to honour his father's request to pass Aquitaine to his brother John, and the family feuding was set to continue.

When Richard acceded to the throne in the summer of 1189, his attention

was centred not on the government of his new kingdom but on leaving for the Third Crusade, whose aim was to recapture Jerusalem from the Saracens. Two years prior to his accession, he had 'taken the Cross' (the symbol of the Knights Templar) and made a vow to fight the Muslim infidels. Now that he had secured the throne he was impatient to leave. He stayed in England just long enough to raise the money for his travels and to bribe his younger brother John to stay out of England while he was away. A deal was struck with William the Lion in which Richard surrendered his feudal superiority over Scotland in return for money – the Quitclaim of Canterbury – and the following summer (1190) Richard and his ally Philip II of France set off to do battle with the Kurdish warrior Saladin.

En route, Philip and Richard quarrelled: Richard was procrastinating over marrying Philip's sister Alice (he had been engaged to her for 20 years but believed that she had been his father Henry's mistress) and Eleanor was instead arranging for Richard to marry Berengaria of Navarre (who would become the only reigning queen of England never to set foot in the kingdom). This in part prompted Philip to return early from the Crusade in order to invade Normandy. To make matters worse, despite several victorious battles in the Holy Land, notably at Acre and Arsuf, Richard didn't achieve his goal of capturing Jerusalem. Instead he was obliged to come to terms with Saladin under

The myths and legends surrounding the folk hero Robin Hood have been associated with Richard the Lionheart and his nefarious brother King John. This Victorian painting by Daniel Maclise is a depiction of Robin and his band of outlaws entertaining Richard in Sherwood Forest and is on display at Nottingham Castle.

the Treaty of Ramla (1192), which agreed that Jerusalem would remain in Muslim hands but stay open to Christian pilgrims. Nonetheless, Richard's crusading exploits became the tales of a hero and bolstered his reputation. On his way home in 1192, the king was captured by Leopold of Austria (Richard had insulted him on the Crusade) and sold to the Holy Roman Emperor who demanded an outrageous ransom.

The government of England had been left in the hands of the Bishop of Ely, William Longchamp, whose high-handed, contemptuous behaviour was very quickly alienating many of the barons. John saw his opportunity. He reneged on his agreement with Richard and, with the support of disaffected barons and the ultimate aim of seizing Richard's throne, he returned to England to set up his own court. Eventually the capable Chief Justiciar Hubert Walter was put in charge. Walter managed to keep John in check and with Eleanor's help raise the huge sum demanded for the king's return. The ransom was the equivalent of three times the annual revenue of the Crown and all the population had to contribute: the tax was almost the only impact Richard's rule had on his realm.

Richard was freed and came to England in March 1194 for what was to be his last visit. After just two months he returned to France to recover the territories forfeited during his captivity. The king successfully re-conquered his lands but was killed by an infected arrow wound in 1199, at Chalus in France. He was buried in France at the same abbey as his father (and mother, who outlived him). The reign of his successor, John, would see the end of Henry II's great Angevin empire.

This illustration is from the 13th-century manuscript Descripto Terrae Sanctae *and shows Crusaders at the gates of Jerusalem. Not long after his succession, Richard I left England on a Crusade.*

John

1199–1216

Born	24 December 1167 at Oxford
Parents	Henry II and Eleanor of Aquitaine
Crowned	27 May 1199 at Westminster Abbey, aged 31
Married	(1) Isabella of Gloucester; (2) Isabella of Angouleme
Children	Five, including Henry III, plus 12 illegitimate
Died	18 October 1216 at Newark Castle, aged 48

King John, power-hungry, petulant, spoiled, cruel and vainglorious, has possibly the worst reputation of any of the kings of England. His reign oversaw the loss of most of the English-held territory in France, which his father and brother had sought to defend, and such immense fiscal pressure on his kingdom that his barons were brought to the point of open rebellion. In 1215 they forced him to sign the Magna Carta, which imposed limits on his power. When John died the following year the country was in the midst of full-scale civil war.

John was his father's favourite son but became one of England's most vilified monarchs. Despite fighting with his barons, John's reign was administratively successful and it was during this time that the first proper records were instigatged.

John, the youngest of the four sons of Henry II and Eleanor, had no inheritance, hence his nickname 'Lackland'. By way of compensation he was invested with the title Lord of Ireland and sent there to rule in 1185, but he returned just months later having alienated both the Irish and the Anglo-Norman barons. After his father's death, he attempted to seize the English throne from his brother Richard the Lionheart. Although unsuccessful, he finally acceded legitimately when Richard, on his deathbed, forgave John and named him his heir. He was crowned six weeks later.

Not long after his accession John's marriage to Isabella of Gloucester, was annulled and he married Isabella of Angouleme. However, the second Isabella had been betrothed to a French count and when Philip II of France heard of the marriage he confiscated all the English-held territory in France. During John's campaign to reclaim his French inheritance, he damaged his reputation further by killing his nephew (the son of his dead brother, Geoffrey), Prince Arthur of Brittany, whom John saw as a rival. Many French nobles then withdrew their support for the king and by 1206 all English-held land north of the Loire had been lost, winning John the even more damning sobriquet of 'Softsword'.

For the next eight years John remained in England, attending to domestic matters and feuding with the Church over his refusal to appoint the papal candidate, Stephen Langton, as Archbishop of Canterbury. As a result, the kingdom was put under a papal interdict: churches were closed and John was excommunicated in 1209. In 1212 the pope declared that John was no longer the legal king of England. This was disastrous, for John needed papal support – to keep his royal authority secure and to gain support for another massive campaign in France – so he agreed to hold his lands as a fiefdom of the papacy.

Enormous sums of money had been extracted from the king's barons by taxation to fund unsuccessful campaigns in France and, when another military offensive to regain the French territories was launched in 1213, the stakes were high. Thus the English defeat at Bouvines in 1214 spelled the beginning of the end for John. The barons broke out in open rebellion and in June 1215 forced the king to sign the Magna Carta. When John reneged on the agreement the barons retaliated by welcoming Philip's son Louis of France into England, which plunged the country into civil war. Louis gained control of the south-east and captured the Tower of London in May 1216. In October of the same year, as John headed for Lincoln, many of the crown jewels and royal treasures were swept away as the royal party crossed the Wash. By the end of the month John was dead from fever and buried in Worcester Cathedral. His nine-year-old son, Henry, was left to rule over a greatly reduced Angevin inheritance and an English kingdom now in turmoil.

Magna Carta

Disagreements with the barons over taxation instigated the drawing up of the Magna Carta (the Great Charter), which John was forced to sign at Runnymede, Surrey, in June 1215. It gave rights to the Church, the barons and the people, and imposed strict limits on royal powers. Although many of the clauses in the document were short-lived, it subjected the monarch to the law of the land – a principle that survives on the statute books to this day.

Feudalism

A key feature of medieval government in much of western Europe was the feudal system, in which the king, at the top of a strict hierarchy, was the only true landowner. The king granted land (a fief) – which included houses, tools, animals and peasants – to favoured noblemen ('tenants-in-chief', who would include barons, earls and bishops). In return, they swore an oath of loyalty to the monarch and agreed to supply him with soldiers, money or advice, and to give accommodation to the king and his entourage on his travels.

The tenants-in-chief divided the land they had been allocated among their knights or lesser lords. This was done in a ceremony that created a feudal relationship conferring

The king was powerful only if he was supported by his nobles. If they changed their allegiance they could threaten the security of the monarch and therefore of the country.

mutual obligations. It consisted of an oath of fealty, in which the vassal stated he would be faithful to the lord and provide him with specific services, such as military support when required to do so; in return, the lord was obliged to provide protection to the vassal and to maintain the land. Since each vassal swore allegiance to the next one up in the hierarchy, all could be said to have sworn loyalty to the king. However, such oaths could be made only by free men so, by definition, women, children and serfs (landless peasants) were excluded as they were essentially classed as the property of their lord.

Below the Crown and the vast estates were the manors. A manor comprised of a lord's manor house or castle, a church, a village, an area of mixed farmland (worked by peasant sub-tenants) and a demesne (the lord's home farm, used to supply his household). Such a community would have been largely self-sufficient and it would have had little contact with the outside world. Eking out a meagre existence at the bottom of the pyramid were the peasantry, comprised primarily of villeins and serfs. Villeins held land but could not sell it and they were not permitted to leave it without the permission of the lord; in return for their use of the land they also worked on the lord's land for a number of days per week. Serfs had no land of their own; instead they worked on the demesne to provide for the manor. There were also peasant freemen, who in effect rented land from the lord; they had more rights and could move elsewhere.

'Unfree' peasants belonged to the lord, so if the lord sold the land the peasants were also sold with it. Disputes were common, and the sheriff assumed the role of judge in the manor court and had the power to fine wrongdoers and administer punishment.

Land was usually managed in a system called open-field farming, in which tenants farmed their own, unfenced strips of land comprising one acre (the area that could be ploughed in a day), typically within two huge fields either side. Laxton, in Nottinghamshire, is a remarkable survival to this day of the open-field system, which virtually disappeared during the great enclosures in later centuries.

When agricultural prices were buoyant and labour was cheap – as they were in the 13th century – the lords of the manor turned to managing their demesne directly by 'high farming' (cultivating land by waged labour) and reaped in sizable profits from wool, dairy and grain products. A century later the devastating effects of the plague, known as the Black Death, meant that there was a huge labour shortage: prices dropped, wages rose, and the lords began to lease the demesne directly to the tenants. The Black Death gave many enterprising peasants opportunities to expand their land holdings, which in time meant that some peasants became relatively well off. In England, the feudal system declined over the next few centuries as the growing number of towns and increasing commerce allowed other forms of class structure to evolve.

Henry III
1216–1272

BORN	13 November 1207 at Winchester
PARENTS	King John and Isabella of Angouleme
CROWNED	(1) October 1216; (2) May 1220 at Westminster Abbey
MARRIED	Eleanor of Provence
CHILDREN	Nine, including Edward I
DIED	16 November 1272, aged 66

Henry III reigned for more than half a century. Yet he had few of the attributes required of a medieval king. He lacked military prowess, he was regarded as high-handed and ineffectual, and he favoured foreigners. His rule is best remembered for the rebellion by his English magnates. Nonetheless, Henry's patronage of the arts and his cosmopolitan mindset expanded England's cultural life, and he oversaw the building of some of the greatest examples of Gothic architecture in the country.

By the time John's young son came to the throne there was little left of the Angevin empire in France; England was in a state of civil war, and Prince Louis of France was in control of London and the south-east. The nine-year-old Henry was hurriedly crowned at Gloucester Cathedral, just ten days after his father's death, and William Marshal, Earl of Pembroke, was appointed as regent. With King John gone – and with him the prime reason

for the English barons' resentment – it was relatively easy for the well-respected Marshall to re-establish order. Louis renounced his claim to England in 1217 and Henry was crowned for a second time in 1220, on this occasion with the appropriate pomp and circumstance at Westminster Abbey.

However, tensions between the magnates and the Crown were still simmering and the Magna Carta was reissued twice before Henry reached his majority and took direct rule in 1227. Perceived as weak and indecisive, the king came under constant criticism. He alienated the English magnates with his arrogance and by bestowing favours and positions of authority on foreigners, particularly after his marriage to Eleanor of Provence in 1236 when an influx of her relatives swelled the ranks of English government. It was an inflammatory situation made worse by the imposition of hefty taxation, defeats in Wales, a disastrous campaign in France to regain lost territories, and Henry's attempts to make one of his sons King of Sicily (by funding a fruitless papal campaign there using the monies he had raised for a crusade). Added to this was the threat of excommunication because of a failed deal with the papacy. The 1259 Treaty of Paris saw the affirmation of the Plantagenet losses when everything but Gascony was signed over to the King of France.

The barons' discontent with Henry reached a climax in 1258. They rallied around Henry's disaffected brother-in-law Simon de Montfort and brought in the Provisions of Oxford, which forced the king to submit to co-rule. Three years later Henry enlisted papal support to overturn the charter and the ensuing crisis erupted into armed conflict. Capturing Henry and his son Prince Edward at the Battle of Lewes in 1264, de Montfort forced the king to acknowledge the magnates' demands and for a short time had command of the kingdom. Royal authority was reinstated thanks to the military prowess of Prince Edward (who had escaped imprisonment and formed an army) at the

Battle of Evesham in 1265. De Montfort was killed, his enemies taking their revenge upon his body by cutting off his hands, feet and genitals.

After Evesham, Edward took an increasingly active role in government leaving Henry free to spend the remainder of his reign pursuing his interests in building and artistic patronage. His zeal and passion for the arts and architecture resulted in a vibrant cultural revival. Henry ordered many buildings to be reworked or newly constructed in the sumptuous continental Gothic style; he personally oversaw the rebuilding of Westminster Abbey and a splendid new shrine for the saintly King Edward the Confessor (whom Henry promoted as something of a cult figure). If little else, when Henry III died in November 1272 he left an important architectural legacy to the country.

Henry's great love for the arts led him to commission the rebuilding of some of England's most outstanding ecclesiastical architecture. He is shown here directing the building of the cathedral at St Albans.

Edward I
1272–1307

BORN	17 June 1239 at Westminster
PARENTS	Henry III and Eleanor of Provence
CROWNED	19 August 1274 at Westminster Abbey, aged 35
MARRIED	(1) Eleanor of Castile; (2) Margaret, daughter of Philip III of France
CHILDREN	Nineteen, including Edward II
DIED	July 1307 near Carlisle, aged 68

England's medieval Edwardian era began with the heroic figure of Edward I, nicknamed 'Longshanks' because of his height. Edward possessed a fiery Plantagenet temper, but he earned the loyalty of his subjects and the devotion of his wife, and he was nothing if not determined. He fought on a crusade; subjugated Wales; defended his territories in France; expanded English administration and its judicial system; established a model of parliamentary practice; and built a string of formidable castles. In the latter part of his reign Edward embarked on a tenacious campaign to bring Scotland under his dominion, possibly the only ambition he failed to achieve.

After the chaos caused by the barons' rebellion against his father, Edward I had to regain royal authority. He achieved this with a remarkable degree of self-confidence and decisiveness, expanding and stablizing his kingdom and finally subjugating Wales.

E dward was far more suited to kingship than his father, Henry III (or his grandfather John), and it was thanks to him that Simon de Montfort's rebellion was subdued and the kingdom returned to order. Edward's skills as a warrior and politician, and his strength of character and self-confidence, secured his position as Henry's heir. When Henry died Edward was away on a crusade, but instead of hurrying to England the new king continued his travels for a further two years. He was 33 when he ascended to the throne of England and 35 at his coronation in 1274, by which time he had an impressive track record as a warrior, having seized victories over the Welsh and the rebel English barons as well as the Muslim infidels on his crusade.

The new king was a force to be reckoned with, so when Llywelyn ap Gruffydd (Llywelyn the Last) squared up to Edward's authority and failed to attend his coronation or to swear fealty (on three occasions), he met with the full force of royal wrath. Edward gathered one of the largest armies ever assembled by an English king and subjugated Llywelyn, allowing him to keep his title, Prince of Wales, but stripping him of most of his lands and any real authority.

At this stage Edward began the first wave of castle building in North Wales to keep Wales in check. The uneasy truce between the two countries lasted until 1282, when an uprising by Llywelyn's brother, Dafydd, obliged Llywelyn to join in another clash with the English, bringing Edward's patience with the Welsh to an end. Acting with characteristic decisiveness, the king ordered his forces into Wales once again, this time with the intention of outright conquest. Llywelyn was killed in battle in 1282 (his head was presented on a platter to Edward) and Dafydd was captured and later executed. Wales was brought under direct rule in March 1284 and became subject to English administration. Irksome Welsh kingdoms were replaced by shires and Edward embarked on a second wave of castle-building.

Ring of Iron

In what was perhaps the most remarkable exercise in castle-building in all medieval Europe, Edward I began constructing defensive castles around Snowdonia, the mountainous heartland of Wales, in 1278.

The first phase of building the fortresses that would collectively become known as the 'Ring of Iron' focused on the north coast and included Flint, Rhuddlan, Builth and Aberystwyth castles. All were based on the latest principles of military architecture and were characterized by huge round towers and curtain walls, concentric defences and a moat. After Wales had been conquered, Edward consolidated his rule with a second batch of castles and French bastide towns designed by the continental master mason James of St George (c. 1230–1309). The last – and largest – of these was Beaumaris, begun in 1295. Edward's crusading possibly influenced some of the architectural features of these monumental fortresses, particularly at Caernarfon (pictured), the centre of English administration in Wales.

Expulsion of the Jews

Jews settled in England after the Norman Conquest and established themselves as money-lenders to the ruling classes, but with the Holy Wars accelerating a growing anti-Semitism in Christian Europe and prospects of an alternative source of income from Italian (papal) bankers and merchants, Edward banished them. By 1290 all the Jews had been expelled from the kingdom.

Although the Welsh campaign diverted his attention, Edward knew that the efficient and straightforward administration of England was essential if he was going to fund his ambitious military campaigns, and he took a great interest in the governance of his kingdom. Early in his reign he tried to check the corruption and extortion that had been enjoyed by his barons under the chaotic reigns of John and Henry, and he was astute enough to recognize the need to gain the barons' assent before imposing measures to raise revenue for costly campaigns. Commissioners were sent out to survey the country, record local administration (known as the Hundred Rolls) and identify any judicial abuses. Edward declared that all rights had to be clearly defined and recorded, and they had to have been established before the reign of Richard I if the landowners wanted to stake a claim to rights under the pretext that they had been held for 'time immemorial'. The 1275 Statue of Westminster codified 51 existing laws, many of which originated from the Magna Carta, and by the end of Edward's reign Justices of the Peace had been introduced and Parliament had evolved to include representation from most stratas of medieval society: barons, clergy, knights and burgesses.

Edward's obsession with Scotland led him to capture the symbol of Scottish kingship, the Stone of Scone (or Destiny) and install it in Westminster Abbey in a specially made Coronation Chair.

Edward had been married at the age of 15 to Eleanor of Castile and, when she died in 1290, he was distraught. Her body was brought from Lincoln to London and Edward ordered that a monumental cross was to be erected at each of the 12 places where her funeral procession rested. These would become known as Eleanor's Crosses, one of which gave London's Charing Cross its name. Nine years later Edward would marry the daughter of Philip III of France, but for now his attention turned towards a Scottish accession crisis, which was spelling the end of his long-standing ambition to unite the kingdoms of Scotland and England.

Alexander III of Scotland had died in 1286 and Edward had betrothed his son to Alexander's granddaughter and heiress, Margaret 'the Maid of Norway'. The infant Queen Margaret died while she was travelling from Norway to Scotland, dashing Edward's hopes of unification. Edward was then invited to adjudicate on the subsequent leadership wrangles: the choice was between John Balliol and Robert Bruce. In November 1292 Edward and his assessors chose Balliol as the Scottish king. Balliol was the weaker candidate but this suited Edward, who was eager to dominate the country and confirm it as a vassal state. The Scots quickly grew tired of Balliol's lack of resistance to English demands and the discontent was inflamed by Edward's insistence that complaints about Balliol's judgements should be heard in England.

By 1294 Edward was facing problems on three fronts: in France, where Philip IV had taken possession of Gascony; in Wales, which had a new resistance leader in Madog ap Llywelyn; and with the Scots. Aside from Edward's ill-disguised intention to subjugate Scotland completely, the Scots were especially resentful at the prospect of having to pay taxes to fight the French. So aggrieved were they that in 1295 they allied themselves with France: this treaty, the Auld Alliance, would endure in various revised forms for centuries.

Once again Edward proved his strong leadership qualities. He had quelled the Welsh rebellion by the spring of 1295, returned to England and summoned the first Model Parliament to get agreement to campaigns in Scotland and France. In March 1296 he led an army of 25,000 north to Berwick. Infuriated by Scotland's alliance with France the previous year, Edward now wanted to conquer rather than just control the country. By the end of June, Balliol had been forced to surrender and Edward had appointed a trio of English magnates to run the kingdom. He seized the symbol of Scottish kingship, the Stone of Destiny, and installed it in the Coronation Chair in Westminster Abbey, where it would remain for the next seven centuries until it was returned to Scotland in 1996. The conflict in France was settled without bloodshed when the pope intervened. Edward renewed relations with the French king and reconfirmed his lordship of Gascony.

Edward's insensitive tactics and constant campaigning against the Scots lasted until the end of his reign and damaged Anglo-Scottish relations for centuries. His quest to subjugate the kingdom earned him the epithet 'the hammer of the Scots'. Old and infirm, he was embarked on yet another Scottish campaign when he fell ill and died in 1307. He was buried at Westminster Abbey.

Prince of Wales

In 1301, with Llywelyn ap Gruffydd defeated and the Welsh thoroughly tamed, Edward I appropriated the title of Prince of Wales and conferred it on his son Edward (the future Edward II). Thereafter, it was bestowed on all male heirs apparent to the English (or British) thrones, and this continues to the present day: Prince Charles is the 21st heir to hold the title.

Edward II
1307–1327

BORN	25 April 1284 at Caernarfon Castle
PARENTS	Edward I and Eleanor of Castile
CROWNED	February 1308 at Westminster Abbey, aged 23
MARRIED	Isabella (daughter of Philip IV of France)
CHILDREN	Four
DIED	September 1327 (murdered) at Berkeley Castle, aged 43

Edward II was like his father only in as much as he was tall and good-looking. He had none of Edward I's leadership qualities and he preferred artistic and aesthetic pursuits to military campaigns and the detail of government. Having inherited a stable and prosperous kingdom, he allowed it to descend into near anarchy as he continually flouted the wishes of his barons and heaped unwarranted riches and glory on unsuitable favourites. Militarily, Edward was incompetent; administratively, he made little mark. His kingship would be defined by anarchy, betrayal, abdication and – finally – by gruesome murder.

It had been Edward I's deathbed wish that his son should continue his campaign against the Scots, but Edward II merely made one desultory foray into Ayrshire before retreating to the amusements and glamour of London, where he was surrounded by a circle of fawning favourites. Chief of

these was the flamboyant and foppish Piers Gaveston, with whom Edward had a controversial relationship. Gaveston received a major earldom (Cornwall) and was appointed regent while Edward left England to marry his redoubtable French bride Isabella. Horrified at Gaveston's behaviour, the barons despatched him to Ireland but he returned within a year. Thomas Lancaster, one of England's most powerful magnates, was so enraged that he formed a council, the Lords Ordainers, which forced Edward to exile Gaveston permanently. When the unrepentant Gaveston reappeared at court he was captured by Lancaster and beheaded. The first years of Edward II's reign had not gone well.

In 1314, partly to divert the barons' attentions, Edward answered a request for help from the governor of Stirling Castle, one of the few English-held castles north of the border and under siege by Robert the Bruce's brother. Edward amassed a vast army and on 23 June squared up to a much smaller Scottish force at Bannockburn. Despite a clear numerical advantage, the two-day confrontation was a disaster for the English, and Scottish independence became to all intents and purposes a reality.

By now Edward's skills as a military tactician were regarded as derisory and England began to disintegrate into pro- and anti-royalist factions. At the head of the royalist supporters were Edward's new favourites, Hugh le Despenser and his son, friends of the late Piers Gaveston. Leading the opposition was Lancaster who, with a large private army, was effectively in control of the kingdom. When the Despensers' growing powerbase (particularly in Wales) became the focus for more discontent, Lancaster and the magnate Roger Mortimer joined forces in a bid to oust them. Edward led a campaign against the royal antagonists, executed Lancaster (in 1322) and took Mortimer prisoner. The Despensers were reinstated at Edward's side, the Lords Ordainers were dissolved, and legislation limiting royal power was annulled or ignored.

In 1324 Mortimer escaped from the Tower of London, became the lover of Edward's queen, Isabella, and joined her in France. When Edward and Isabella's son and heir arrived in France to pay homage to the French king, Isabella refused to allow him to return to England. Isabella and Mortimer planned to overthrow Edward and install the prince on the English throne: they raised a mercenary army and landed in England in September 1326. By December Edward II had been forced to abdicate in favour of his son and was imprisoned, first at Kenilworth and then at Berkeley Castle in Gloucestershire. Here, in September 1327, on the orders of Roger Mortimer and with the acquiescence of Queen Isabella, Edward II was murdered. To make his death appear natural it was necessary to avoid leaving any obvious marks of violence. When starvation proved to take too long, the murderers' aim was achieved by inserting a red hot poker up into his bowels.

Edward's favourites lost their lives whern Isabella and Mortimer rebelled. Shown here is the execution of Hugh le Despenser, at Bristol on 27 October 1326. His son was hanged at Hereford in November of the same year.

Birth of Parliament

The modern British parliament has a legacy that stretches back to just after the Norman Conquest, when an informal group of nobles and high-ranking clergy met to advise the kings of England. Soon it developed into a more formal assembly, the Great Council, meeting three times a year to assist the king in governing his kingdom and making laws.

Limping from crisis to crisis, Henry III unwittingly brought about the beginnings of modern parliament with his bad decisions, punishing taxation and high-handed manner. Antagonizing the barons at every turn, he finally drove them to rebel. In 1258, a group led by Henry's brother-in-law, Simon de Montfort (6th Earl of Leicester), unable to tolerate the situation any longer, forced the king to accept the Provisions of Oxford (the plan was drawn up in Oxford). This created a Privy Council of 15 members selected by the barons to act as an advisory body to the king, with elected officials overseeing the administration. The council met in parliaments held three times a year and for the first time the monarch had to share power. In the following year the Provisions of Oxford was replaced by the more detailed Provisions of Westminster, which included inheritance and tax reforms, but it was not to last and with papal support Henry was able to overthrow the charter.

Civil war followed. De Montfort defeated Henry at the Battle of Lewes in 1264, a victory so complete that de Montfort was effectively able to take control of the realm.

Alexander rey Scotore & ... lewellin princeps wallie

PARLIAMENT
OF EDWARD I

The future Edward I defeated Simon de Montfort in battle but he embraced the idea of a parliament. Depicted here is a session of parliament under Edward. By the end of Edward's reign, parliament (which comes from the French work parler 'to talk') usually had representation from most upper levels of medieval society: the barons, clergy, knights and burgesses.

But in 1265 he was killed at the Battle of Evesham and the rebellion collapsed. His innovation was to last for posterity, however: his summoning of knights, burgesses and commoners – the first time the people had been represented – to attend Parliament can be said to be the origin of the concept of modern representative parliament, though variations in membership continued well into the 14th century. Although, with de Montfort's loss, Henry was restored to power, the growing importance and power of Parliament was now irrefutable and Henry was forced to make some conciliatory moves, which were recognized under the Statute

The seal of Simon de Montfort (c.1150–1218) who tired of Henry III's poor leadership and believed that Henry needed a council of nobles to advise him. Although Henry agreed to a council, he soon started to ignore their advice. De Montfort defeated the king in battle and set up what was in effect the first parliament.

of Marlborough, passed in 1267. Many of the clauses in that document remain in force today.

Edward I went one stage further in 1295 in summoning to Parliament two knights and lesser Church figures from each county and, from each of various towns, two representatives that did not belong to the clergy or aristocracy. His motive was to gain more widespread support and raise money for his military campaigns. Termed by historians in the 19th century as the Model Parliament, this set the pattern that was to follow. Two years later he consented not to collect taxes without parliamentary consent.

Further refinements took place in the 14th century under Edward III. From 1341 two houses of parliament were emerging – the 'lower house' and the 'upper house' – which sat separately and would eventually be defined as the Commons and the Lords. Later in Edward's reign, in 1376, a parliament was called to halt growing corruption associated with Edward's mistress and to curb taxation and high expenditure at court and on foreign campaigns. This came to be known as the Good Parliament. It lasted nine weeks and during it, the first speaker, Sir Thomas Hungerford, was elected to represent the Commons. Shortly after the concept of impeachment emerged, in which the House of Commons had the power to accuse officials of abusing their authority.

Later, under Henry V, the Commons and the Lords had equal power in passing legislation, sealing the right of the masses to be heard in government.

Edward III
1327–1377

BORN	13 November 1312 at Windsor Castle
PARENTS	Edward II and Isabella of France
CROWNED	1 February 1327 at Westminster Abbey, aged 14
MARRIED	Philippa of Hainault
CHILDREN	Thirteen plus at least three illegitimate (by Alice Perrers)
DIED	June 1377 at Sheen Palace, Surrey, aged 64

Edward III's 50-year reign saw the restoration of good relations with the English barons, who flocked to his colourful and cultured court with renewed respect for the monarchy. For a time at least, Edward and his son Edward, the Black Prince, expanded England's holdings in France to the extent that they nearly matched those of the great Angevin emperor Henry II. However, Edward outlived his successes: by the time he died, plague had ravaged his kingdom, most of the French territory was lost, and the enormous cost of his campaigns had made him unpopular and indebted. Nevertheless, he is remembered as one of England's greatest warrior kings.

The forced abdication of Edward II put his son on the throne of England when he was still a boy of 14, and for the first few years of his reign Edward III was in the thrall of his father's murderers

– his mother, Isabella, whom history labelled 'the she-wolf of France', and her ambitious lover, Roger Mortimer, who had virtual rule of the kingdom. But three years after his accession Edward III felt compelled to assert himself when Mortimer had his uncle, the murdered king's younger brother, executed. Edward had Mortimer executed for treason and Isabella was banished to Norfolk where she lived harmlessly for the rest of her days, out of the political limelight. Edward was now free to rule, which he did with the support of the barons who welcomed a leader showing all the qualities required of a great medieval king. There would be no favourites or louche behaviour in the court of this third Edward; his interests lay firmly in the direction of most red-blooded Plantagenet males – war and women, with a little culture, pageantry and high living thrown in for good measure.

The king's main tactic to reunite the Crown and his subjects was to use Parliament as an arena for debate and consultation and so secure backing from his barons to raise the resources for expansionist campaigns. His ambitious plans started with Scotland. Shortly after his accession he had been forced to sign over Scottish independence at the Treaty of Northampton (1328), but this didn't suit his aspirations and he was anxious about the Scottish-French alliance. A child-king, David II, had replaced Robert the Bruce on the Scottish throne, and Edward used this as an opportunity to support Edward Balliol's claim to the kingdom. King David was overthrown in 1332, but Balliol's hold on rule was tenuous, and it became clear that he could not continue without the help of the English king. It came in July 1333, when Edward effectively ended the Wars of Scottish Independence by inflicting a crushing defeat on the Scots at Halidon Hill, near Berwick-upon-Tweed. Nevertheless Balliol failed to maintain his grip on the kingdom and was deposed for a third (and final) time in 1336.

By now though, Edward's attentions were on France as his Gascony lands had been seized and the French were making incursions on the English coast. Through his mother, Edward was a legitimate rival to the French throne; although it was a prize that he had not pursued in 1324 when his uncle Charles IV had died, it now seemed wise to assert his claim.

A propaganda campaign was launched in England and resources (both money and men) were raised for the campaign for the French throne; thus at the start of November 1337 Edward stated his intentions to fight for his right to France, and the extended Anglo-French conflict, later known as the Hundred Years War, began.

Early attempts to overcome the French were inconclusive, partly because Philip VI refused to fight – even when Edward offered him the chance to settle their rivalry in one-to-one combat. English fortunes turned in 1345 when the Earl of Derby swept through Gascony, successfully reclaiming territory. Bolstered by this, Edward launched a major invasion of Normandy in

Windsor Castle has been a home to the English monarchy for more than 900 years. Edward III greatly extended the residence and built St George's Hall.

July 1346. His armies inflicted terrible destruction and this time Philip was compelled to act. In August, French forces faced up to the English at Crécy. The French had the numerical advantage but superior English battle tactics won the day and Edward's army moved on to besiege Calais for several months; the town would remain in English hands for the following two centuries.

Meanwhile, under the terms of the Auld Alliance, Philip appealed to the Scots to create a diversionary tactic on English soil. David II (who had been restored to the Scottish throne) responded in October 1346 by invading the north of England with the ultimate goal of taking Durham. The English army under William la Zouche, Archbishop of York was, once again, greatly outnumbered, but the clash at Neville's Cross brought another resounding English victory and the King of Scotland was taken prisoner.

In 1348 Edward – inspired by Arthurian ideals – founded the Most Noble Order of the Garter, an exclusive chivalric order that has its spiritual home in Windsor Castle's Chapel of St George. It bound Edward and his barons together as partners 'both in peace and war'. In the same year, there were the first cases of bubonic plague in England. The social, spiritual and economic toll of the pestilence was profound; and fighting with the French was brought to a temporary halt. It resumed after French rule passed to Philip VI's son, Jean (the Good), in 1350. Edward's son the Black Prince, was responsible for the second of the great English victories in the Hundred Years War, at Poitiers in 1356. King Jean II was captured and brought to England, where now two foreign kings were imprisoned.

The French campaign reached its height in 1360 with the Treaty of Brétigny. Edward had to renounce his claim to the French throne, although English dominion over nearly 25 per cent of France was recognized. However, keeping a hold of such a vast amount of land was to prove impossible. The toll of the plague (which returned again in 1361) and the accession of an aggressive Charles V to the French throne began to undermine English territories in France; by 1375 the French had retaken everything but Calais and a part of Gascony.

During the last years of his reign Edward lost his grip on the country and was increasingly unpopular. Contributing to this was the death in 1369 of his wife of 40 years, Queen Philippa, which allowed Edward's power-hungry mistress Alice Perrers to wield her malign influence. Eventually, the Good Parliament, which sat in 1376 in order to moderate the growing royal corruption, banished Perrers. But political unrest caused by rivalry between the Black Prince and John of Gaunt (another of Edward's sons) continued. When the Black Prince died, Parliament recognized the king's grandson Richard as heir to the throne.

The Black Death

A seismic change in Europe occurred with the advent of the plague. In Britain it killed something between 30 and 50 per cent of the population. Carried by rat fleas, this lethal infection spread mercilessly. First it devastated Bristol, before hitting London in September 1348, then continuing to East Anglia, Wales and the Midlands in 1349; it reached Scotland in 1350. According to an observer, 'The plague raged to such a degree that the living were scarce able to bury the dead.' Renewed outbreaks continued over the next 50 years. For some of the peasant class the Black Death improved their lot: land was cheap and they were able to increase their holdings. In particular, the number of yeoman farmers increased, which was significant when they later protested at an excessive poll tax: their riots culminated in the Peasants' Revolt of 1381.

Hundred Years War

This drawn-out conflict between England and France in fact lasted for more than a hundred years – from 1337 to 1453. The term 'Hundred Years War' was coined in the 19th century, and conveniently weaves together a series of campaigns and battles of a seemingly endless power struggle either side of the Channel.

By the early 13th century England had lost Normandy, Anjou, Maine and Poitou but it had held on to Gascony, which had supplied England with most of its wine. During the Hundred Years War, England first increased its lands in France, then lost all of them apart from Calais. At its height the English territory included the whole of western France from Brittany down to the south-west corner, as well as Ponthieu and Calais in the north. Many castles built by the English in France survive to this day.

The war started with the attempted seizure of the French throne by Edward III, whose claim was derived from his mother. Philip VI of France retaliated by trying to take back the English gains. Edward invaded Normandy in 1346 and defeated the French at Crécy; meanwhile the Scots, allied to the French cause against a common enemy, invaded northern England but met with defeat at Neville's Cross near Durham.

A year later Calais was captured for the English, and during the following decade Edward's son, the Black Prince, raided Bordeaux and elsewhere in the south-west. Jean II of France was captured among many others, which paved the way for negotiation through the Treaty of Brétigny in May 1360: Edward renounced his claim to the throne but took sovereign control of more territories – Calais, Ponthieu, Poitou and Aquitaine. The Black Prince ruled from Bordeaux until his death in 1376.

In the aftermath of victory, Parliament agreed to pay for the costs of the war, and peace was at last made with the Scots. For some years all seemed well. But in 1369, the new French king, Charles V, claimed those lands over which

The Black Prince was an outstanding military leader who fought with his father at Crécy at the age of 16. In his day the prince was referred to as Edward of Woodstock, later he became known as the Black Prince possibly because he wore black armour. Here, Edward III is granting the principality of Aquitaine to the Black Prince.

Edward asserted sovereignty. The French navy outpowered the English, and raids were made across the Channel and along England's southern and eastern shores. The threat of the Auld Alliance between France and Scotland again reared its head. In France, however, the English still had some control, and civil war between Burgundian and Armagnac groups made France – by now ruled by the insane king Charles VI – even more vulnerable. Henry V invaded in 1415, captured Harfleur and was massively victorious at Agincourt. He followed up his successes with another wave of conquests in Normandy. Rouen fell to him in 1419.

Henry VI was the only king of England ever to have also been crowned King of France – in Paris in 1431. But holding the French territories proved increasingly expensive and Henry VI signed a truce in 1444, at which time he married French heiress Margaret of Anjou. The French recovered – thanks in no small measure to the efforts of Joan of Arc – and blockaded Bordeaux in 1451. Normandy had been retaken in 1450 and two years later Gascony was also lost. The battle at Castillon heralded the end of the Hundred Years War. Only Calais was left under English control, remaining so until the reign of Mary Tudor.

This map shows France as it was in the late 1420s, with much under the control of the English and Burgundians. The name is misleading, since there was not a hundred years of continuous war, but rather a series of campaigns, battles, setbacks and victories by both sides, and changes of sides and allegiances. Crucial battles: Sluys 1340, Crecy 1346, Poitiers 1356, Agincourt 1415 and Castillon 1453 (the last) are marked. French fortunes began to turn in their favour with the taking of Orleans by Joan of Arc in 1429.

Legend:
France in the 1420s
Held by the English and Burgundians
Held by the French

ENGLAND

River Thames

London

Southampton

Sluys

Calais

Agincourt

Crécy

Ponthieu

Harfleur

River Seine

Rouen

Normandy

Burgundy

Paris

Brittany

Orléans

Troyes

River Loire

FRANCE

Poitou

Poitiers

Aquitaine

Bordeaux

Castillon

Quercy

River Gironde

Rouergue

Gascony

Navarre

Aragon

Catalonia

HOLY ROMAN Empire

Richard II
1377–1399

BORN	6 January 1367 in Bordeaux
PARENTS	Edward, the Black Prince, and Joan of Kent
CROWNED	16 July 1377 at Westminster Abbey, aged ten
MARRIED	(1) Anne of Bohemia; (2) Isabella of France
CHILDREN	None
DIED	February 1400, Pontefract Castle, Yorkshire, aged 33

The reign of Richard II was a dichotomy. He was a well-educated, shrewd and supremely cultured monarch and a great patron of the arts, but he was also an extravagant, dogmatic and despotic ruler who took little notice of his barons' interests and eschewed Parliament. Richard's unshakeable belief in absolute royal power and his inability to gain the loyalty of his most powerful subjects inevitably led to rebellion. In 1399 Richard II was deposed, imprisoned and then starved to death.

Richard II's coronation was celebratory and splendid, a welcome diversion from the turbulent last years of Edward III's reign. England was tense though: the effects of the plague had been catastrophic in every way, the wars in France and Scotland had bled the kingdom dry, and the new king was still a minor. Four years into Richard's reign, in what was coined the Peasants' Revolt, he faced an uprising by yeomen who could no longer endure

the burden of extortionate taxation. The 14-year-old Richard's courage in facing them and quelling the rebellion enhanced his authority immeasurably. It seemed he might, after all, make a worthy king. For him, the incident served only to reinforce his conviction that he was God's representative on earth and that his right to rule was absolute.

This attitude antagonized the barons, who were also dismayed by the king's appointment of his favourites, including Robert de Vere, Earl of Oxford, as his closest advisors; furthermore, his interests lay in the patronage of arts and culture rather than in military conquest. In 1385, in an attempt to placate them, Richard led a military campaign (the only one of his reign) into Scotland, but it was a disappointing affair: the Scottish army were never encountered and the king quickly returned to England. Opposition to Richard's government reached its height when in 1386, without parliamentary consent, de Vere was appointed as Regent of Ireland. Five magnates, including the king's uncle (the Duke of Gloucester) and his cousin Henry Bolingbroke (the son of John of Gaunt, Edward III's son), formed a council known as the Lords Appellants. They presided over the 'Merciless Parliament' of 1388, effectively seizing control of England by banishing or executing Richard's circle of cronies.

When the king reached his majority in 1389, he was able to assume direct rule and choose his own advisers. With this new independence, Richard's court became cultured and extravagant. He relentlessly promoted his image and majesty but, cleverly, he also kept his cool, inflicting no serious reprisals on those who had opposed him. In 1394 he launched a semi-successful campaign to subdue Ireland – Richard II was the only reigning monarch to set foot in Ireland between 1210 and the late 17th century – and he negotiated a 30-year truce with France, taking the seven-year-old daughter of the king of France as his wife in 1396.

With these successes, Richard's authority strengthened and the treacherous magnates were in increasing danger. In the summer of 1397 the five former Lords Appellants were arrested and executed or exiled and their forfeited estates were divided up among royal favourites. Henry Bolingbroke, Gaunt's son, was banished for ten years. Free from restraint, the king lost the last vestiges of wisdom and became a paranoid, power-crazed despot. When, in 1399, John of Gaunt died, Richard seized his lands and extended Bolingbroke's banishment to life. This alarmed his barons to such an extent that when, shortly afterwards, Richard and his supporters left for a second campaign in Ireland – giving Bolingbroke the opportunity to land in England with a small army – allegiance to the absent Richard collapsed. Bolingbroke saw the chance not only to reclaim his father's legacy but to claim the throne. By August 1399 Richard had been forced to surrender to Bolingbroke and was imprisoned in the Tower of London. In September Richard abdicated and was moved to the castle at Pontefract where, within a few months, he died of starvation.

The Peasants' Revolt

In June 1381, a mutinous rabble of disaffected yeoman from Kent and Essex marched on London. Plundering, ransacking and murdering as they went, the rebels advanced on the Tower of London where the king was taking refuge. Courageously Richard met with the dissenters and managed to diffuse the situation, even though a member of the royal entourage killed one of the rebel leaders, Wat Tyler. Richard made promises to his subjects that he never kept but from then on, although pockets of further insurrection were brutally dealt with and the rebellion achieved little, Richard was regarded as a champion of the people.

Meanwhile...

1154   1178   1191   1203   1212

1296   Edward seizes the Stone of Scone, symbol of Scottish nationhood. It remains in Westminster Abbey until 1996.

1305   The Scottish nationalist William Wallace is executed in London.

1311   Robert the Bruce of Scotland leads forces into Cumbria where they ravage the English.

1312   Throughout Europe, members of the Knights Templar are arrested and their property seized on the pope's orders.

1314   Completion of 'old' St Paul's Cathedral in London

1316   Torrential rain causes a grain harvest failure, leading to soaring prices, fear of famine and civil unrest.

1318   A council is established to oblige the king to call a parliament and to accept the 'Ordinances', or barons' demands.

1235   1296   1318   **1386**   1399

1338   The French use Genoese troops to attack ports on the south coast of England.

1353   Fifteen 'staples' are set up in English towns to collect, store and tax wool and resolve disputes about quality.

1382   The Peasants' Revolt, protesting against Richard II's taxes, begins in southern England.

1386   Rough seas confound the plans of a 100,000-strong French force trying to invade England.

1388   The English under Henry Hotspur suffer huge losses as the Scots rout them at the Battle of Otterburn.

1394   Winchester College opens. Founded by William Wykeham it provides students for his New College, Oxford University.

Lancaster & York
1399–1485

The acquisition of the English throne by the Duke of Lancaster's son, Henry Bolingbroke, perpetuated Plantagenet rule. However, the questionable legitimacy of Henry's incumbency not only tarnished this able king's reign but it rocked the firmly established principle of inherited kingship, thereby undermining the stability that strict rules of succession had helped to ensure since the early 13th century. The consequences of this only became apparent when the madness of Bolingbroke's grandson, Henry VI, opened up a window of opportunity for the York dynasty to stake a rival claim. So began three decades of internecine fighting – the Wars of the Roses – which ended with the demise of the centuries-old Plantagenet line. Throughout the reigns of the Lancastrian and Yorkist monarchs the fortunes of England waxed and waned. During the short but remarkable reign of Bolingbroke's son, the indomitable Henry V, the House of Lancaster regained the French throne, a prize that would be lost by his son Henry VI – whose ineptitude would finally also lose him the English Crown to the first Yorkist king, Edward IV. Under Edward's able and focused rule, the kingdom enjoyed a period of economic prosperity and modest expansion, but his untimely death led to the rise of the English monarchy's most vilified incumbent, Richard III and, with his death, the succession of the House of Tudor.

Henry IV
1399–1413

BORN	1366 or 1367 at Bolingbroke Castle, Lincolnshire
PARENTS	John of Gaunt and Blanche of Lancaster
CROWNED	13 October 1399 at Westminster Abbey, aged 32
MARRIED	(1) Mary of Bohun (d. 1394); (2) Joan of Navarre
CHILDREN	Six, including Henry V
DIED	March 1413 at Westminster Abbey, aged 45

Henry Bolingbroke came to the throne by the simple expedient of seizing it from Richard II. His claim was tenuous, and the means by which he asserted it were questionable to say the least, but he was undoubtedly better equipped for medieval kingship than his predecessor had been. In his youth, Henry had all the vigour, charm and accomplishments of the most successful of his Plantagenet ancestors. However, the incessant opposition to his rule, the phenomenal cost of the campaign to subdue his opponents and his own remorse for his treatment of Richard II took their toll on Henry's health. He left his kingdom and the succession secure, but he died a wasted, broken man.

Henry was intelligent, literate and cultured, extremely pious and politically astute, and a master warrior whose adventurous spirit had taken him to Lithuania to fight alongside the Teutonic Knights. Clearly, he

Henry 4.ᵗʰ
K. of Eng.ᵈ

also had great strength of character, for in his bid to depose Richard he secured the support of important magnates – despite the existence of a designated heir, Edmund, 5th Earl of March. Edmund was a direct descendant of Edward III's second son, Lionel, Duke of Clarence; Henry, on the other hand, was the son of Edward's younger son, John of Gaunt, Duke of Lancaster. But, Henry was persuasive, and since Edmund was still a boy Parliament accepted him.

Consolidating his kingship was not so easy, however. Just months after his proclamation as king in September 1399, he was facing rebellion from the supporters of the imprisoned Richard. He responded by ordering Richard's death (by starvation, so there would be no brutal marks) and then having his corpse publicly displayed so he would no longer be a focus for dissent. Then, in 1400, a revolt in Wales began when Owain Glyn Dwr declared himself Prince of Wales and persuaded Edmund Mortimer (uncle of the Earl of March) to join his rebellion. Even more seriously, Henry's erstwhile supporters, the Percy family – which included the Earl of Northumberland, the Earl of Worcester, and Northumberland's son, the hot-headed Henry Percy ('Harry Hotspur') – began a determined campaign to bring Henry down. As ever, Henry reacted swiftly and decisively. At the Battle of Shrewsbury in July 1403 the king and his army defeated the Percy forces. Hotspur was killed and Worcester was executed soon after but this did not stem the opposition. The Earl of Northumberland schemed with the Archbishop of York, Edmund Mortimer and the Earl Marshal of England – as well as with Owain Glyn Dwr – to remove Henry and divide the kingdom between them. Henry discovered the conspiracy and Northumberland escaped to Scotland, but Mortimer was imprisoned and both the archbishop and the earl marshal were executed. (The killing of the archbishop was regarded as scandalous and did nothing for Henry's popularity.)

When the Welsh rebellion came to an end in 1409, Henry's position seemed secure: the rebels in England and Wales had been subdued; James I of Scotland was captive in England (Henry had taken him prisoner two years earlier); and France, although it had never recognized Henry as king and it had offered real support to the Welsh, was too occupied with its own internecine conflicts to pose a threat. But Henry was not at ease. Prematurely aged, and unable to reconcile his position or the manner in which he came to it, his last years were spent struggling with severe ill health, a guilty conscience, and the misery of living in the shadow of his more popular son, the future Henry V. In 1413, the once vigorous monarch died, disfigured from disease – the result, it was alleged, of divine retribution for the overthrow and murder of a legitimate king.

Owain Glyn Dwr

Owain Glyn Dwr was a prosperous Welsh squire whose loyalty to the English Crown seemed well established. But then a minor dispute with an English neighbour sparked local trouble that escalated into national rebellion. Owain proclaimed himself Prince of Wales in 1400 and persuaded his son-in-law, Edmund Mortimer (who was also the brother of Hotspur's wife), to side with him against the king. He also managed to gain support in both Scotland and France. In 1404, he called the first Welsh parliament. But his ambition was not merely to oust the English from Wales and secure Welsh independence: through his pact with the English rebels, his ultimate aim was to take a share in the spoils when Henry was finally overthrown. It was not to be. After years of guerrilla warfare, besieged Welsh forces in Harlech Castle were finally forced into submission in 1409. Owain Glyn Dwr himself was never captured. His end is unknown.

Henry V
1413–1422

BORN	16 September 1387 at Monmouth Castle
PARENTS	Henry IV and Mary de Bohun
CROWNED	9 April 1413 at Westminster Abbey, aged 25
MARRIED	Catherine of Valois (d. 1437)
CHILDREN	One (Henry VI)
DIED	August 1422 at Bois de Vincennes, France, aged 35

Henry of Monmouth, son of Henry IV, was the last of the great warrior kings of the Middle Ages. In his short but extraordinary reign he expanded England's territory in France, became the heir to the French throne and led his army in one of the most iconic victories in English history at Agincourt. Skilful military leadership was matched by his abilities as administrator and politician: despite requiring enormous sums for his campaigns he held the support of his barons and Parliament throughout his reign. Premature death robbed Henry of his chance to wear the crown of France but he passed straight into legend as one of England's most heroic leaders.

Despite tales of Henry's boisterous youth, the king was intensely pious and ascetic, taking a hard line against lawlessness and heretics. Nevertheless, Henry was a champion of the people and ruled that government documents were to be written in English for the first time.

Shortly after his father deposed Richard II, Henry was created Prince of Wales and put under the guardianship of Henry Percy and his son Harry Hotspur. When the Percys' friendship with the king turned to rebellion the young prince fought valiantly (despite a serious arrow injury to his face) alongside his father at the Battle of Shrewsbury in 1403, where his erstwhile friend and mentor Hotspur was killed.

Henry had been commanding military campaigns from an early age. Under the expert tutelage of the Percys he developed into an exceptionally able soldier, learning strategy during the Welsh campaign against Owain Glyn Dwr. When Henry IV's health worsened the prince involved himself in the administration of the kingdom and did it so impressively that there was talk of the king abdicating in favour of his son. The tension this created between the pair was exacerbated by their quarrels over France. The French king's bouts of madness had resulted in a state of anarchy, and the ensuing hostilities over the regency and guardianship of the royal children was presenting an almost irresistible opportunity to try to reclaim some English territory. Henry and his father disagreed about which of the French factions to back: Charles VI's cousin, the Duke of Burgundy, or Charles's brother, the Duke of Orleans (who had the support of the Armagnacs). Two modest expeditions were launched: one led by the Prince of Wales to aid the Burgundians and the other instigated by Henry IV in favour of the Armagnacs; neither of them reached a conclusive outcome.

Thus the final years of Henry IV's reign were fraught with conflict and accusation, a potentially lethal situation that was diffused only with the king's death and his heir's unopposed succession to the throne in March 1413. The newly crowned Henry V was free to draw a line under the doubts over his father's accession and to pursue what he believed to be England's rightful heritage in France. His plans, which were far from diffident, had the almost

Agincourt is remembered as one of England's most iconic battle victories. Against enormous odds in October 1415, Henry V succeeded in destroying the chivalry of France: the victory was not only a military success, it also engendered the whole ideal of English nationhood.

universal approval of his barons and of Parliament and, much to Henry's credit, he held on to their support to the end of his reign. His political acumen and statesmanship matched his talents as a military strategist, and one of his first acts as king was to reinstate the lands and power of many of his father's opponents, including those of the Earl of March. This paid dividends: a couple of years later the earl demonstrated his loyalty by reporting a conspiracy against the king; the plotters were executed. It was the only baronial revolt that Henry would face. In another shrewd move he arranged a state burial for the body of Richard II and had it reinterred in the tomb that Richard had built for himself in Westminster Abbey. This may have been an act of loyalty (Henry was a guest at Richard's court while his father was in exile and accompanied the king on the fateful trip to Ireland in 1399, and Richard refused to take him hostage), but in any case it was a masterstroke in terms of propaganda.

Henry in France

Nearly all Henry's actions during the first two years of his reign were mindful of his ultimate aim to reinstate an empire and claim the French throne, just as Edward III had done. Astutely, he opened negotiations with both factions in the French conflict and played them off against each other, giving the appearance of having tried diplomacy even though he had every intention of going to war. By the time negotiations ended in the early summer of 1415 Henry had secured funding and raised an army for his campaign. In August an English force of around 10,000 invaded Normandy and besieged the naval port of Harfleur. The siege, which lasted a little over a month, was ultimately successful but took its toll on the English troops. They were weary and weakened by dysentery, and winter was approaching. Henry decided to head for the English stronghold of Calais.

While the English were occupied with Harfleur, Charles d'Albret, the Constable of France, amassed a feudal army of over 20,000, and it was this vast fighting force that confronted the depleted English troops (of around 6,000) at Agincourt on 25 October 1415. The battle took place in a sea of mud, which favoured the more lightly armoured English troops as it allowed them to move more freely than their opponents; and the English had their longbows, which had in the past proved an advantage. Nevertheless, the odds against an English victory were so tremendous that their triumph was nothing short of astounding. Estimates of the French losses have been put as high as 7,000 men or more against less than 500 of Henry's army. In terms of territory, Henry's Agincourt campaign gained little, but the destruction of the French military nobility made the success of his subsequent campaigns far easier, if not a foregone conclusion. In addition it boosted Henry's support at home and most importantly earned him the backing of the Holy Roman Emperor.

By August 1417 Henry was back in France making the most of his previous success. Two years later, with Normandy already under his control, Henry was outside the walls of Paris, which was at the time in the hands of his tacit supporter the Duke of Burgundy. In September the duke was murdered while he was at a meeting with the dauphin (Armagnacs); the Burgundians gave their wholehearted support to Henry's claim to France and cemented it with the Treaty of Troyes in May 1420. The treaty stated that Henry V would inherit the French throne after the death of Charles VI and marry Charles's daughter Catherine of Valois; in return, Henry was to avenge the murder of the duke by continuing the war against the disinherited dauphin. The wedding took place at Troyes Cathedral in June 1420 and Henry resumed his war with the dauphin and the Armagnacs. Henry was now the dominant power in western Europe, and in February of the following year he returned to England with his queen for her coronation and an exultant tour of the country. The couple's only child, a boy, the future Henry VI, was born at Windsor early in the December of 1421.

Henry never saw his son, for by the time of his birth he was back campaigning in France. Earlier in the year, his brother Thomas, Duke of Clarence, had been killed in the Battle of Baugé, one of the first English defeats of the Hundred Years War, and Henry had been keen to return to France and resume the conflict himself. His last victory was at the dauphin's stronghold of Meaux in May 1422. At the end of August, weakened by dysentery and a hard winter of campaigning, Henry died at Vincennes, outside Paris, having first made plans for his son's minority. His body was brought back to England and buried at Westminster Abbey.

In his short reign Henry had proved himself to be not only an exceptionally competent military strategist but an inspirational leader whose energy, iron will, piety and strong sense of justice earned him wide respect and admiration. Had he lived for another six weeks he would have realized his ambition and inherited the throne of France; instead he left that legacy to his infant son.

The wedding of Henry V to Catherine of Valois, the daughter of Charles VI of France, took place at Troyes Cathedral on 2 June 1420. After Henry's death Catherine began a secret relationship with the Welsh courtier Owen Tudor and through him became the grandmother of the first of the Tudor kings, Henry VII. In 1428 Parliament forbade Catherine from marrying without the consent of the king and council, but Catherine and Owen married anyway and went on to have five children.

R · DE · FRANCE · ꝏ ꝶ · LE · CINQVIESME ·

Henry VI
1422–1461; 1470–1471

BORN	6 December 1421 at Windsor
PARENTS	Henry V and Catherine of Valois
CROWNED	(1) November 1429 at Westminster Abbey, aged seven; (2) October 1470 at St Paul's Cathedral, aged 48. (Also as Henri II of France, December 1431 at Cathedral of Notre Dame de Paris, aged ten)
MARRIED	Margaret of Anjou (d. 1482)
CHILDREN	One
DIED	May 1471 (murdered) at the Tower of London, aged 49

Henry VI was less than a year old when he inherited the crowns of both England and France, and almost immediately his father's empire began to shrink. When Henry reached his majority he was overwhelmed by the demands of kingship, and his reign oversaw the loss of virtually all of England's territories in France. In 1453 he was plunged into the first episode of insanity that allowed the York dynasty to stake a claim on the throne. Henry VI lost his crown, his son and eventually his life.

On his deathbed in France, Henry V had made provision for his son's minority by appointing his brother the Duke of Gloucester as Protector of England and another brother, the Duke of Bedford, as regent in France. However, since the disinherited dauphin, Charles VI's

son, was also declared King of France, hostilities were set to continue. Neither Bedford nor his opponent had the strength to end the stalemate. Then in 1429, Joan of Arc reversed French fortunes by leading an army to victory in the besieged city of Orleans. The dauphin was crowned Charles VII at Rheims in June. In response the ten-year-old Henry was taken to Paris to be crowned Henri II; he was the only king ever to be formally crowned in both kingdoms.

Henry's coronation failed to rally the French to his side: in 1435 the Burgundians ended their alliance with England and followed Charles VII. Paris fell to Charles the following year. Meanwhile, in England, the huge cost of the war in France and Gloucester's unpopularity caused squabbling among the barons and in Parliament. Things did not improve when Henry reached his majority in 1437. The king was uninterested in government and had no control over the majority of his magnates, so he invested authority in a few favourites, primarily the Earl of Suffolk, who in 1444 negotiated a five-year truce with France. Under the treaty Henry would marry Charles's niece Margaret of Anjou (in April 1445), and the territory of Maine would be returned. This second condition was kept secret from Parliament until Margaret and Suffolk succeeded in pressing the king to honour it, which he did in 1447. This caused popular outrage and angered the pro-war magnates, including Gloucester; and it did not even achieve the king's aims, for it failed to placate the French.

The situation in France was turning to crisis in England, and Henry was beginning to fear for his life. So when Suffolk and Margaret persuaded the king that Gloucester was plotting against him, Gloucester was immediately arrested. He died a week later. Suffolk then shifted his anti-war stance and invaded Brittany, precipitating the loss of Normandy, which fell in 1450. For this the earl was impeached and executed. Paying no heed to increasing discontent about corruption and weakness among the king's advisers, Henry stirred the situation even further by replacing Suffolk with another favourite, Edmund Beaufort, Earl of Somerset. Notwithstanding previous military successes, Somerset now found himself associated with English losses, particularly Rouen, which had fallen to the French under his command.

In less than two decades, everything that Henry V had achieved had vanished and the Hundred Years War had ended. Gascony, held by the English for three centuries, fell in 1453, and Calais became the sole English stronghold. In August of the same year, Henry began to suffer his first bout of insanity, and the Duke of York was made Protector of the Realm in March 1454. York and Somerset despised each other, and finally the enmity between them would escalate into the Wars of the Roses. In 1461, Henry lost his crown to York's son Edward, whose promotion had been engineered by the Yorkist 'Kingmaker' Earl of Warwick. For a brief period from October 1470, after Edward quar-

relled with Warwick, Henry was reinstalled on the throne; it lasted only until the following April when Edward returned with an army. In the ensuing battles, Henry was taken prisoner again and his only child was killed. In May 1471, on the day Edward re-entered London, Henry was stabbed to death in the Tower.

It was under the command of Joan of Arc that the siege of Orleans was ended and French fortunes were reversed. In 1432, at the age of 19, the 'Maid of Orleans' was convicted of heresy and burned at the stake. She was later found innocent and sanctified.

Wars of the Roses

Had the Lancastrian Henry VI been a king after the fashion of his father, it is quite possible that the Wars of the Roses would not have come about. As it was, corruption at court, the loss of English territories in France, the king's ineptitude and bouts of insanity, and – in particular – his favouritism of Edmund Beaufort, Earl of Somerset, created such friction and rivalry that armed conflict became all but inevitable. The deep resentment that the king's behaviour fostered among many of his magnates was felt most keenly by his cousin, Richard Duke of York, with whom Somerset had a long-standing feud. Both York and Somerset had claims on the throne, and both were determined to be recognized as Henry's heir (Henry and Margaret had so far produced no children). York was a direct descendant of Edward III and a nephew of the Earl of March (the legitimate heir of Richard II, ignored by Henry IV); Somerset was also a descendant of Edward III, via a younger son, John of Gaunt, Duke of Lancaster. From the rivalry of these two men and their respective supporters stemmed the Wars of the Roses, a drawn-out civil conflict between the House of Lancaster (symbolized by a red rose) and the House of York (symbolized by a white rose).

A 15th-century illustration of the Battle of Barnet which took place in April 1471. This pivotal encounter saw the Earl of Warwick facing his former ally Edward IV. The day ended in victory for Edward and death for Warwick. With 'the Kingmaker' out of the way, Edward was ready to regain his throne.

Et vous dire noſtre ſouuerain
ſeigneur Edward lequart
par la grace de dieu roy den
gleterre et de france / et ſeigñ
Dirlande / departiſt du pais de zeſlande et

In 1453, the king fell into one of his periods of madness. The Duke of York, seeing this as an opportunity to dislodge Somerset, assumed the role of Protector of the Realm and had Somerset put in the Tower. In early 1455, Henry recovered himself sufficiently to take control again, dismissing York and restoring Somerset. Within weeks, the skirmish that signalled the start of the Wars of the Roses was taking place at St Albans, where Somerset was killed. Since the primary aim of most of York's supporters at this stage had been the removal of Somerset, not the overthrow of the king, conciliation should have been possible. The fact that the conflict continued for another 30 years – despite the king's own efforts to reconcile the two houses – was largely down to Margaret of Anjou's intense personal hatred of York. In 1459 she and her army marched on York's stronghold at Ludlow, where the Yorkists were routed. They had their revenge in 1460 at Northampton, where they defeated Margaret's forces and captured the king. Although Henry and Margaret had by now produced a son (1453), York succeeded in getting Henry to name him as heir. But then, in December, the two sides met again at Wakefield. This time, the Yorkist forces were defeated and York himself was killed. However, York's son Edward was victorious at the

Battle of Towton the following year and, with the assistance of Richard Neville, Earl of Warwick ('the Kingmaker'), he was crowned Edward IV, the first of the Yorkist kings. When Warwick later changed sides, allying himself with Margaret, Edward was forced into exile. But he returned in 1471 to emerge victorious at the battles of Barnet (in which Warwick was killed), and of Tewkesbury, three months later, where Henry's son, Edward, was slain. Margaret was rounded up and Henry was murdered in the Tower of London.

Edward was succeeded in 1483 by his 12-year-old son Edward V. But he was never crowned. His uncle, the Duke of Gloucester, disputed the boy's legitimacy, claimed the throne for himself and was crowned Richard III. His rule was short-lived: it ended when he was defeated at Bosworth Field in 1485 by the Lancastrian Henry Tudor, Earl of Richmond, who became Henry VII. The Wars of the Roses ended here.

The years of actual fighting had not been many, but the damage done to the stability of the monarchy was great. Henry Tudor's marriage to Elizabeth of York, daughter of Edward IV, went some way to reconciling the two houses. But Yorkist claimants to the throne still existed, and in 1513 the last serious contender, Edmund de la Pole, Earl of Suffolk, was executed.

Edward IV
1461–1470; 1471–1483

BORN	28 April 1442 at Rouen, France
PARENTS	Richard, Duke of York, and Cecily Neville
CROWNED	28 June 1461 at Westminster Abbey, aged 19
MARRIED	Elizabeth Woodville (d. 1492)
CHILDREN	Six surviving, including Edward V and Richard, Duke of York (the Princes in the Tower)
DIED	April 1483 at Westminster, aged 39

Edward IV, the first king of the House of York, consolidated his claim to the throne by defeating the Lancastrians at Towton in March 1461, the bloodiest battle in the Wars of the Roses. Henry VI was deposed and Edward was crowned soon afterwards. With Henry's death in 1471, the drama of Edward's early years on the throne came to an end, and the king went on to enjoy a stable, peaceful reign. Under his careful administration the Crown enjoyed its first period of solvency for several centuries and the kingdom's economy thrived. His unexpected death left England in the control of his brother, the Duke of Gloucester.

E dward IV was tall, handsome, charming and generous, interested in the arts and deservedly popular. Politically and financially savvy, he proved to be a fine statesman as well as an able soldier, although

in his private life he let his heart rule his head. This caused problems with his mentor, chief ally and cousin, Richard Neville, Earl of Warwick, who was livid when he discovered that Edward had, in May 1464, secretly married Elizabeth Woodville (who was from a family of Lancastrian sympathizers). At the time Warwick was negotiating with Louis XI of France for a marriage between the king and Princess Bona of Savoy. A humiliated Warwick lost the lands and titles that would have come to him for brokering the alliance; it was the first in a series of irritations that led to a major falling out between Warwick and the king.

The rift culminated in Warwick's defection to the Lancastrian cause and Edward's overthrow in October 1470. Henry VI was released from the Tower and reinstalled on the throne. Edward fled to Burgundy, regrouped and invaded England in March 1471; by May, Edward had defeated Warwick's forces at Barnet (Warwick was killed) as well as the Lancastrian army, led by Margaret of Anjou, at Tewkesbury. Shortly after Tewkesbury – where Henry VI's son, the Prince of Wales, died – Edward returned to London and Henry VI was murdered in the Tower. Edward was back as ruler, firmly in control

Caxton and Printing

The introduction of printing had far-reaching consequences for the literary development of the English language, and the spread of ideas. Previously, all books had been copied by hand. Hearing of Gutenberg's success in printing from moveable type in Germany around 1450, Kent-born merchant William Caxton (c. 1422–c. 1491) travelled there to learn about it. Around 1475 in Bruges he published the first book in English, *The Recuyell of the Historyes of Troye*. Returning home, he produced the first printed book in England, *Dictes or Sayingis of the Philosophres* (1477) and the poems of Chaucer.

of his kingdom. The one remaining problem was his brother George, Duke of Clarence, who had allied himself with Warwick in 1470, quarrelled with his other brother Richard, Duke of Gloucester, and harboured ambitions of taking the throne himself. Although he had since sworn allegiance to Edward, he was proving to be an unpredictable menace. In the end the monarch had him arrested and tried for treason. Tradition has it that George's subsequent execution was by drowning in a vat of malmsey wine.

Restoring the fortunes of the Crown was Edward's priority, and he took a high level of personal control as he set about increasing the efficiency of the kingdom's administration, improving the justice system and delivering the promises of the Yorkist manifestos that had gained him the support of his subjects. Edward's reforms boosted England's economy to unprecedented levels. The Crown was freed from decades of debt, and for several years Edward was able to rule without subsidies from Parliament. Alliances with Burgundy and Brittany were sought with the aim of re-conquering the former English lands in France. But when Edward's allies failed to deliver support, he realized his objective was unachievable and so agreed to a financially beneficial peace with Louis XI in 1475. Some of the English magnates saw this as defeat, but it swelled England's coffers and avoided years of expensive campaigning. The king's only military assault was in Scotland in 1482: led by Richard, Duke of Gloucester, it ended with Berwick being permanently returned to English control.

Edward's love of food matched his insatiable appetite for women and eventually the king became corpulent and inactive. Several military campaigns had been postponed but Edward planned a renewed assault on France which never took place as he died unexpectedly in April 1483. Edward's heir was still a child so the Duke of Gloucester was appointed Lord High Protector. His treachery would provoke one of the most tragic events in the history of the monarchy.

Richard III
1483–1485

BORN	2 October 1452 at Fotheringay Castle, Northamptonshire
PARENTS	Richard, Duke of York, and Cecily Neville
CROWNED	6 July 1483 at Westminster Abbey, aged 30
MARRIED	Anne Neville, widow of Edward, Prince of Wales
CHILDREN	One son (plus at least four illegitimate priot to his marriage)
DIED	22 August 1485 at Bosworth Field, Leicestershire, aged 32

Richard's reputation as one of the most villainous kings in the history of English monarchy is largely owed to Tudor propagandists and Shakespeare's monstrous portrayal of his character. Undoubtedly Richard was ruthlessly vicious on occasion, he may have been guilty of some or all of the historical accusations against him, and he failed to inspire loyalty among his magnates. But Richard also had his attributes: he was a courageous soldier, an excellent administrator, almost fanatically pious, decisive, fair, loyal and a devoted husband and father. His short two-year reign gave him little chance to prove himself among the ranks of English sovereigns. His death marked not only the end of the Plantagenet dynasty but also the transition from medieval to modern kingship.

Portrait of Richard III painted in oil.

Richard: Rex tertius

E dward IV's younger brother Richard, Duke of Gloucester, had been at the king's side through the Yorkist campaigns for the throne. Accompanying Edward into exile after Warwick switched allegiance and had Henry VI readopted, he assisted with the successful attempt to defeat Warwick's army and remove Lancastrian opposition once and for all. On Edward's restoration to the throne in 1471, Richard was made Constable and Lord High Admiral of England, and he was granted many of the forfeited estates and titles of the treacherous 'kingmaker' Warwick, who had been killed at the Battle of Barnet. Richard married Warwick's daughter Anne Neville (she was Richard's childhood friend and the widow of Henry VI's son Prince Edward) and the couple installed themselves in the north of England where Richard, now one of the most powerful landowners in the realm, ruled as king in all but name.

Despite his terrible historical reputation Richard was well respected in this role; popular with his peers and his subjects he proved to be a clever, just and decisive leader. The duke was an infrequent visitor to Edward's court but he accompanied the king on his 1475 campaign to France, which ended with the Treaty of Picquigny with Louis XI. Richard was one of several magnates who disapproved of the peace with France, regarding it as defeatist, but unlike his other brother George, Duke of Clarence he remained steadfastly loyal to Edward and the Yorkist cause. Clarence, who was married to Anne's sister, co-heiress of the Warwick estates, had menaced both Richard and Edward for years. When the king's patience finally ran out, George was tried for treason and executed. Despite the animosity that had existed between the brothers, Richard was said to have been devastated at the extreme punishment and held Edward's haughty queen, Elizabeth Woodville, responsible for encouraging it. From then on the pious duke had little contact with what he regarded as Edward's increasingly dissolute court. He was in any case taken up with the task of securing and subduing the northern territories. This included the 1482 campaign in Scotland against James III, which saw the permanent return of Berwick to English hands. Richard's unswerving loyalty was rewarded a year later as Parliament made his Wardenship of the West March, an hereditary office, and the duke was given sovereign powers over his territory.

All this changed when Edward died unexpectedly in April 1483 and named Richard as Lord High Protector of the Realm in his will. The widowed queen and her Woodville relatives reacted swiftly. Prince Edward, the 12-year-old heir to the throne, was in their care at Ludlow and they immediately set up a regency council. The Woodvilles knew that once Edward had been crowned the protectorship would lapse, and since they also knew that the Duke of Gloucester was hostile to them they planned a hasty coronation for late June. Wise to this, Richard hurried south. He and the Duke of Buckingham intercepted the prince, who was on his way to London under the escort of Elizabeth's brother Earl Rivers. The earl and several others in the party were arrested and Elizabeth fled to sanctuary at Westminster with her younger son the Duke of York. In May Richard, Buckingham and the uncrowned king entered London, and Edward was taken to the royal apartments at the Tower of London where his brother soon joined him, after he was removed from his safe haven at Westminster.

Rebellion and Plot

The princes were not kept strictly as prisoners – the Tower was a royal residence, not just a prison – but their movements were restricted and Edward's coronation was postponed. Whether Richard made this move for his nephews' protection or, as history tells it, for their elimination so he could claim the throne himself has been the subject of much controversy. What is known is that Edward and his brother were not seen outside the Tower again.

It must have been clear to Richard that in order to protect the House of York and his own position against the Woodville influence he needed to have control, and that would require him to be king. To this end Richard instigated a campaign to bring Edward IV's marriage into disrepute and bastardize his children. Claiming that the union with Elizabeth Woodville was bigamous, as Edward had entered into a prior marriage contract with Lady Eleanor Butler, Richard put himself up as the legal heir to the throne. However spurious the argument, Edward IV's promiscuity gave credence to it and Parliament accepted it. The uncrowned Edward V was declared illegitimate and deposed on 25 June 1483, and by the 6 July the Duke of Gloucester was being crowned King Richard III at Westminster Abbey.

Unsurprisingly Richard's tactics lost him the support of some Yorkist devotees; Lord Hastings, an ally of Edward IV, was summarily executed when he protested at the princes' disinheritance. Shortly after the coronation it became clear that the king was under threat from the remaining Lancastrian claimant, the exiled Henry Tudor, who was in alliance with the Woodvilles. Buckingham turned traitor and joined the Woodville/Tudor camp. A rebellion was plotted, but bad planning meant it ended in Buckingham's capture and execution at Salisbury in November 1483. Consequently Henry Tudor's small invasion fleet turned tail in the Channel and headed back to Brittany. However, Henry's position was strengthened when Richard's son died in April 1484: without an heir the grief-stricken king was left in a vulnerable position. Meanwhile his rival was successfully courting the support of Charles VIII for another attempt at a coup: Richard's antipathy towards Picquigny and his attacks against their Scottish allies had earned him the mistrust of the French. Things were looking bleak for Richard, even more so when his queen, Anne, died in March 1485. Propagandists put it out that the king had poisoned his wife so that he could marry his niece, Edward IV's eldest daughter, and so prevent her planned union with Henry Tudor.

In August 1485 Henry launched his inevitable assault on Richard's throne. Landing near Milford Haven with an army of French mercenaries he gathered reinforcements as he marched eastwards. On 22 August, Richard's army met with Henry's forces near Market Bosworth in what was to be the final battle of the Wars of the Roses. Richard was slain, the last of the English monarchs to die in battle. He was killed in the thick of the action after being deserted on the field by his key allies and while trying to eliminate Henry personally. Naked, the dead king's body was put on a packhorse and taken away for burial at Greyfriars Abbey, Leicester. His crown, supposedly found under a hawthorn bush, was placed on the head of Henry Tudor.

The Princes in the Tower

The fate of the young Edward V and his brother, the Duke of York, has never been proved beyond doubt, but evidence indicates that they disappeared some time in the late summer of 1483. The skeletons of two young males of a corresponding age to the boys were discovered during repair work at the Tower in 1674, and Charles II had these remains buried at Westminster Abbey. It seems most likely that the princes were murdered, but no one knows exactly when it happened or who was responsible. Both Richard Duke of Gloucester and Henry Tudor had much to gain from their removal. Unsurprisingly, Tudor propagandists blamed Richard, and their version of events has remained the favoured one, but there is no certainty that this heinous act – if it took place at all – was truly Richard's doing.

Meanwhile...

1400 Writer Geoffrey Chaucer dies, leaving *The Canterbury Tales*, begun some 15 years earlier, incomplete.

1401 The Lollard preacher William Sawtrey is the first heretic to be burned at the stake in the British Isles.

1404 Owain Glyn Dwr calls a Parliament, declaring himself the true Prince of Wales.

1409 The Scots destroy the castle at Jedburgh in the Scottish Borders, to deny its use to the English.

1411 Work begins on building the City of London Guildhall, completed 1426, as the centre of the City's government.

1413 Henry V agrees to enact a 1404 Statute expelling all aliens (including Welsh and Irish) from England.

1399 1411 **1416** 1421 1440

1414 Sixty Lollard supporters are hanged in London for an attempted coup, but the leader, Sir John Oldcastle, escapes.

1415 Dancers, musicians and cheering crowds greet Henry V in London for his triumphal return from Agincourt.

1416 Henry V fêtes the Holy Roman Emperor Sigismund at Windsor to enlist his support for the English claim to France.

1417 Margery Kempe, a celebrated holy visionary and mystic, is arrested for heresy but acquitted on trial at Leicester.

1421 Thomas, Duke of Clarence, Henry V's brother and heir, is killed by French cavalry at the Battle of Baugé.

1440 Henry VI founds Eton College, giving free education to 70 resident scholars.

1441   Sir Roger Fiennes starts building Herstmonceux Castle in Sussex, one of the country's first major works in brick.

1446   Work begins on King's College Chapel, Cambridge – one of the greatest examples of Perpendicular Gothic style.

1450   Jack Cade leads a rebellion in the south-east against war taxation, and defeats royal forces at Sevenoaks.

1453   The Duke of Somerset is sent to the Tower, but when Henry VI's health returns in 1455 he is released and reinstated.

1455   Beginning of the Wars of the Roses. Henry VI is captured by the Yorkists at the Battle of St Albans.

1463   Edward IV signs a treaty with France in which both sides agree not to assist each other's enemies.

1450   1455   1464   **1469**   1485

1463   Edward IV of England signs a truce with Scotland at York.

1464   The Lancastrians are defeated at the Battle of Hexham. The Duke of Somerset is executed.

1469   Warwick has the queen's father and one of her brothers executed at Warwick Castle.

1469   The future Richard III is made Constable of England and given Sudeley Castle in Gloucestershire.

1474   Completion of the north-west tower of York Minster, the final phase of its majestic west front.

1476   William Caxton returns to England and sets up a printing shop at the sign of the Red Pale in Westminster.

Scotland
1329–1567

The Stewart family succeeded to the Scottish throne in 1371. Hereditary stewards to the kings of Scots, hence their surname, they were originally from Brittany, went to England with the Normans and then to what was later Renfrewshire in Scotland in David I's time. James the Steward was a supporter of Robert the Bruce, and it was through his marriage to Robert the Bruce's daughter that the Stewarts inherited the throne. The Stewart kings survived long periods of war with England. They had also to wrestle with their own over-mighty subjects, who were not easily kept in check, but the Stewarts were more successful than earlier historians tended to recognize. They built up their own position as powerful landed magnates to such effect that by the 1390s, 12 of the 16 Scottish earldoms were in Stewart hands. The later Stewart kings had their troubles with their aristocracy, including their own relatives, but they commanded enough general support to ensure that the fact that every monarch from James I to James VI inherited the throne as a minor did not cause Scotland to implode. On the contrary, the dynasty survived and in the person of James VI would succeed to the throne of England itself.

David II
to James I
1329–1437

The Scottish Succession 1329–1437

KING	BORN	REIGN	RELATIONSHIP TO PREDECESSOR	AGE AT DEATH
David II	1324	1329–71	Son	46
Robert II	1316	1371–90	Nephew	about 74
Robert III	c. 1340	1390–1406	Son	about 70
James I	1394	1406–37	Son	43

David II was three when his mother died, four when formally married to the seven-year-old Joan, sister of Edward III of England, and five when he succeeded his father, Robert the Bruce. A small sceptre was made specially for him to hold when he was crowned at Scone. The Balliol family renewed its claim to the throne in league with Edward III, who renewed his claim to overlordship. So menacing was the situation that in 1333 David and his queen were sent to France for safety. They returned seven years later. In 1346 David led a Scottish army to defeat by the English near Durham. Wounded in the head by arrows, he was held prisoner in England for 11 years.

An unknown artist's portrait of James I. One of his murderers was a younger Stewart who hoped for the throne and for his pains was given a red-hot iron crown to wear instead.

IACOBVS I D GRAT
REX SCOTORVM

Meanwhile, Robert Stewart (the son of Robert the Bruce's daughter, Marjorie), coped as governor of a Scotland torn by disputes between powerful nobles and reduced in population by around a quarter to a third by the Black Death. Shrewdly building up his own estates and power base, he kept the English at bay while making sure that King David's suggestions that the English royal house should be recognized as heirs to Scotland were not accepted. David was released in 1357 for a substantial ransom and when he died childless in 1371, Robert Stewart succeeded him.

Robert Stewart had been born by Caesarian section after his mother suffered a fatal riding accident. He came to the throne at the age of 55, a shrewd, experienced politician dedicated to the advancement of the Stewarts, of whom he ensured an ample supply by fathering 21 or more children, both legitimate and illegitimate. He and his crippled son John, crowned as Robert III in 1390, faced renewed tension with the English. In 1396 Robert III presided over a notorious clan battle at Perth, in which, to settle a dispute between the Mackintoshes and the Mackays, 30 men from each clan fought to the death before a throng of spectators. The Mackintoshes won.

The gentle, ineffective Robert III had two formidable younger brothers, Robert, Duke of Albany, who largely managed matters in the Lowlands, and Alexander, 'the Wolf of Badenoch', who held the north in his grip. The king was keenly aware of his inability to keep control. He allegedly said that he should be buried in a dunghill as 'the worst of kings and the most wretched of men in the whole realm'. In 1399, because of the king's ineptitude, the royal council appointed as his lieutenant his flamboyant 20-year-old eldest son David, who was soon brought down by Albany. David was imprisoned at Falkland, where according to a widely believed report he was left in a solitary cell to starve slowly to death while Albany ruled as regent. Not long before Robert III died, he packed his remaining heir, his younger son James, off to France, to be safe from Albany, but the 12-year-old was captured at sea off Flamborough Head by the English. He was held prisoner in England for 18 years while the English tried in vain to take control of Scotland. Albany, enjoying power in Scotland, made no ardent attempt to bring him back.

Albany died in 1420, and in 1424 at the age of 30 James I returned to Scotland at last with his English wife, Lady Joan Beaufort, whose beauty he praised in his poem 'The Kingis Quair'. He was a talented musician and a skilled jouster and archer. He executed the leading members of his uncle Albany's family, eliminated other nobles whom he considered a threat, had a number of Highland clan chiefs dispatched, increased taxes and, while he was at it, banned fishing out of season and football at any season. So domineering was he that his uncle the Earl of Atholl organized his murder in the royal apartments at Perth. A later story told how one of the court ladies bravely tried to protect him by bolting the door with her arm, which was broken when the assassins burst in. They stabbed the fleeing king to death in a sewer under the floor, but were caught and tortured to death.

Seal of Robert II, showing him crowned and seated on the throne, holding his sceptre, beneath a richly carved and turreted Gothic canopy. Descended from Robert the Bruce through his mother, he was the first and one of the shrewdest of the Stewart kings.

James II
to James V
1437–1542

The Scottish Succession 1437-1542

KING	BORN	REIGN	RELATIONSHIP TO PREDECESSOR	AGE AT DEATH
James II	1430	1437–60	Son	29
James III	1452	1460–88	Son	35
James IV	1473	1488–1513	Son	40
James V	1512	1513–42	Son	30

The kings from James II to James V inherited the throne as minors and died at an average age of 34, three out of the four of them by violence. James II, nicknamed 'fiery face' after his birthmark, was six when his father was murdered. The dominating figures during his minority were the rival Crichtons and Livingstons, in shifting alliances with the Black Douglases, the powerful Borders branch of the family (their cousins the Red Douglases were earls of Angus). James was ten when the teenaged Earl of Douglas and his younger brother were entertained to dinner with him in Edinburgh Castle

James IV and his young English Tudor queen dressed in their fashionable finery, from the Seton Armorial of 1591. James holds his royal sceptre and the red lion standard of Scotland, while his queen's costume ostentatiously displays the royal arms of England.

Margaret eldest dochter
of Henry the [...] schint[...]

by Sir William Crichton. The severed head of a black bull was placed in front of the earl as a grim sign of what was to happen: the two Douglas boys were seized and beheaded.

Forceful and fiery-tempered, James loved hunting, but banned golf, and was fascinated by the new-fangled artillery. He married Mary of Gueldres, a Burgundian protégé who brought a pleasing supply of up-to-date cannon with her to Scotland, possibly including the famous Mons Meg. When he came of age in 1449, James gave the Livingstons short shrift and in 1452 summoned the new Earl of Douglas to Stirling Castle under a safe conduct but then angrily stabbed the earl, who was finished off by the courtiers. Civil war with the Douglases followed, which James won partly by using his artillery against their castles and partly because many other lords were jealous of the Douglas predominance. It ended with the confiscation of the Black Douglas estates in 1455, and the Crown was substantially richer in consequence. Five years later James was besieging the English in Roxburgh Castle when, to impress his visiting queen, he touched off a cannon that burst and killed him. Mary of Gueldres took charge and saw the siege successfully through.

Mary was not to be trifled with and very efficiently protected her eight-year-old son, James III. However, she died in 1463, and three years later, when the boy king was out hunting, he was kidnapped by two courtiers, Robert Boyd and his brother Alexander, keeper of Edinburgh Castle. They forced James to pretend they had his approval for the abduction, and used their spurious authority to organize their charge's marriage to the King of Norway's pious daughter Margaret, which would eventually bring Orkney and Shetland into the Scottish kingdom. However, when James came of age in 1469, the Boyds were found guilty of treason. Robert Boyd fled to England but Alexander was caught and beheaded.

James III was interested in the arts, astrology and alchemy. He was too grasping and greedy for money, too fond of low-born musicians and artists, and too intent on peace with England to suit some of his magnates, and also his two younger brothers, John and Alexander. James had his brothers arrested in 1479. John died mysteriously in prison – he apparently bled to death in the bath – while Alexander, after killing his guards, escaped down a rope and fled to France. There remained, however, many disaffected nobles who disliked the low-born royal favourites. In 1482 James was taken prisoner at Lauder, north of Melrose, by conspirators led by the Earl of Angus, head of the Red Douglases. Some of the king's favourites were hanged on the spot. James survived, but there was another rising against him three years later, in which his son and heir, the future James IV, was involved. Defeated in a skirmish of 1488 at Sauchieburn, near Stirling, the fleeing king was killed, possibly by accident. He 'happened to be slain', it was said at the time. His son, horrified, wore an iron chain round his waist next to his skin for the rest of his life as a mark of remorse.

The Auld Alliance

An understanding between Scotland and France from the 13th to the 16th centuries was the natural consequence of the vexed relationship of both countries with England. The Scottish kings frequently received help from the French and in return invaded England when it suited France, often with damaging consequences for the Scots. Flodden was the most dramatic example. The relationship gave Scotland closer contact with continental Europe and a taste for things French, including claret. It was an obstacle to peace with England, but it helped to fuel Scottish nationalism and a sense of identity, and consequently to strengthen the monarchy.

Copy of an original double portrait of James V and his French queen, Mary of Guise, from Falkland Palace. Mary of Guise came from one of the most important Catholic families in France and would play a major role in the history of Scotland as the mother and regent of Mary, Queen of Scots.

James IV, who succeeded at 15, was the most engaging and most popular of the Stewart kings. Intelligent, handsome, chivalrous and recklessly brave, he was a Renaissance man, open-minded and responsive to new ideas. He spoke seven languages, including Gaelic. William Dunbar was his court poet and he encouraged architects and artists. He created a Scottish navy, of which the Great Michael was the biggest warship afloat, and he travelled widely to impress his subjects and see justice done. He was interested in alchemy-cum-chemistry, paid volunteers to let him practise his skill at taking teeth out, and encouraged his pet alchemist's attempt to fly with wings off the battlements of Stirling Castle, which ended in his landing in a dungheap. He sponsored the first Scottish university medical faculty, at Aberdeen, and in 1507 he approved the installation of Scotland's first printing press. James loved hunting, hawking and jousting. The laws against football and golf were reissued in 1491 – because too many people were playing them

MARIA LOTHORINGIA ILLIVS IN SECVNDIS
TIIS VXOR ANNO ÆTATIS SVE Z 4

TORVM REX
S SVE

instead of practising archery – but James himself seems to have enjoyed both, as well as card games. He also enjoyed the company of prostitutes and a succession of mistresses.

In the north the lords of the Isles were brought low in the 1490s by a succession of royal expeditions, while in the Highlands the government relied mainly on the Campbells and the Gordons to keep things quiet. James gave the English pretender Perkin Warbeck a refuge for a while at his court, but later signed a treaty of 'perpetual peace' with Henry VII of England in 1502 and the following year married Henry's daughter, Margaret Tudor. The groom was 30, the bride 13. The new queen soon discovered the nursery in Stirling Castle, where seven of her husband's illegitimate children were being brought up under their fond father's eye. Few of her own babies by James survived, but the marriage would eventually bring their great-grandson to the English throne. Henry VII had foreseen this possibility but pointed out that, if it happened, England would inevitably be the dominant partner.

James longed to lead a European crusade against the Turks, but nothing came of it. Relations with England deteriorated after Henry VIII's accession, and in 1512 James renewed the 'auld alliance' with France. When Henry invaded France the next year, James kept his obligations to the French by taking an army of 20,000 or more strong into England, only to be killed with the flower of the Scots nobility at Flodden. His corpse was embalmed and sent eventually to London, where years later some workmen are said to have cut off the head and used it as a football.

Unlike his father, James V has had a bad press. The persecution of Lutherans set Protestant writers decisively against him. He was only a year old when his father was killed, and his mother Margaret Tudor was age 23. Within a year she married the Earl of Angus, of the Red Douglases. The council sent to

France for John Stewart, Duke of Albany, grandson of James II, to act as regent, and the king's minority saw a tug-of-war between his mother and his regent, and their pro-English and pro-French attitudes. Margaret fell out with Angus, who held James a virtual prisoner for almost three years until 1528, when at 16 he escaped and took over the government.

James was a keen musician and introduced the consort of viols to Scotland. Also a tennis player, archer and enthusiastic jouster, he had many mistresses and at least nine illegitimate children. He married Magdalene, the daughter of Francis I of France and, after her premature death, took another aristocratic French wife, Mary of Guise in 1538. James liked to go about in disguise and find out for himself what his subjects thought. It was not a characteristic his magnates welcomed, and in desperate need of money he aroused opposition by sharply increasing taxes. Determined to bring the Borders to order, he hanged some of the Armstrongs of Liddesdale, who were notorious raiders and rustlers. He later had Angus's sister, Janet, burned to death in Edinburgh on a trumped-up charge of plotting to poison him. Her forfeited estates boosted his income.

Defeat and Decline

Tension developed with the English after James's uncle succeeded to the English throne as Henry VIII and tried unsuccessfully to draw the Scots away from their traditional alliance with France. The two sides fell out and in 1542 the English crossed the border. The Scots held the off at first but were then soundly beaten by the English at Solway Moss, near Carlisle. James went into a decline at Falkirk Palace, Fife, and died within a month, leaving as his heir a baby girl who was only six days old. His last words were reported as, 'It cam' wi' a lass and it'll gang wi' a lass.' A reference to the Stewarts' descent from Marjorie Bruce, the prophecy proved inaccurate.

High Road and Low Road

The Scottish kings established their authority in Lowland Scotland – the area south of the Clyde and the Forth plus the North Sea coastlands – far sooner than in the Highlands. The MacDonalds, with their fleet of fast war galleys, were Lords of the Isles, ruling the Western Isles and the western seaboard as virtually independent potentates, while authority in the Highlands was wielded by clan chiefs. A clan was theoretically an extended family (the word means 'children' in Gaelic), with the chief as its patriarch, but in practice it included everyone who lived on the clan's lands. Medieval clan chiefs included men of Norse (MacLeod), Norman (Gordon and Fraser) and Flemish (Murray) origins, but the Highlands and Islands were pre-eminently the refuge of the old Celtic culture of Scotland. Scots Gaelic survived there after it had ceased to be used in the Lowlands, along with traditional costume, poetry, music and lore.

Lowland Scotland came to fear and dislike the Highlands. In the 1380s the chronicler John of Fordun called the Highlanders 'a savage and untamed race, rude and independent', and later Lowland writers echoed the theme of lawlessness and barbarism prevalent in the Highlands. Fuel was added to the flames by the notorious 'Wolf of Badenoch', a younger brother of Robert III and royal lieutenant north of the Moray Firth. He kept rough and ready order with his own army and burned Elgin Cathedral down in 1390 with a crew of 'wild Highlandmen' after quarrelling with the

This tomb effigy at Dunkeld Cathedral is believed to be that of Alexander Stewart, the notorious 'Wolf of Badenoch', who ruled the northern Highlands for his brother Robert III.

local bishop. To Lowland Scots he was alarmingly typical of Highland brutishness.

The Lords of the Isles were brought down in James IV's time when James forced the last lord, John MacDonald, to submit to him and forfeit his lands. As royal power strengthened in the Lowlands, clan chiefs were held accountable to the Crown for their clansmen's activities. However, the chiefs in their Highland fastnesses retained immediate, unchallenged authority over their own people into the 18th century.

Mary,
Queen of Scots
1542–1567

BORN	8 December 1542 at Linlithgow Palace
PARENTS	James V of Scots and Mary of Guise
CROWNED	9 September 1543 in Stirling Castle, aged nine months
MARRIED	(1) Francis II of France (d. 1560); (2) Henry Stewart, Lord Darnley (d. 1567); (3) James Hepburn, Earl of Bothwell (d. 1578)
CHILDREN	One son, James, by Darnley
DIED	Executed 8 February 1587 at Fotheringhay Castle in England, aged 44

One of most romantic figures in British history, Mary was queen within a week of her birth. In her mother, the 27-year-old Mary of Guise, Scotland had yet another strong-minded foreign widow in charge of a minor on the throne, but as a Roman Catholic she had to contend with the rise of Protestantism. There were also the English, who invaded Scotland in 'the rough wooing', a vain attempt to force a marriage between the baby queen and the young Edward VI.

Mary was never on easy terms with her mother-in-law, the formidable Catherine de Medici.

The marriage was a prospect Mary of Guise detested. In 1548 she and the Scots regent, James Hamilton, Earl of Arran, a descendant of James II and currently the heir presumptive, sent little Mary to France. There she was brought up as a Catholic Frenchwoman by her mother's family, the Guises, and given an appropriate education in the classics, literature, drawing, singing, dancing and music. French became her favourite language – and she always styled herself Marie Stuart, in the French fashion – but she also learned Spanish and Italian. At 15, as planned, she was married to the 14-year old French dauphin. He became king as Francis II in 1559, which made Mary briefly Queen of France until his premature death in 1560. Her mother, Mary of Guise, died of dropsy the same year and in 1561 Mary was sent back to Scotland. It suited the French to maintain that as Margaret Tudor's grand-daughter she was the rightful queen of England (Elizabeth I being illegitimate on this hypothesis). She vainly hoped to be accepted as Elizabeth I's heir, but she almost instantly found herself in a confrontation with John Knox, the aggressive Calvinist divine, who maintained that subjects owed no obedience to a ruler mistaken in religion. He had earlier attacked Mary of Guise because he thought no woman should hold power, and gleefully rejoiced at her death.

It was the first of many confrontations. Attractive, vivacious and charming, Mary made a delightful impression at first, and came cheap with a substantial French income, but the Reformation was proceeding at full tilt in Scotland, and the so-called 'lords of the congregation' – Protestant nobles who had formally committed themselves to 'the Congregation of Christ Jesus in Scotland' – feared Catholic France and favoured Protestant England. They were deeply suspicious of their Frenchified Catholic queen and her glamorous court at Holyroodhouse, which went riding and hunting by day, and by night danced and played cards, chess and billiards.

Mary tried to conciliate them. She had the mass said privately in her own chapel, but forbade it in public and officially recognized the Reformed Church. Despite this, the Protestant lords were distrustful. They feared the influence of an Italian musician, called David Rizzio (or Riccio), a Catholic, in his thirties, who became Mary's secretary and confidant in 1564. They also disliked Mary's tall, handsome, worthless cousin Henry Stewart, Lord Darnley, who arrived at court the following year. Related to both the Scots and English royal families, he had his eye on the Scots throne. She fell in love with him and they married – she was 22, he was 19. Darnley was ostensibly a Protestant, but the wedding ceremony was Catholic and he was soon loudly announcing his return to the mass. After fathering Mary's only surviving child, the future James VI of Scotland (James I of England), he jealously connived at the murder of David Rizzio. The Italian was knifed to death by a group of conspirators at Holyroodhouse in 1566 when Mary was six months' pregnant. He clung desperately to Mary's skirts, begging for his life, but was dragged away and killed on the stairs.

Darnley himself had not much longer to live. Mary was sick of him and early in 1567 he was recovering at a house in Edinburgh from an illness, possibly syphilis, when at two o'clock in the morning the building was blown up by a huge explosion – barrels of gunpowder had been unobtrusively packed in the cellar – and the corpses of Darnley and his valet were found in the garden, apparently strangled. Suspicion centred on James Hepburn, Earl of Bothwell, a swaggering adventurer (Protestant but anti-English), in whom Mary had been showing interest. Whether she knew about the murder in advance, nobody knows, though her opponents certainly wanted to believe it. The famous Casket Letters from Mary to Bothwell, which were supposed to prove her guilt, disappeared in James VI's time and may well have been forgeries.

Two months later, in April, Bothwell carried Mary off to Dunbar Castle and allegedly raped her. She issued an equivocal statement about it and in May she married him at a low-key Protestant ceremony in Holyroodhouse. The turn of events was too much even for Mary's sympathizers. In June an alliance of nobles led by James Douglas, Earl of Morton, confronted her and Bothwell and their small army at Carberry Hill, east of Edinburgh. Mary's soldiers mostly found reasons to be elsewhere and she surrendered without a blow struck. Bothwell got away to Orkney (and would ultimately die insane in Norway). Mary was taken to Edinburgh, where a mob screamed at her captors to 'burn the whore', and was then imprisoned on an island in Loch Leven, where she miscarried twins, presumably Bothwell's. In July 1567 she was forced to abdicate in favour of her baby son. James Stewart, Earl of Moray – a bastard son of James V – was made regent.

Mary escaped the following year. After one failed attempt in which she disguised herself as a washerwoman, but was given away by her smooth, white hands, she was finally successful in getting away in a boat. She gathered an army with support from the Hamiltons, Campbells and Gordons, but was defeated in the battle of Langside by the Regent Moray. She fled to England, asking for Elizabeth I's protection. Now 25, she would spend the last 19 years of her life as a prisoner in England, where she became the focus of Catholic plots against Elizabeth, some of them initially encouraged by English government secret agents. She fostered an image of herself as a Catholic martyr, while her enemies depicted her as a Jezebel enslaved to her passions.

Mary and Elizabeth never met. Elizabeth's advisers repeatedly urged her to have Mary executed, but she demurred until, in

1586, Mary's involvement in Anthony Babington's assassination plot against her, when she reluctantly gave way. Mary was beheaded at Fotheringhay Castle in Northamptonshire in 1587. It was done with some haste, before Elizabeth could change her mind. Mary, whose personal motto was *En mon fin est mon commencement* ('In my end is my beginning') went bravely to the block, where three strokes of the axe took off her head. She was buried in Peterborough Cathedral. Her son, James VI, who had not stirred a finger to help her, had her body moved to a magnificent tomb in Westminster Abbey in 1612.

The death mask of Mary, Queen of Scots, from Lennoxlove House, near Haddington in East Lothian. Charming and vivacious, considered a beauty in her own time, she was no match for Elizabeth of England. Contrary to Schiller's play and Donizetti's opera, the two queens never met.

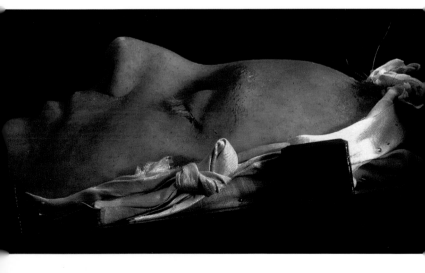

The Tudors
1485–1603

After Richard III's death, England was ruled in turn by Welsh, Scottish and German dynasties. The Tudors were landowners in North Wales – in Caernarfonshire and Anglesey – who rose to prominence and two earldoms in England in the 15th century through Owen Tudor's romantic love affair with Henry V's French widow. A distant link with the House of Lancaster put them on the throne for 119 years, 49 of which were the reigns of two queens. The Tudors saw the transition from the medieval to the modern world, the discovery of America, and the Reformation. Between them they created the Church of England and the Royal Navy, set the modern relationship between Crown and Parliament on course, and boosted English national pride. Three of the five Tudor monarchs were among the most effective ever to wear the English crown. Henry VII settled the Wars of the Roses. Henry VIII broke with Rome, declared himself head of the Church of England, closed down the monasteries and, notoriously, beheaded two and divorced two more of his six wives. The dynasty's brilliant apogee came under Elizabeth, with the defeat of the Spanish Armada, a Protestant religious settlement and an explosion of literary genius, involving Shakespeare, Marlowe, Sidney and Spenser.

Henry VII
1485–1509

BORN	28 January 1457, Pembroke Castle
PARENTS	Edmund Tudor, Earl of Richmond, and Margaret Beaufort
CROWNED	30 October 1485, aged 28
MARRIED	Elizabeth of York (d. 1503), daughter of King Edward IV
CHILDREN	Eight, only four of whom survived infancy: Arthur, Margaret, Henry and Mary
DIED	21 April 1509, Richmond Palace, Surrey, aged 52

Henry VII liked to claim descent from the legendary King Arthur – he named his eldest son Arthur accordingly – but his real claim to England was distinctly slender. He was the son of Edmund, Earl of Richmond, who was the son of Henry V's widow, Catherine of France, who fell in love with a Welsh courtier named Owen Tudor. When he was 14, Henry was taken to Brittany to escape the triumphant Yorkists. Living in exile, in danger and dependent on the uncertain goodwill of his hosts, he developed as a reserved, secretive, inscrutable character, shrewd and cautious, and extremely acquisitive in money matters. A story grew up later that when Henry had an audience with King Henry VI in 1470, the king prophesied that the 13-year-old boy would rule England. The story was told with the benefit of hindsight and as a Lancastrian tribute to Henry VI's supposed saintliness.

Whether or not Owen Tudor ever married Catherine of France, their sons Edmund and Jasper were half-brothers to Henry VI, who liked them and created them earls of Richmond and Pembroke respectively. Edmund married Margaret Beaufort, the great-great-granddaughter of Edward III by way of John of Gaunt. She was 13 when their son Henry was born. He never knew his father, who had died a few weeks earlier. His mother was soon married off again and the little boy was brought up in Wales by his uncle Jasper and by the Herbert family at Raglan Castle.

A succession of fortuitous deaths left Henry Tudor, improbably, as the House of Lancaster's claimant to the throne, in right of his mother, who began scheming on his behalf. In 1485 defeated Richard III at Bosworth, and was crowned in Westminster Abbey two months later, with his mother watching in floods of tears. He married Elizabeth of York, eldest daughter of Edward IV, to unite Lancaster and York, and the red rose and the white mingled in the Tudor rose. Elizabeth was 19, tall, blonde and gentle, and was bossed about by her mother-in-law. Although it was a political match, Henry and Elizabeth enjoyed a loving marriage. Neither of them apparently ever looked at anyone else.

It may seem obvious now that the Wars of the Roses were over, but it was not obvious at the time. The new king had to cope with a succession of plots and two pretenders claiming to be Yorkist princes. Lambert Simnel was beaten in battle in 1487 and contemptuously put to work as a menial in the royal kitchens. Perkin Warbeck was a greater threat in the 1490s, but he was captured and executed. The last Yorkist claimant, the Duke of Suffolk, was not caught until 1506.

Most people wanted peace and order, and Henry enjoyed the support of his parliaments and most of his aristocracy. An excellent businessman, a good judge of men and picker of subordinates, he used the existing system ruthlessly to build up the royal revenue from taxation, rents and feudal dues. The Crown's income more than doubled during the reign. Heavy fines cut down dangerous private armies and aristocratic families faced severe financial penalties for misbehaviour. Royal income from customs was raised by stimulating English exports and merchant shipping, and advantageous commercial treaties were signed with the Netherlands, Spain, Portugal and Denmark. Hope of profit was a motive for Henry's encouragement of the Bristol merchants and the Italian adventurers John and Sebastian Cabot voyaging to North America in the 1490s.

Henry had a shrewd grasp of public relations and spent lavishly on a brilliant court and spectacular pageantry. Besides Westminster, he had palaces at Richmond and Greenwich, reached by river, and he improved Windsor Castle and the Tower of London. He collected books, encouraged scholars, poets and artists, and enjoyed hunting, hawking, tennis and mild gambling. His children's glittering marriages indicate how firmly the new dynasty was established. A Spanish princess, Catherine of Aragon, was acquired for the heir to the throne, Prince Arthur. After his premature death she was passed on to his younger brother Henry, with fateful consequences. Margaret became Queen of Scots and Mary Queen of France.

Henry and Elizabeth were loving parents, and Prince Arthur's death at 15 in 1502 was a bad blow to them both. They comforted each other as best they could, but when Elizabeth died the following year on her 37th birthday, Henry was appalled. He shut himself away alone and would not speak to anyone. In his last years his sight began to fail, he was often ill, and his rapacious greed for money was arousing resentment. Replacement queens were dangled in front of him, but he did not marry again and he chose to be buried next to Elizabeth when he died.

Henry VIII
1509–1547

BORN	28 June 1491 at Greenwich Palace
PARENTS	King Henry VII and Elizabeth of York
CROWNED	24 June 1509, aged 17
MARRIED	Six times
CHILDREN	Three legitimate who survived infancy – Mary, Elizabeth and Edward; at least one illegitimate
DIED	28 January 1547 at Whitehall Palace, London, aged 55

Historians still disagree about Henry VIII – some consider him a failure, others a major architect of modern England – but his father had left him the undisputed succession to a prosperous country at peace and he was crowned to an almost hysterical outpouring of approval. Over six feet tall and well-built, he was a boisterous extrovert with a magnetic charm that made everyone he met feel special. He was also highly intelligent, clean, unalterably convinced of his own rightness and, when necessary, ruthlessly unscrupulous. In short, he was every inch a king.

In his youth, Henry VIII was not the irascible, overweight tyrant that he is famed for having been in middle age. The young Henry was an able athlete with a strong sense of fun, a fine horseman and a crack archer and tennis player. He enjoyed dressing up and play-acting, and he wrote poetry and

songs. He was well educated, speaking French and Latin, and some Spanish and Italian, and he was particularly interested in theology.

Henry had been betrothed to his brother's widow, Catherine of Aragon, since he was 11 and they were married two months after his accession. She was now 23 and, like all his wives bar one (Anne of Cleves), he married her because he wanted her. Neither of them seems to have had much, or perhaps any, sexual experience, but they got on happily and she would bear him six children. Unfortunately, the only one who survived was a girl, the future 'Bloody' Mary, not the son that Henry and his country thought they needed.

Henry was eager to flex his muscles and the Scots were smashed at Flodden in 1513. Invasions of France came to nothing, however, and in 1520, just outside Calais, Henry staged a wildly expensive but empty spectacle of reconciliation with Francis I of France – such was the extravagance that it became known as the Field of the Cloth of Gold. More effectively, he developed his navy and built some of the greatest warships of the age, including the *Harry Grâce à Dieu* and the *Mary Rose*. Like his father, he understood the public relations value of

Henry's Wives

Five of Henry VIII's marriages ended unhappily for his wives. His sixth wife, Catherine Parr, outlived him. Wife one was Catherine of Aragon, his brother's widow – the reason Henry used to divorce her to marry Anne. After a short, turbulent marriage, Henry learned of Anne's apparent adultery and she was executed. Her successor Jane Seymour died after giving Henry his heir, Edward. Anne of Cleves' appearance disappointed Henry and he swiftly divorced her. Catherine Howard, wife five, was executed after accusations of adultery.

magnificence and he created the palaces of Whitehall and St James's in London and he grandified Hampton Court.

New families from the aristocracy's lower ranks came to prominence at Henry's court, more dependent on royal favour than the old-style feudal grandees, who thought them upstarts. They would play leading roles in the future. Henry picked able ministers, who could be blamed for unpopular policies and things that went wrong. The chief minister from around 1513 was Thomas Wolsey, the Ipswich butcher's son who became Cardinal Archbishop of York and had hopes of being pope. Henry himself was a convinced Catholic, awarded the title of Defender of the Faith by the Pope in 1521 for his treatise attacking Lutheranism.

By this time Catherine of Aragon was in her forties, and still Henry had no male heir. He had discovered he could sire a son – Henry Fitzroy, Duke of Richmond – but the boy was illegitimate, by a beautiful mistress, Elizabeth Blount. Henry now fell in love with a witty, black-eyed charmer in her twenties called Anne Boleyn, whose older sister Mary had already been his mistress. But Anne would not go to bed with him unless he agreed to marry her. Henry wanted her and he wanted a legitimate son. By 1527 he was determined to divorce Catherine and, to this end, he conveniently discovered that their children's deaths were proof of divine displeasure with him for marrying his deceased brother's wife in defiance of the prohibition in the Old Testament. Pope Clement VII was asked to annul the marriage but he was under the thumb of Catherine's nephew the Emperor Charles V who was the most powerful monarch in Europe, and he refused.

The consequence was the transformation of the Church in England into the Church of England. Wolsey's failure to get the annulment turned the king and Anne Boleyn against him. Accused of treason, he died on his way to trial

Henry's Realm

Henry was no dictator. His drastic changes in English life were carried out by act of parliament, which meant that royal power was tacitly acknowledged to have limits. Parliament was strengthened and so were English national identity and pride. There was increasing centralization of government in England and in Wales, which was made part of England and divided into English-style counties. English was made the official language, the Marcher lords established by William the Conqueror lost their power, and the border between England and Wales was fixed. Henry was less successful in making Ireland part of England rather than a separate province, but he called himself King of Ireland not Lord of Ireland (as his father had been).

in London in 1530. His place was taken by the driven, power-hungry Thomas Cromwell, a blacksmith's son who steered the separation of the English Church from Rome through Parliament in the 1530s. Anne Boleyn began sleeping with Henry in 1532 and became pregnant late that year. She and Henry were secretly married in January 1533. Archbishop Cranmer of Canterbury annulled the king's marriage to Catherine in May and crowned Anne queen in June. Their daughter, Elizabeth, was born in September. The Pope eventually excommunicated Henry, who logically enough took no notice.

The Act of Supremacy of 1534, which declared Henry supreme head on earth of the Church of England, confirmed his profound conviction that his only superior was God. But he could also claim that he was responding to his people's demand. Personally introducing into Parliament a bill to dissolve the monasteries in 1536, Henry asked the members not to be influenced by him, but to do what the good of the realm required. The monasteries were duly closed down, and in a redistribution of landholdings unseen since the Norman

Conquest their estates and massive wealth went to the Crown and the Crown's supporters. Cromwell, Cranmer and Anne Boleyn were all Reformation-minded, but Henry was not. His religion became a baffling mixture of his inherited Catholicism and whatever suited him. He kept a balance between religious conservatives and Reformers, and executed some 50 people who failed his balancing act.

The regime poured out a flood of tracts glorifying the king, and his picture was everywhere. Anne, however, failed to bear him a son. After Elizabeth, her babies were stillborn and Henry began to look elsewhere. Charges of incest with her brother, adultery with four other lovers and attempted murder were trumped up against her, along with whispers of witchcraft, and she went to the block in 1536. At her request a specialist was imported from France to cut through her slender neck with a sword rather than an axe (her brother and the others got the axe). The same month Henry married Jane Seymour. She was

Heir to Arthur

Henry VIII was a younger son, and the history of England might have been very different if his elder brother had survived to become king. Arthur was a premature baby, undersized and sickly. He was married at 15 in 1502 to Catherine of Aragon and the pair were ostentatiously put to bed together, but whether the marriage was ever consummated is uncertain. Catherine insisted it was not, though Arthur boasted about having been 'in Spain'. They lived at Ludlow Castle in the Welsh Marches where Arthur died a few months later. To retain Catherine's ample dowry and the valuable connection with Spain, she was transferred to Henry, from which followed the break with Rome and the English Reformation.

a docile relief after Anne and when she died the following year after giving Henry his son, Edward, the king was genuinely grief-stricken. Meanwhile, with the support of his great lords, he had easily survived the Pilgrimage of Grace, a serious uprising in the north in which thousands of Catholics demanded an end to the breach with Rome. More than 200 of them were executed.

In 1539, with the Catholic powers of Europe threatening war, Henry reassured his conservative subjects with the Act of Six Articles, which upheld traditional Catholic doctrine on the mass, clerical celibacy and confession. The Act was intended to show that Henry's being head of the Church of England did not require fundamental changes in belief, and he wrote the final text himself.

In 1540 at Cromwell's urging, he married a foreign Protestant princess, Anne of Cleves. Holbein's portrait of her proved to have been far too flattering, and Henry swiftly divorced her. Cromwell's enemies at court moved against

him and he was executed for treason. Henry, now 48, married the enticing 19-year-old Catherine Howard, but she was much too free with her favours and was executed for adultery in 1542. The following year the king married his sixth wife, the already twice-widowed Catherine Parr, who was in her early thirties. Humorous and kind, she established friendly relationships with his children, and she contrived to soothe her husband and survive him.

In 1544 Henry decided that if his son left no children, he would be succeeded by Mary and then if necessary by Elizabeth. By this time Henry was an ogre and a physical wreck. He suffered agonies from an ulcerated leg and grew so bloatedly fat that he had to be pushed about in a specially constructed cart. Suspicious and distrustful, he had become menacingly paranoid. It must have been a relief to those close to him when he died. He was buried at Windsor next to Jane Seymour.

Henry VIII and his family, by an unknown artist. This allegorical painting at Hampton Court, dates from about 1545. The king is shown on his throne beneath the royal coat of arms. Jane Seymour is standing demurely to his left, despite the fact that she was long dead by this time. She is there as the mother of the future Edward VI and the king has his right arm firmly about the boy. The Lady Mary, Henry's daughter by Catherine of Aragon, is further to the king's right and on the opposite side is Elizabeth, his daughter by Anne Boleyn. The figure to the far right of the picture with a monkey on his shoulder is the king's jester, Will Somers.

Edward VI
1547–1553

BORN	12 October 1537 at Hampton Court Palace
PARENTS	Henry VIII and Jane Seymour
CROWNED	20 February 1547, aged nine
MARRIED	Unmarried
CHILDREN	None
DIED	6 July 1553 at Greenwich Palace, aged 15

After a three-day labour, Henry VIII's precious male heir was born on the eve of the feast of St Edward the Confessor, hence his name. The little boy's mother died 12 days later. He was quartered at Hampton Court, where his food was routinely tested for poison and strict standards of personal hygiene were required of his attendants. However, the fastidious care lavished upon him could not change what later became apparent: that the prince had a weak constitution. Though he succeeded his father and showed signs that he might prove to be a strong and assertive monarch, he did not live to reach his majority.

Henry VIII liked small children and enjoyed playing with Edward, his 'most precious jewel', when he could. Short-sighted, with fair hair and grey eyes, the precious jewel had an intensive education in the classics, languages, scripture, philosophy and sciences, and lessons in horse-

manship, archery, fencing, tennis, dancing and music. Being royal, he had a whipping boy to take most of his beatings for him. His father had him educated as a Protestant, presumably to make sure that there would be no retreat from the royal supremacy when Edward succeeded him.

On Henry's death a council of regency assembled and Edward Seymour, Earl of Hertford, was appointed Protector of the Realm and created Duke of Somerset. He was Edward's uncle and the leader of the Reform faction in the council, supported by Archbishop Cranmer and John Dudley, Earl of Warwick, and opposed by such conservatives as bishops Gardiner and Bonner of Winchester and London. Somerset and Cranmer altered the coronation oath to commit the king firmly to the Reformation. To Somerset's disapproval, the widowed Catherine Parr promptly married his brother, Lord Thomas Seymour, the Lord High Admiral. The admiral was a noted charmer, but he tried too hard to gain the affections of both the young king and his sister Elizabeth, and his suspicious brother had him executed for treason.

As the reign went on, the council ordered church services to be conducted in English and popish images to be removed from churches. Much of the English heritage of medieval art was destroyed: stained-glass windows, figures and murals were smashed or painted over. Mystery plays and maypoles vanished, Catholic altars were gradually replaced by communion tables and the clergy were permitted to marry. There were threatening uprisings against religious changes and also against sharply rising prices and the enclosure of land, which was steadily destroying the medieval pattern of agriculture. They were so threatening that in 1549 Somerset was overthrown and the council had him arrested.

Warwick now took charge. A shrewd politician, he ran the country efficiently, won Edward's trust and affection, and had himself created Duke of Northumberland in 1551 on the day before Edward's 14th birthday. He used to visit the boy secretly at night in his bedchamber and prime him with speeches for the next day's meeting of the royal council, whose other members were amazed at their young master's precocious intelligence.

Edward was beginning to display something of his father's determination to have his own way, but in 1552 he had measles and smallpox, and by March the following year he was dying of tuberculosis. He drafted a plan for the succession. He did not want his ardently Catholic half-sister Mary to inherit the throne. At Northumberland's urging, he left the throne to his cousin Lady Jane Grey, who could be trusted to carry the Reformation forward. On his deathbed, Edward prayed for England to be preserved from papistry. His death was kept secret for a few days while Northumberland moved to install Jane as queen. A rumour went around that the young king had been poisoned on Northumberland's orders, although there is no evidence that this was true.

The Nine Days' Queen

An intellectual and bookish Protestant, Lady Jane Grey was the Duke of Northumberland's daughter-in-law (and Henry VII's great-granddaughter). After Edward VI's death she was proclaimed queen in London, against her inclinations, and took up her quarters in the Tower of London, where she tried the royal crown on for size. It made her feel faint, appropriately enough, for a message arrived from the Lady Mary, Edward's elder sister, asserting her right to the throne. Northumberland had miscalculated the amount of support for his scheme, for most of the royal council deserted him and proclaimed Mary queen. Jane was delighted and asked if she could please go home now, but she was held prisoner in the Tower and went to the block the following February. She was 16 years old.

Mary I
1553–1558

BORN	18 February 1516 at Greenwich Palace
PARENTS	Henry VIII and Catherine of Aragon
CROWNED	1 October 1553, aged 37
MARRIED	Prince Philip of Spain (d. 1598)
CHILDREN	None
DIED	17 November 1558 at St James's Palace, London, aged 42

Edward VI's deathbed prayers went unanswered, for his successor ushered England back to Rome. Mary was 17 when her mother's marriage to Henry VIII was annulled. She was declared illegitimate, demoted to dance attendance on the baby Elizabeth, her father's daughter by Anne Boleyn, and persistently humiliated. Convinced that Anne had bewitched her father, she vainly plotted to escape abroad. Like her mother, she was a staunch Catholic, and despite the considerable pressure that had been brought to bear upon her during her half-brother's regime, she refused to accept the Protestant Reformation. She wanted England restored to the Roman Church.

When Northumberland attempted to put Lady Jane Grey on the throne, Mary was in Norfolk. She gathered an army and marched on London, greeted with loyal support and rejoicings all the way.

ANNO DÑI · 1544

LADI MARI DOVGHTER TO
THE MOST VERTVOVS PRINC
KINGE HENRI THE EIGHT

THE AGE OF XXVIII YERES

The stability of England and the Tudor dynasty were demonstrated by the fact that Northumberland's plan failed because the majority of the English nobility and gentry, and the common people, regarded Mary as the rightful successor. That was what Henry VIII had wanted and that was what should happen.

Since neither Jane Grey nor Henry I's daughter Matilda had been crowned, Mary was the first anointed queen to rule England of right, and she worked hard at it. Some 800 Protestants betook themselves abroad, no doubt to the new regime's relief. Mary's inevitable restoration of Catholic worship restored the position as it had been at the end of Henry VIII's reign. As such, it met little opposition, but her decision to renounce the royal supremacy and return to obedience to the Pope was another matter. So was her plan to marry Philip of Spain, the son and heir of the powerful Catholic Charles V: this was another

The Menace of Spain

All the Tudor monarchs were confronted with the might of Spain, and Mary I married it. Ferdinand and Isabella, Catherine of Aragon's parents and Mary's own grandparents, united Spain in the 15th century. They backed Christopher Columbus, the discoverer of America, and founded a Spanish empire that included Mexico, Central America, large areas of South America, and most of the West Indies. Quantities of gold and silver from the New World made Spain the richest country in Europe and from 1519 it was part of the Holy Roman Empire under Charles V, who also ruled the Netherlands, the hub of England's foreign trade. He retired in the 1550s and handed Spain over to his son Philip, a zealot for the Catholic Counter-Reformation, who would launch the Spanish Armada against Elizabeth I's Protestant England.

offence against English nationalism, and it provoked an armed rebellion in Kent in 1554, led by Sir Thomas Wyatt, who objected to England being turned into 'a cockleboat towed by a Spanish galleon'. He was defeated and went to the block, as did the unfortunate Lady Jane Grey, but the rising was a danger signal.

Philip of Spain duly arrived in England and their marriage in Winchester Cathedral in 1554 was possibly the happiest day of Mary's life, but he was 27 and she was a virgin of 38. He preferred his women younger, and one of Mary's ladies-in-waiting had to beat him off with a stick. He left England the following year and came back only once for a few weeks in 1557. He had become king of Spain as Philip II the year before, which made Mary Queen of Spain. She twice joyfully imagined she was with child by him, but they turned out to be false pregnancies.

Meanwhile, the queen was earning herself the nickname 'Bloody' Mary, for in just four years she had some 300 Protestants burned alive. Most of the victims were humble folk, but Archbishop Cranmer went to the stake and so did bishops Latimer and Ridley. Whether Latimer really said, as the gorse branches and wood faggots were lit, 'We shall this day light such a candle by God's grace in England as shall never be put out' is uncertain, but the burnings gave many English a lasting distaste for 'popery'.

A new policy was adopted to bring Ireland more under control by planting English colonists there. On the Continent, Mary aligned England with her husband's Spain in a failed war against France, which in 1558 resulted in the loss of Calais, England's last French possession. It was a blow to English pride, though the story that Mary said Calais would be found written on her heart when she died is apparently apocryphal. Her second false pregnancy, which brought her such joy, turned out to be the stomach cancer that killed her.

The Tudors and the Reformation

Henry VII was a conventional Roman Catholic, who was on amiable terms with practically all the bishops he inherited from his predecessors and with successive popes. His 23 years in power saw the Church burn an average of two heretics a year at the stake. It was not until after his time that Martin Luther nailed his theses to the church door at Wittenberg, in 1517, and the Reformation became a matter of critical importance to every crowned head in Europe. Rome for Luther was the seat of the Great Beast of Revelation and the new ideas fed on disillusion with the Church and the clergy. The fundamental impulse was to return to the simplicity of Early Christianity and sweep away the Roman Church's accretions. These could include the doctrine of transubstantiation (the transformation of the bread and wine in the mass into Christ's body and blood), prayers for the dead, altars and vestments, confession and clerical celibacy. Protestants found their authority in the Bible and wanted it translated into the vernacular languages so that ordinary people could read it for themselves, not be told what to think by priests. John Calvin would tolerate no form of religious devotion not authorized in scripture.

The principle that each country's religion should be determined by its ruler was promulgated in 1526 by the Lutheran princes of Germany, who were the first to be called

Protestants (because they protested against the Catholics three years later). Henry VIII was a cradle Catholic, but he took a sceptical view of the clergy, dismissed the idea of purgatory, and had his doubts about relics and miracles.

Towards Protestantism

The fact that Henry was able to push his changes through fairly easily suggests that majority opinion in England was with him. There was a strong feeling that too many priests and monks were no credit to their calling and that the Church was too rich. In 1536 a report to the House of Commons spoke of 'manifest sin, vicious, carnal and abominable living' in the monasteries, to justify their dissolution. In that same year Henry VIII approved an English translation of the Bible and under Edward VI the Reformers were able to advance their agenda. It was not until then that the word Protestant was commonly used in England. A new prayer book in English was issued in 1549, but it did not go as far in a Protestant direction as Archbishop Cranmer would have liked and a more radical one came out in 1552. It rejected the concept of transubstantiation and attacked 'the bishop of Rome'. Fanatical Protestants and Roman Catholics were both intolerantly certain of their own rightness, but there were not many of them. Most people in England, including many of the lower clergy, seem to have been basically Catholic in their sympathies, but broadminded and generally ready to go along with what the authorities decided.

The pendulum swung back easily at first under Mary I, but Parliament flatly turned down any question of restoring Church land, and acceptance of the pope collided with English nationalism. The burning of Protestants was a gift to anti-Catholic propaganda, exemplified by Foxe's *Book of Martyrs* with its gruesome illustrations, and would damage Roman Catholicism in England for centuries. Elizabeth and her advisers reintroduced the royal supremacy and the 1552 Book of Common Prayer and created a lasting Protestant settlement, while the English parliament's role in the Reformation enabled it to grow stronger at a time when its equivalents abroad were falling to the power of monarchies. Scotland, where Calvinism became the established religion under the name of Presbyterianism, chose a more austere path.

The execution of four Protestants, John Bland and John Sheterden, who were both clergymen, and John Frankish and Humfrey Middleton, who were laymen. They were burned alive for heresy at Canterbury in 1555. Canterbury Cathedral can be seen in the background. Agonizing executions like this earned Queen Mary her nickname of 'Bloody' Mary and pictures in books like Foxe's Book of Martyrs, *which came out in 1563 and ran to numerous later editions, fastened a lasting fear and hatred of Roman Catholicism in many English minds.*

Elizabeth I
1558–1603

BORN	7 September 1533 at Greenwich Palace
PARENTS	Henry VIII and Anne Boleyn
CROWNED	15 January 1559, aged 25
MARRIED	Unmarried
CHILDREN	None
DIED	24 March 1603 at Richmond Palace, aged 69

Like her grandfather Henry VII, Elizabeth survived an edgy, dangerous youth. She grew up a survivor, with a wary, inscrutable streak, but she also inherited the enormous charm of her father. Like both of them, she grasped the importance of public relations, of which she was the most consummate exponent ever to occupy the English throne. She knew how to inspire loyalty and how to keep her options open, and in a man's world she spurned masculine domination and used her femininity to maximum effect. Wilful, theatrical, shrewd, vain, obstinate, often maddeningly indecisive, she danced rings round her devoted if anxious councillors.

Queen Elizabeth's coronation portrait of 1559 by an unknown artist. The portrait once hung in the Great Hall of Warwick Castle but was acquired by the National Portrait Gallery. The painting shows the queen in the Mantle of Estate and kirtle.

Elizabeth I was a fascinating figure in her own time and she has remained a fascinating figure ever since. More books have been written about her than about any other British monarch. During her 44-year reign, England would begin to emerge as a world power, and she would give her name to an era that would be remembered as a golden age. And yet the baby Elizabeth was a disappointment to her parents: they wanted a son. Named after her paternal grandmother, Elizabeth of York, she grew up motherless after Anne Boleyn was executed in 1536. She was declared illegitimate and, although she was only two years old, she was aware of a change, asking why she was Lady Princess yesterday and only Lady Elizabeth today. She was formidably intelligent, and a thorough education had her learning French and Italian in addition to Latin by the age of ten, with classical Greek added later. It was translating Calvin into English that gave her a lasting distaste for his opinions.

In 1544 Henry restored her to the line of succession, after Edward and Mary, and she presently went to live in the household of her last stepmother, Catherine Parr, who was kind and affectionate. Elizabeth was 14 when her father died. Her stepmother's replacement husband, Lord Thomas Seymour, was a dashing figure who liked to romp with the teenaged Elizabeth in her bedroom. Catherine Parr thought it was innocent fun and joined in, but what effect these attentions from a handsome man of the world in his thirties had on Elizabeth's attitude to sex is a question. She was moved away the following year, but after Catherine Parr's death in 1548 Seymour renewed his attentions. The royal council suspected a plot, and Elizabeth and some of her household were interrogated. She was far too smart to give anything away, even if there was anything. Seymour, however, was executed in 1549.

During the rest of Edward VI's reign Elizabeth kept out of politics. She lived mainly at Hatfield in Hertfordshire, with her own household of 120 people or more, enjoying a substantial income under her father's will and investing heavily and profitably in property. Danger reappeared with the accession of Mary I, when Elizabeth was 19. Mary suspected her of involvement in Sir Thomas Wyatt's rebellion and sent her to the Tower of London. Landed by boat in pouring rain at Traitor's Gate, Elizabeth protested she was no traitor, but she was held there for two months and then put under house arrest in Oxfordshire. The half-sisters were formally reconciled and Elizabeth returned to Hatfield in 1555, but it must have been a huge relief when Mary died.

Elizabeth immediately appointed her trusty friend and adviser William Cecil, later Lord Burghley, as her secretary. He would be her chief minister for the next 40 years. Another reliable friend, Robert Dudley, future Earl of Leicester (a son of the executed Duke of Northumberland), was also taken on

The Worship of Gloriana

Pride in England and the queen helped to inspire a brilliant outpouring of the arts in music, painting and architecture, and especially in drama and poetry, with Shakespeare in the van, his history plays glorifying the Tudor dynasty. Elizabeth liked her subjects to flatter her and they did. A cult of her as a demi-goddess developed and she was hailed in wildly extravagant tributes as Diana, virgin huntress and goddess of the moon, or Astraea, personification of a golden age. In a court spectacle of 1581 she was represented as the Fortress of Perfect Beauty, unsuccessfully besieged by the cannon of Desire, which fired sweets. In Edmund Spenser's interminable 1590s poem *The Fairie Queen* she appeared in two roles as the chaste and beautiful Belphoebe and as Gloriana, majestic queen and empress, while Thomas Dekker called her Eliza who had made her land Elysium.

Portrait of Robert Dudley, Earl of Leicester a-swagger in his fashionable finery, painted in the 1560s by Steven van der Meulen. There has always been talk of a love affair between Dudley and Queen Elizabeth, and there is no doubt that she loved her Robin dearly, at least as a sterling friend. It is doubtful whether it ever went any further than that.

board. The burnings at the stake stopped at once, the royal council was purged of its most zealous Catholics and an astrologically propitious date was chosen for the coronation in January 1559. Elizabeth laid out £16,000 of her own money (equivalent to £6 million or more today) on a coronation of staggering magnificence with processions and propaganda pageants.

The main item on the new regime's agenda was inevitably religion. What exactly Elizabeth's religious convictions were, nobody knows. During Mary's reign she had dutifully followed Catholic forms, but she now approved a return to Protestantism and reassertion of the royal supremacy, and a return to the situation much as it had been at the death of Edward VI. It did not satisfy fervent Catholics, and still less did it satisfy Calvinists, but it suited the majority of people.

Another pressing question was the queen's marriage. A Protestant heir to the throne was needed, and in any case everyone took it for granted that a woman should marry. For years her advisers and her parliaments would plead with Elizabeth to wed, partly out of concern for the succession but also out of genuine affection for her in the belief that she could only be unhappy and unfulfilled without a husband and children. She thought differently, and tantalizingly wove her way through all proposals and out the other side. She was very close to Robert Dudley, but he was politically impossible. Philip II of Spain offered himself in 1559 and was rejected. King Erik XIV of Sweden sent lavish presents in vain, and two Hapsburg archdukes were considered. The 1570s saw the arrival of a promising new foreign suitor, François, Duke of Alençon, youngest son of Henry II of France. He was ugly, charming and amusing, and Elizabeth was fond of him and called him her frog. Marry him she did not. That such proposals were contemplated but never accepted was not capriciousness on the queen's part. She and her council found the deceptive encouragement of foreign suitors a useful ploy to ward off interference from the Roman Catholic powers of Europe.

The Calvinists assumed, mistakenly, that things were moving their way and were content to wait on events. From the official Catholic point of view, Elizabeth was illegitimate and had no right to the throne, but there was no anti-Catholic witch hunt, and closet Catholics were left undisturbed. In 1568, however, the arrival of Mary, Queen of Scots seeking sanctuary in England provided a tempting focus for Catholic plots. A rising in the north by the Catholic earls of Northumberland and Westmorland was defeated without difficulty and the Duke of Norfolk was arrested in 1569 and executed at the demand of Parliament in 1572 after being drawn into an idiotic plot for a

The Master of Horse

Robert Dudley was Elizabeth I's friend and supporter from before she came to the throne. In 1560 he was suspected of murdering his wife, Amy Robsart, who died in mysterious circumstances. He dodged Elizabeth's plan to marry him to Mary, Queen of Scots, by pleading that he could not bear to be parted from his sovereign lady. She made him Earl of Leicester in 1564 and he used to entertain her in style at Kenilworth Castle. He was put in command of the troops gathered at Tilbury to defend the country against the Spanish Armada in 1588. He died a few months later, in his fifties.

Spanish invasion. In 1570 Pope Pius V had excommunicated and deposed Elizabeth, releasing her subjects from their oaths of allegiance. The subjects, very sensibly, paid him no mind.

England was prosperous and peaceful, and the queen was popular with her subjects and took trouble to remain so. Her Accession Day on 17 November was celebrated as a national holiday and she made progresses round the country in summertime to show herself to her people, on horseback or in an open litter so that she was easy to see. Country people flocked to cheer her and she took apparent, and probably perfectly genuine, pleasure in events staged in every town in her honour – parades, tableaux, recitations by the local schoolchildren, welcoming speeches by the local dignitaries – and would wave cheerfully to the crowds. In appearance and bearing, Elizabeth was the personification of majesty. She dressed in the height of fashion, and it took two hours to get her ready to be seen at court every day. After a smallpox attack in 1562, which almost killed her and left her scarred and partially bald, she relied heavily on wigs and cosmetics. Moving between Whitehall, Greenwich, Richmond, Hampton Court and Windsor, her court enjoyed dancing and card games for high stakes. To the queen's irritation it was also a hive of romantic intrigue and sexual liaisons.

Elizabeth summoned Parliament far less often than her predecessors – she was not enamoured of masculine authority, after all – but Parliament was still treated as a necessary and useful, if sometimes irritating, element in the governing of the country. In the 1580s the country was drawn into a long conflict with Spain, partly by a rebellion in the Netherlands, which was vital to English commercial interests, and partly because after the execution of Mary, Queen of Scots in 1587 Philip II of Spain considered it his religious duty to bring England back to the embrace of Rome. The English regime backed

Francis Drake and other piratical adventurers in preying on Spanish shipping and Spain's New World colonies, and Elizabeth invested money in some of the ventures. In 1587 Drake 'singed the King of Spain's beard' with an attack on Cadiz harbour and the following year he took a leading part in the defeat of the Spanish Armada.

The menacing Spanish fleet of some 130 vessels was intended to ferry an invasion army from the Netherlands across to England, to bring the English forcibly to heel, but as the big galleons sailed up the Channel from Spain they were harried by the smaller, handier English ships. When they anchored, fire-ships were sent in and the weather intervened decisively for England with a fierce westerly gale. The Spaniards had to run for it through the North Sea and all the way round Scotland and Ireland to get home and more than half their ships were wrecked. Meanwhile Elizabeth joined her troops, which had mustered at Tilbury to defend London. She rose to the moment with a superb speech: 'I know I have the body of a weak and feeble woman, but I have the heart and stomach of a king, and a king of England too ...' The Spanish defeat was hailed in England as a divine deliverance, and the wind was a Protestant wind. 'God breathed and they were scattered.' Two more attempted Spanish invasions were defeated by the weather in the 1590s.

Since her subjects could not persuade her to marry, they took to hailing her as the Virgin Queen instead and Elizabeth became almost a Protestant substitute for the Virgin Mary. Her sex life is a total mystery, but she was not

The 'Ermine Portrait' of Queen Elizabeth I (from the ermine on her arm) belongs to the Cecil family, Marquesses of Salisbury, who are descended from Lord Burghley, the queen's principal minister. It hangs at Hatfield House and shows 'Gloriana' in all her royal magnificence. Her portraits were not intended as likenesses, but as icons and images of a semi-divine being.

Shakespeare and History

The history play was a new idea in Shakespeare's time and it was his plays of the 1590s on the kings from Richard II to Richard III that made him a popular dramatist. Telling the audience what it wanted to hear, the plays were a persuasive endorsement of the Tudors as England's saviours after the nightmare of civil war. There were stirring statements of pride in England – 'this royal throne of kings, this sceptered isle … this precious stone set in the silver sea' – and the plays both reflected and contributed to English nationalism, as they have done ever since (witness the Laurence Olivier film of *Henry V* made during World War II). In *Richard III* the last Yorkist king was unfairly but unforgettably portrayed as a twisted monster of evil from whose tyranny England was rescued by Henry Tudor. Shakespeare may have seen Elizabeth entertained at Kenilworth Castle (pictured).

displeased when Sir Walter Raleigh named a bit of North America Virginia in tribute to her. A rival to Raleigh at court in the 1590s was Robert Devereux, Earl of Essex. He was in his twenties and Elizabeth, now in her fifties, was taken with his boyish good looks and showy charm. She liked to play cards with him until the dawn chorus and he was given a succession of military commands. In 1599 he was sent with a sizeable army to put down a rebellion in Ireland, where resistance against the planting of English Protestant settlers had been growing and Hugh O'Neill, Earl of Tyrone, had offered the Irish throne to Philip II of Spain. Essex made a hash of it and instead of defeating Tyrone signed a truce with him. He was put under house arrest by the furious queen and council, and in 1601 staged a characteristically incompetent abortive coup. He paid with his head.

Elizabeth had reached the age of 65 in 1598. Her looks had gone, her teeth were falling out, she was often depressed, and time was robbing her of faithful councillors and friends. Robert Dudley had died in 1588 and William Cecil in 1598. His place was taken by his highly capable son Robert, later to be the principle minister of James I but things were turning sour. Inflation, a succession of poor harvests and the high taxes needed to pay for the long struggle with Spain were causing resentment. Parliament was fractious, though the queen made a superb speech to the members in 1601, which reduced many of them to tears. 'And though you have had, and may have, many mightier and wiser princes sitting in this seat, yet you never had, nor shall have, any that will love you better.'

In her last illness, in which she was brought down by bronchitis and perhaps pneumonia, Elizabeth seems finally to have given up on her life. She refused to eat or go to bed or see a doctor, and for days lay propped up on cushions, sighing miserably, until early one March morning death came for her at last.

Meanwhile...

1493   The Holy Roman Emperor backs Warbeck's claim to the throne; Henry VII begins a trade war with the Low Countries.

1496   The king authorizes Italian navigators John and Sebastian Cabot to find new lands and establish a trade route to Asia.

1502   James Tyrrell is executed for plotting to overthrow Henry VII and confesses to the murders of Edward V and Richard.

1504   Thomas More takes a prominent role in effecting Parliament's huge cuts to the king's spending.

1526   The bishops order an English translation of the New Testament to be burned outside St Paul's Cathedral.

1536   The Pilgrimage of Grace begins with a revolt in Lincolnshire against the Dissolution of the Monasteries.

<table>
<tr><td>1485</td><td>1502</td><td>**1536**</td><td>1549</td><td>1552</td></tr>
</table>

1540   The last of the monasteries to be dissolved, in March of this year, is Waltham Abbey in Essex.

1545   Henry VIII sees his flagship the *Mary Rose* sink in the Solent. At least 500 men drown.

1548   Catherine Parr, the surviving wife of Henry VIII, dies from complications of childbirth at Sudeley Castle.

1549   Rebellions break out. At Mousehold Heath, rebel Norfolk Robert Kett establishes a 'commonwealth'.

1550   England makes peace with France and Scotland, and the Treaty of Boulogne finally returns Boulogne to France.

1552	Archbishop Cranmer publishes the Second Book of Common Prayer, confirmation of the move to Protestantism.
1553	Hugh Willoughby and Richard Chancellor set out from England to discover a northeast passage to China.
1554	Four months after Mary I's accession, English parliament meets to re-establish Catholicism in England.
1557	A burlesque titled *The Sack-Full of Newes* becomes the first play in England to be completely censored.
1557	Following Mary I's marriage to Philip of Spain, England becomes an ally of Spain and declares war on France.
1562	Milled coins replace hand-hammered ones, and are produced in a screw press powered by a horse-drawn mill.

1557   1571   1576   **1593**   1603

1563	John Foxe publishes *Actes and Monuments* (or Foxe's *Book of Martyrs*), highlighting persecutions during Mary I's reign.
1571	Sir Thomas Gresham founds the Royal Exchange in London, to establish the capital as a financial power base.
1576	James Burbage opens London's first playhouse – The Theatre – in Shoreditch.
1593	William Shakespeare writes *Romeo and Juliet* and *A Midsummer Night's Dream*.
1598	John Stow publishes a survey of the city of London and creates a survey of Tudor life for posterity.

The Stuarts
1603–1714

The Stuarts were the first sovereigns of the whole island of Britain. Under the Tudors the English Parliament had grown stronger, with royal support. Under the Stuarts it grew stronger still – against the royal will. James I and Charles I clashed with their parliaments because of their belief in royal absolutism and the divine right of kings. James was too prudent to endanger his throne, but Charles fought a civil war that cost him both his crown and the head on which he had worn it. High Churchmen and Puritans fell out over religion, but the Commonwealth period gave most people their fill of Puritanism and Charles II was welcomed back in 1660. Cynical and shrewd, he kept his throne for 25 years. His younger brother, James II, was a Catholic throwback to Stuart autocracy and was soon driven out of the country. The 'glorious revolution', which replaced him with his daughter Mary and her husband, William of Orange, decisively limited the power of the monarchy. The reign of the last Stuart ruler, Mary's sister Anne, saw Britain triumphant in war on the Continent and the development of something beginning to resemble modern party politics.

❧

Blenheim Palace in Oxfordshire was built between 1705 and 1722 for the Duke of Malborough and his formidable duchess. The duchess detested it, considering it absurdly expensive, and was constantly quarrelling with the principal architect, Sir John Vanbrugh.

James I
1603–1625

BORN	19 June 1566 at Edinburgh Castle
PARENTS	Mary, Queen of Scots, and Henry Stewart, Lord Darnley
CROWNED	(1) as James VI of Scots: 29 July 1567, at Stirling Castle aged one; (2) as James I of England and Ireland: 25 July 1603 at Westminster Abbey, aged 37
MARRIED	Anne (d. 1619), daughter of Frederick II of Denmark and Norway
CHILDREN	Seven, of whom three survived infancy: Henry, Elizabeth and Charles
DIED	27 March 1625 at Theobalds Park, Hertfordshire, aged 58

The three most momentous products of James I's reign in England were probably the Authorized Version of the Bible, the Pilgrim Fathers' voyage to America in the Mayflower, and the introduction of golf. During Elizabeth's last years, sharp politicians in England had kept their lines open to the King of Scots, the obvious candidate to succeed Elizabeth, and within minutes of Elizabeth's death a horseman rode full tilt for Edinburgh. The new King of Great Britain, as he styled himself, took the road to London with an entourage of Scots looking forward to rich pickings in England. In his remaining 22 years he would return to Scotland only once.

James I as painted by Daniel Mytens in 1621. For the portrait he wore the insignia of the Order of the Garter.

L ike Elizabeth, James had grown up without a mother. However, he had grown up without a father either, and his difficult and dangerous youth left him so terrified of violence that in later life he wore thickly padded clothes to protect him from assassination. Baptized a Roman Catholic, he was brought up a Protestant and four Protestant regents in succession, three of whom died violent deaths, ruled Scotland during his childhood. His education was sadistically beaten into him and gave him both an appetite for scholarship and nightmares for the rest of his life. Inevitably, powerful figures contended to control him. In 1582, at the age of 16, he was kidnapped by a group of conspirators led by William Ruthven, Earl of Gowrie, and held prisoner. He got away the following year and Gowrie was hanged. In 1600, when James believed that the new Earl of Gowrie and his brother were plotting to murder him, the two Ruthvens were killed.

James had discovered how to run Scotland by steering a middle course between Protestants and Catholics. He refrained from persecuting Catholics, managed to keep the Presbyterian Kirk on a leash and collected a substantial annual allowance from Queen Elizabeth in England while impatiently awaiting her demise. In 1599 he published his book *Basilikon Doron*, upholding the divine right of kings.

On his way south to accept the English throne hopeful English Puritans – Calvinists who wanted to 'purify' the Church of England – presented him with a petition calling for an end to popish practices such as bowing at the name of Jesus, the use of the ring in weddings and the sign of the cross in baptism. They wanted stricter Sabbath observance and more sermons but, surprisingly, shorter services. The new king presided over a conference of Anglicans and Puritans at Hampton Court, which came down mainly on the Anglican side and also originated the Authorized Version of the Bible. James found the

Church of England with its moderate temper and himself as its supreme head very much to his liking. The Puritans were disappointed, but it became clear that what the new regime most wanted was peace and quiet, and it had no wish to proceed against anyone who was not an infernal nuisance. The same principle applied to English Catholics as well.

James VI of Scots, as he told his first English Parliament, was an old hand at kingship but he lacked Elizabeth's charm and glamour. If not as shambling and slobbery as he was sometimes maliciously portrayed, he was uncouth and

The King James Bible

The Authorized Version of the Bible was the outcome of the Hampton Court conference of 1605, chaired and dominated by the king himself, which decided that there were too many English versions of the scriptures. There was the 1539 Great Bible of William Tyndale and Miles Coverdale, the 1560 Geneva Bible by English Protestants who had taken refuge in Switzerland in 'Bloody' Mary's time (also called the Breeches Bible because it had Adam and Eve making themselves breeches out of fig leaves), and the rival Bishops' Bible of 1572. They were now to be replaced by a translation that would be undertaken by scholars, reviewed by the bishops, and ratified by the king. The new Bible was the work of some 50 translators, working together in six teams. Among them were some of the greatest scholars of the day. Lancelot Andrewes, for instance, knew 15 or more languages, among them Hebrew, Syriac, Greek and Latin, and was later Bishop of Winchester. The Bible came out in 1611, with a dedication to the king, and was for centuries the translation known and loved in all English-speaking countries.

undignified, and his court was a coarser place than Elizabeth's. His Scottish speech was sometimes incomprehensible to the English, he was wildly extravagant financially and, although he was an affectionate husband and father who sired seven children, he had an unconcealed enthusiasm for good-looking young men. Far worse, he lacked the Tudors' understanding of English politics and the English way of doing things. In 1614 he told the Spanish ambassador that he could not understand how his predecessors had allowed the House of Commons to come into existence at all. On the other hand, he was no fool, he had long experience of coping in Scotland, and on the whole he managed religious and political tensions in England skilfully and successfully.

Peace and Diplomacy

With James's arrival in England, the expensive war against Spain was halted and the years of raiding and looting across the Anglo-Scottish border came to an end. The situation in Ireland was also brought under control and thousands of Scots Protestants were subsequently settled in Ulster on land taken from the native Irish. However, the new king was short of money and his attempts to raise it roused parliamentary opposition. Parliament also disliked both the king's views on royal predominance and the predominance of Scots in his household, and turned down James's attempts to unite England and Scotland. The two countries had the same king, but they remained separate entities, although a combined flag, the Union Jack, was adopted in 1606.

James and his queen, Anne of Denmark, gave their first two children Tudor names, Henry and Elizabeth. The promising Prince Henry died of typhoid fever at 18 in 1612, leaving his unpromising brother Charles as the heir. Robert Cecil's death the same year robbed James of his ablest minister, and his handsome young favourites were resented, less from disapproval of homosexuality than because they interfered in politics. This was particularly true of George Villiers. Born to a minor Leicestershire landed family, he had great influence with the king in James's last ten years. Besides feathering his own nest and enriching his relations, he dominated the court and largely controlled access to the king, who fondly called him Steenie and made him Duke of Buckingham.

Various rejected designs for the new union flag of 1606, combining the English cross of St George with the Scottish saltire of St Andrew, and used to identify British ships at sea. King James had hoped to achieve a formal union of England and Scotland, but he failed and the two countries remained separate entities for another hundred years.

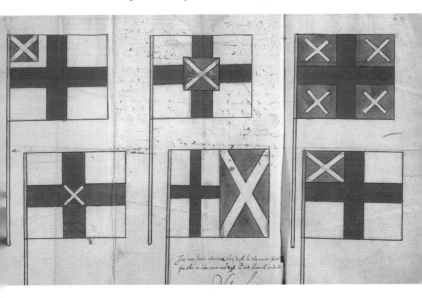

In foreign affairs, as in religion, James believed in peace and quiet, but he was attacked for conciliating Spain, especially after the outbreak in 1618 of the Thirty Years War between Catholics and Protestants, fought mainly in Germany. The alliance of Spain with the Hapsburg emperor on the Catholic side sent shivers down Protestant English spines. In the Protestant camp was Frederick V, Elector Palatine of the Rhine and for a mere four days in winter King of Bohemia, the 'winter king', who was married to James's beautiful daughter Elizabeth. When he was driven from his realm, English opinion was firmly for him and against Spain. James considered his son-in-law an idiot, and his relations with Parliament became strained. Characteristically, he hoped to proceed by diplomacy, by marrying Prince Charles to a Spanish princess and persuading Spain to get the Elector Frederick restored. Parliament demanded all-out war against Spain and James sent the members home. The marriage plan failed in any case.

James adored hunting and disliked music. A prolific author, he translated the Book of Psalms and wrote poems, Bible commentaries, and books on political philosophy. He also wrote on witchcraft and smoking, both of which he disapproved of. A sneering critic called him 'the wisest fool in Christendom'. There's a recent suggestion that he suffered from attention deficit hyperactivity disorder, but he took an intelligent interest in science and encouraged the Dutchman Cornelius Drebbel, who developed a kind of submarine. He is said to have taken the king for a trip along the Thames in it, making James the first sovereign to travel underwater. In his last years, however, the ageing king suffered from gout, arthritis and kidney problems until finally carried off by a stroke.

Gunpowder, Treason and Plot

Guy Fawkes was a Roman Catholic soldier of fortune who went abroad to fight for Spain. Drawn into the Catholic plot that made him famous, he returned to England in 1604 when he was in his mid-thirties. A small house was taken near the palace of Westminster. From here the conspirators began digging a tunnel, from which they intended to blow king and Parliament to smithereens when Parliament was opened by the king on 5 November 1605. The tunnel was abandoned when they discovered they could instead rent a vault beneath the Lords' chamber. However, word of the conspiracy leaked to the royal council and a search was ordered on the night of the 4th. About midnight, Guy Fawkes was discovered in suspicious proximity to a length of slow match and 36 barrels of gunpowder. He was arrested, and the citizens of London were encouraged to light bonfires to salute the deliverance. They merrily did and bonfires have celebrated the event ever since.

Charles I
1625–1649

BORN	19 November 1600 at Dunfermline Palace, Scotland
PARENTS	James VI of Scots and Anne of Denmark
CROWNED	2 February 1626, at Westminster Abbey, aged 25
MARRIED	Henrietta Maria (d. 1669), daughter of King Henri IV of France
CHILDREN	Nine, of whom six survived infancy: Charles, Mary, James, Elizabeth, Henry and Henrietta
DIED	Executed in London on 30 January 1649, aged 48

A cult of the 'royal martyr' grew up after the beheading of Charles I. To this day, on the anniversary of his execution, wreaths are placed on his statue in Trafalgar Square, which looks down Whitehall to the site of his execution. Charles was remarkably unlike his father, which was to prove a fatal disadvantage. He was of finer clay altogether and his court was far more civilized, but unlike the garrulous James he was reserved and shy, with no sense of humour and a very limited understanding of other people.

Charles I's portraits by Van Dyck make him look kingly (and disguise how short he was at 5ft 4in), but he lacked his father's political skill. One thing he did inherit from James, unfortunately, was an adamant belief in the divine right of kings and in his people's duty to obey him – an attitude that was probably made all the more unyielding by his own lack of self-confidence.

Born in Scotland, Charles was two when his father succeeded to the English throne and four when he was brought to England. A sickly little boy, slow to walk and talk, he grew up with a stammer and in the shadow of his elder brother Henry, the heir to the throne, who was six years his senior. Henry was much admired, and Charles idolized him. He was 11 when Henry died. Charles was left with the impossible task of living up to his brother, in his own mind as well as in English opinion.

When Charles was in his early twenties, his father was still fondly calling him 'my baby'. Needing a guide, philosopher and friend, he attached himself to the most detested person in the country, George Villiers, Duke of Buckingham, his father's favourite. They went to Spain together in 1623, incognito as Thomas and John Smith, to angle for a Spanish princess as a bride for Charles. The Spanish court found them embarrassing. Charles decided that the Infanta Maria was for him and, seeing her walking in a garden one day, jumped over the wall to press his suit in person, at which she promptly ran away. Having acquired two Titians, but no infanta, Charles and Buckingham returned to England, where they began calling for war with Spain.

That went down nicely with Parliament at first, but Charles followed Buckingham along the wrong paths. A marriage was arranged for him with an attractive French Roman Catholic princess, Henrietta Maria, who was guaranteed the free exercise of her religion and control of the children. She arrived with a small army of priests, and the wedding was held soon after Charles succeeded to the throne, when he was 24 and she was 15. She did not seem to enjoy the wedding night and Parliament did not enjoy the prospect of a Catholic heir. Expensive wars with Spain and then with France led to humiliating English defeats, and Buckingham's assassination by an oddball naval officer in 1628 was greeted with rejoicing in London. Charles and Henrietta Maria began to get along much better after that and the following year their first child was born, though the little boy lived for only a few hours.

The relationship with Parliament, however, did not sweeten. Many of the country gentlemen, town businessmen and lawyers in the House of Commons disapproved of the regime's high-handed measures to raise money, including taxation without parliamentary consent, forced loans and the imprisonment of people who refused to pay. In 1628, Parliament passed the Petition of Right against these practices. Needing money, Charles accepted it grudgingly, but then there was trouble over religion. The king took the High Church attitude, broadly for Catholicism without the pope, valuing continuity with the past. He had no time for the Puritans in the Commons, who in 1629 condemned 'popish practices'. Charles adjourned Parliament, but in an unprecedented scene the Speaker of the Commons was held down in his chair by force while the members passed resolutions condemning the king's behaviour. At this point they had no idea whatever of dethroning him, but it was ominous.

A King's Road to War

Despairing of getting his way in Parliament, Charles decided to rule without it, which he did for 11 years from 1629 to 1640. He felt much happier. He and Henrietta Maria were now a loving couple, and he relied on her advice: she was his substitute for Buckingham (though her influence unfortunately was to stiffen his absolutist spine). Their sons Charles and James, both future kings, were born in 1630 and 1633. Charles loved hunting and enjoyed tennis and chess. Whitehall Palace was his principal residence, but he was especially fond of Hampton Court. The court's stately formality expressed his belief in an ordered hierarchy, with himself at the summit, and he spent money on the navy and on art. He bought the Raphael cartoons, and Inigo Jones helped to design the court masques, which Henrietta Maria loved acting in. Anthony Van Dyck was appointed court painter.

The king enjoyed the support of the High Church bishops he had appointed. They accepted the principle of divine right and obedience to the royal will. Led by the Archbishop of Canterbury from 1633, William Laud, they were suspected by many landowners of wanting to reclaim the estates that had been taken from the monasteries in the Reformation, a hundred years previously. Some Puritans thought bishops an abominable papist relic in any case, and feared Henrietta Maria's Catholic influence. The regime began persecuting extreme Puritans in England and, disastrously, tried to introduce the Anglican prayer book into Scotland. Charles and his advisers were badly out of touch with the Scots, and their action provoked a riot in Edinburgh Cathedral. Led by Archibald Campbell, Earl of Argyll, Presbyterian Scots signed a National Covenant of resistance in 1638 and gathered an army to defend the Kirk.

The long period of autocracy without a parliament, religious tensions and the regime's methods of raising money had roused determined opposition. In 1640, needing funds to fight the Scots, Charles was forced to summon Parliament. This was the Short Parliament – so called because the members were soon dismissed when they insisted on sulkily rehearsing their piled-up grievances. The Scottish army crossed the border, occupied Newcastle and demanded to be paid to go back home. Charles was now forced to summon Parliament again, but this time the king would not be permitted to dissolve it. The Long Parliament, as it became known, realized the strength of its hand, condemned the king's actions and sent his chief minister, Thomas Wentworth, Earl of Strafford, to the block. The king had to accept, or pretend to accept, drastic limitations on his royal prerogative. Changing tack completely, he went to Scotland to gather support there, and agreed to the abolition of bishops in Scotland and the establishment of root-and-branch Presbyterianism. In January 1642, when he was back in London and feeling that there were some in Parliament who supported him, Charles personally led a force of soldiers to Westminster to arrest five of the most objectionable members of the House of Commons and one member of the House of Lords for treason. When he got there, 'the birds had flown'. The action turned many potential supporters decisively against him.

Charles had reached a position where assertiveness had failed and his attempts at conciliation were rightly distrusted. The crunch was coming and

The Divine Right of Kings

In his book *Basilikon Doron* James I proclaimed that God made the king 'a little God to sit on his throne and rule over other men'. The idea that the king had a God-given right to rule and subjects a corresponding obligation to obey was not new in England. From Anglo-Saxon times there was a solemn moment in a king's coronation when his head was anointed with holy oil, signifying that God had made him king. This ritual remained in the ceremony ever afterwards. The recognition of Henry VIII as supreme head of the Church of England bolstered the idea of divine right, which both Catholics and Calvinists disliked. Fundamentally it rested on the widespread belief that human society was a hierarchy with the monarch at the top, a hierarchy that was seen as a vital protection against anarchy. Charles I's execution did not behead the notion of divine right. It remained part of the outlook of High Churchmen into the 18th century.

The Execution

King Charles spent his last night at St James's Palace. Up by 5 o'clock on an icy January day, he put on two shirts so that he would not shiver and be thought afraid. At about 10 o'clock, soldiers escorted him through the park to Whitehall Palace, but there was difficulty in finding an executioner: no one wanted the job. In the early afternoon the king was led to the scaffold, outside the Banqueting House in Whitehall. He made his last speech, blaming his opponents for the war, forgiving them, and saying that he died a Christian of the Church of England. Then he took off his doublet and Order of the Garter insignia and put his hair up under a white satin cap. He knelt at the block and, when he spread his arms to signal he was ready, the hooded, anonymous executioner severed his head with one axe-blow. It fell into the basket and a huge groan went up from the crowd. The head was sewn roughly back on to the body and the corpse was taken to Windsor for burial.

both sides began preparing for war. Henrietta Maria raised money from her Catholic connections. Charles toured the north and the Midlands, making speeches and issuing proclamations and pamphlets that maintained that by defending the constitution of the country, the law and the Church of England against the power-hungry Parliament he was defending his people's freedom and keeping anarchy at bay. After waiting for the harvest to be in, Charles raised the royal standard at Nottingham in August 1642.

The Civil War split the country, split families and split old friends. The advice Charles's father had given him about battle was always to wear lightweight armour, so he could run away fast if need be. Charles was too brave to run, but he had no experience of war and he was no strategist. At critical moments he was too often indecisive. Parliament had the wealth of London at its disposal and an unexpected military genius in a Huntingdonshire squire named Oliver Cromwell. The Scots Covenanters allied themselves with Parliament in 1643 and crossed the Tweed. Cromwell's army – the Roundheads – won the crucial battles of Marston Moor in 1644 and Naseby in 1645, and Charles surrendered to the Scots in 1646. Under house arrest, the king enjoyed reading and playing bowls, while taking part in a complicated game of cat-and-mouse as all parties tried to turn the situation to their advantage. The Scots handed Charles over to Parliament in 1647, but after secret negotiations with the king they changed sides in return for his promise to make England Presbyterian. They were defeated in battle by Cromwell and at last, in January 1649, Charles was tried in Westminster Hall for 'high crimes against the realm of England'. He maintained that no court on earth could try a king, but 'Charles Stuart' was duly sentenced to death as 'a tyrant, traitor, murderer and public enemy'. At the end of the month, with exemplary courage and dignity, he went to his beheading in Whitehall.

The Commonwealth

There was no king in England between the execution of Charles I and the restoration of the monarchy with Charles II, or not in theory. But after centuries of monarchy there was no practical possibility of suddenly doing without it: Oliver Cromwell would be king in all but name, with the backing of Parliament's godly New Model Army. Parliament declared the existence of something called the Commonwealth and Free State of England and abolished the monarchy and the House of Lords. Cromwell went to Ireland in 1649 to put down Irish Catholics and royalists, which he did with a ruthlessness that was to rouse enduring hatred. He went on to defeat the Scots who had come out for the future Charles II. The navy was put to good use against the Dutch.

Cromwell was a godly Puritan, but not nearly as intolerant as some. He tolerated closet Anglicans and Catholics, allowed Jews to immigrate, and once told a deputation of bothersome, ranting Presbyterians to think it possible that they might be mistaken, which must have come as a shock to them. He was a man of commanding ability and character and like Charles I, ironically, he could not work with parliaments. He summoned them and irritably dismissed them when they would not do what they were told. Late in 1653 he was declared Lord Protector and introduced various new constitutional arrangements that failed to work.

A portrait of Sir Oliver Cromwell by Sir Peter Lely, who went on to paint the beauties of Charles II's court. Cromwell was no beauty, but a plain man who liked to be depicted 'warts and all'.

The title of king was urged on Cromwell, who lived in Whitehall Palace and was addressed as 'Your Highness', but he refused it. After his death in 1658 his son Richard succeeded him as Lord Protector, but he resigned the next year. It was clear to almost everyone that the political experiment had failed and the army brought back Charles II, who was waiting anxiously abroad.

Charles II
1660–1685

BORN	29 May 1630 at St James's Palace
PARENTS	Charles I and Henrietta Maria
CROWNED	(1) as King of Scots: 1 January 1651 at Scone, aged 20; (2) as King of England and Ireland: 23 April 1661 at Westminster Abbey, aged 30
MARRIED	Catherine (d. 1705), daughter of the Duke of Braganza
CHILDREN	Three, who died in infancy, plus 16 by at least eight mistresses
DIED	6 February 1685 at Whitehall Palace, aged 54

Fleeing from defeat at the Battle of Worcester in September 1651, the young Charles II spent a day hiding high in an oak tree at Boscobel, in Shropshire, while Roundhead soldiers beat the bushes below in search of him. With the help of faithful royalists, he reached the south coast disguised as a manservant and got away by boat across the Channel. There was a tempting price on his head, but not a soul betrayed him. After his restoration in 1660 the oak tree flourished as the Royal Oak of many an inn sign, while the day of Charles's return to London was celebrated as Oak Apple Day.

As Charles I had been unlike his father James I, so Charles II was unlike Charles I. Worldly and easygoing, he was charming, humorous, devious, highly likeable, and highly sexed. He had knocked about

a bit and learned how to take care of himself. He was not one to let his principles cost him his head. He kept his head and his country together through years of turmoil, and his throne was never seriously challenged again. As he remarked to his brother James once, no one was going to kill him to make James king.

Charles started his life in the royal nursery at St James's Palace, where he would not go to sleep without his favourite bit of wood to cuddle. He was joined by a growing number of siblings as time went by, and one of his nursery companions was George Villiers, 2nd Duke of Buckingham, son of James I's favourite. George, who was two years older, would be a lifelong friend. When he was eight Charles was moved to Richmond with his own household under the Earl of Newcastle, who taught him horsemanship and to be a gentleman, not too religious nor too studious. He spent the first years of the Civil War with his father, seeing action at first hand. At 14 he was sent to the west country and, to keep him out of Parliament's hands after the Cavaliers' defeat at Naseby in 1645, Charles I ordered him to join his mother in exile in France.

Life with mother was not comfortable. A 'black' man, with black hair and a swarthy complexion, Charles was considered passably good-looking, but he was a penniless outsider who spoke no French, and the French court took little notice of him. He and Buckingham and other royalist young bucks in exile amused themselves with amateur scientific experiments and the pursuit of women. Charles acquired his first known mistress, the bold and beautiful Lucy Walter, who bore him a dearly loved son, James, future Duke of Monmouth.

Charles was 18 when his father was executed – the news reduced him to tears – and he succeeded to the throne, theoretically at least. He was invited to Scotland, where he found the Presbyterians detestable (and Presbyterianism 'not a religion for gentlemen'), but by accepting the Covenant he gained a coronation at Scone and an army to invade England. It was defeated at Worcester.

Escaping back to France after the Boscobel episode, he returned to Paris where he and his few courtiers were so poor they could afford only one meal a day and were besieged by creditors in the street. Charles presently moved to the Netherlands. Oliver Cromwell's death in 1658 changed the situation and secret negotiations began with General George Monck, commander of the parliamentary army in Scotland. Monck marched his men south to London, summoned the remnants of Charles I's Long Parliament and, to general approval and relief, secured the restoration of Charles II.

Return of a King

Parliament sent a fleet to the Netherlands and on a May morning the king embarked for the voyage to England. He had with him his household, the royal spaniels, and his new mistress, Barbara Villiers (of Buckingham's family), a young beauty with a complaisant husband and a taste for men. He arrived at Dover, to be met by Monck, and moved slowly with his retinue through Canterbury, Rochester and Deptford to London, greeted by cheering crowds all the way. He arrived in London on his 30th birthday to a tumultuous welcome, with church bells ringing, trumpets blasting, fountains running with wine, streets strewn with flowers and draped with tapestries, and women waving from balconies as the appreciative king raised his hat to them. So many people joined the parade that it took seven hours for it to pass through the City on the way to Whitehall. People were cheering not just the king's return but the end of Puritan grimness and dreary disapproval of pleasure.

All the rest of his life Charles loved to tell stories of his youthful adventures. His experiences had evidently toughened him and given him a survivor's resilience and a determination never to go on his travels again. Arrangements had to be worked out with a new parliament, which was naturally dominated by royalists. Oliver Cromwell's corpse was disinterred and hung on a gallows at Tyburn, and the head was stuck up on a pole at Westminster Hall. The surviving regicides – the judges who had condemned Charles I to death – were executed or imprisoned, but otherwise the past was not pursued. Many Commonwealth officials remained in their posts and most of the land deals made during the Commonwealth were retrospectively legalized. The New Model Army was paid off. The religious settlement, however, was less tolerant than Charles himself wanted. Parliament insisted on the supremacy of the Anglican Church as a guarantee of order and a bulwark against chaos.

In 1662 Charles married a 23-year-old Portuguese princess, Catherine of Braganza. With protruding teeth she was no beauty, but she came with a gratifying dowry and possession of Tangier and Bombay. England was beginning to dominate worldwide maritime trade, and commercial rivalry set off wars with the Dutch. A by-product was the acquisition in 1665 of New Amsterdam, renamed New York after the Duke of York, the king's brother. With New Jersey as well, there was now a chain of English colonies down the American north-eastern seaboard. At home, the country survived the Great Plague of 1665 and the Great Fire of London which followed the year after.

Charles's court was notoriously extravagant and licentious. Charles had such a bevy of mistresses that he was popularly nicknamed 'Old Rowley' after one of the stallions in the royal stud. Besides Barbara Villiers, eventually Duchess of Cleveland, there was the delightful actress Nell Gwynne, another actress named Moll Davies, and Louise de Kéroualle, a French charmer who was a spy for Louis XIV of France. Charles called her 'Fubbs' and made her Duchess of Portsmouth. A beauty who did not succumb to him, Frances Stewart, was the model for Britannia on his coins. The dukes of Buccleuch, Grafton, Richmond and St Albans are all descended from Charles's bastards.

He liked to stride across St James's Park with his courtiers and his little yappy dogs, and enjoyed tennis and a croquet-like game called pall mall as well as fishing and horse-racing. The court went racing at Newmarket twice a year, and Charles was the first monarch to have his own yacht, which was wittily christened *The Royal Escape*.

It was a flourishing period for literature, the theatre, the arts and science. *Paradise Lost* and *Pilgrim's Progress* were products of Charles's reign, if not of his spirit. John Dryden was poet laureate from 1668 and later defended the king against his political antagonists. The theatres reopened after being closed during the Commonwealth and, with the court's encouragement, Restoration comedy came into its own. Sir Peter Lely painted the court beauties; Sir

The Great Fire of London

The fire started in a bakery in Pudding Lane in the City on 2 September 1666 and spread with terrifying rapidity from one wooden building to another. London's mayor, Sir Thomas Bloodworth, who at first said dismissively that 'A woman might piss it out' did not prove competent to cope. King Charles and his brother James, Duke of York, arrived on the scene and took charge, as families fled with whatever possessions they could carry. The duke directed the fire-fighters and the king himself, black with smoke, encouraged soldiers who were demolishing buildings to create a fire-break. The Guildhall and St Paul's blazed and a stream of molten lead from the cathedral's roof poured down Ludgate Hill. When the fire was finally contained it had destroyed 13,000 buildings, including 87 churches, though only nine people had died.

Godfrey Kneller was court painter. Charles founded the Royal Hospital in Chelsea for old soldiers and laid the foundation stone for its stylish building by Sir Christopher Wren, who by royal appointment was rebuilding St Paul's and the City churches which had been destroyed in the fire.

In politics the king and his ministers struggled to cope with bitter religious divisions between Anglicans, Catholics and Puritans of various brands. Persistent shortage of money enabled Parliament to influence policy in ways the king disliked and to frustrate his attempts to extend greater toleration to Catholics. The Treaty of Dover, signed in 1670 with Louis XIV of France, allied England with the French against the Dutch, but there were secret clauses, known only to the king and a handful of advisers: in return for a subsidy

The Royal Society

Charles II was interested in science, in the aristocratic fashion of the day, and had his own laboratory in Whitehall Palace. In 1662 he conferred a charter on the Royal Society, which promoted research and met to discuss scientific ideas, witness experiments and demonstrations, and peer interestedly at new gadgets. The king found the Society's efforts to weigh air richly comic, but its presidents in his reign included Sir Christopher Wren and Samuel Pepys, and the prodigious Robert Hooke was curator of experiments. Among prominent members were Sir Isaac Newton, the pioneer chemist Robert Boyle, the expert on blood transfusions Richard Lower, Prince Rupert of the Rhine, and the astronomer Edmond Halley. Another was the king's astronomer royal, John Flamsteed, and the king supported the building of the Royal Observatory at Greenwich.

Astronomers at work in the Old Royal Observatory in Greenwich, one using a quadrant and the other a telescope. Charles II, who was interested in science, appointed John Flamsteed as Astronomer Royal in 1675 and helped to pay for the observatory, which was sited in Greenwich at the suggestion of Sir Christopher Wren. The Octagon Room was specially designed to contain pendulum clocks by Thomas Tompion. Further buildings were added in subsequent centuries and the time ball, put on the tower of the Octagon Room in 1833, was timed to drop every day at 1pm precisely.

Charles committed himself to re-establishing Roman Catholicism in England with the assistance of French troops. Charles never carried through with it and probably never meant to.

The queen's children were all stillborn and, by the end of the 1660s attempts to produce an heir had petered out. One of the king's problems was that his brother and heir apparent, James, Duke of York, was a known Catholic and it was widely suspected that the king was, too. Parliament's suspicions and prejudices prompted the passing of the Test Act of 1673, which excluded

Catholics from all public offices, although it stopped short of barring James from the succession. The duke resigned as Lord High Admiral, and Samuel Pepys, though not a Catholic, lost his position as Secretary of the Admiralty where he and the duke were building up the navy.

In 1678 anti-Catholic feeling rose to a frenzy when a loathsome, ex-Catholic opportunist called Titus Oates revealed a supposed Jesuit conspiracy to murder the king, replace him with the Duke of York and make England Roman Catholic again. The king saw straight through Oates, but most people wanted to believe him and the Popish Plot resulted in the execution of more than 30 Roman Catholics as well as attempts to exclude the Duke of York from the succession. The terms Whig and Tory first emerged at this time: the former were those who wanted James barred from the throne; the latter were opposed to them. Charles supported his brother to the hilt. He kept his nerve, dissolving three parliaments in succession to prevent the passing of a bill to exclude James, and turned the mounting fear of another civil war to his advantage. The discovery in 1683 of a real conspiracy, the Rye House Plot, to murder both the king and the duke, and put the Duke of Monmouth on the throne, caused revulsion. Some of the Whig leaders were implicated and executed, and the hysteria died down.

In his last years, Charles's income was boosted by a booming economy, so 'the Merry Monarch' had no need to summon any more parliaments. At the end, the king suffered an unexpected stroke. The doctors' efforts were useless and he gracefully apologized 'for being such an unconscionable time a-dying'. He sent for a Catholic priest to give him the last rites of the Church and after five days he fell into a coma; his breathing stopped and his brother James hurried from the bedside to take over the reins. There were the usual rumours of poisoning.

The Protestant Whore

The best-remembered of the Merry Monarch's many mistresses, Nell Gwynne was a poor London girl who reputedly grew up in a brothel. In her teens she got a job selling oranges in theatres and was soon on the stage herself, being particularly admired in comedy parts. She became King Charles's mistress in 1668 or thereabouts, when she was 17 or so, and retired from the stage in 1671 when the king provided her with a smart house in Pall Mall. Cheerful, good-natured, saucy and high-spirited, disdaining social niceties, she seems to have come as a breath of fresh air to the man she called her Charles III because she had had two Charleses before him. There was a famous occasion in 1681 when her coach was surrounded by a hostile crowd

who thought she was her French rival, the Roman Catholic Duchess of Portsmouth. Nell stuck her head out of the window and said, 'Pray good people be silent. I am the Protestant whore.' Charles II's last words on his deathbed were reported as, 'Let not poor Nelly starve.' James II treated her generously, but she had only two more years to live: she died in 1687, aged about 36.

James II
1685–1688

BORN	Born 14 October 1633 at St James's Palace
PARENTS	Charles I and Henrietta Maria
CROWNED	23 April 1685 at Westminster Abbey, aged 51
MARRIED	(1) Anne (d. 1671), daughter of Edward Hyde, Earl of Clarendon; (2) Mary (d. 1718), daughter of the Duke of Modena
CHILDREN	Eight by his first wife, of which only his successors Mary and Anne survived; many more by his second, but only a son James (the Old Pretender) and a daughter Louise Maria survived; seven or more by mistresses
DIED	16 September 1701 at St Germain-en-Laye in France, aged 67

The future James VII of Scots and II of England and Ireland was created Duke of York in 1643. He was with his father and brother in the early days of the Civil War, but in 1646 he was caught in Oxford when the city surrendered to the Roundheads. With his servants all dismissed – even his favourite dwarf – he was taken to London and confined in St James's Palace. He was a resourceful boy and in 1648, under cover of a cheerful game of hide-and-seek, he slipped away to helpers who disguised him in girl's clothes and got him on a boat to Holland.

Portrait of James II in garter robes, painted by Sir Peter Lely.

The 14-year-old James moved uneasily between relatives in the Netherlands and his mother in Paris. Four years later he took a commission in the French army. He made a good officer, and he would surely have been more successful in a career in the armed forces, giving orders and having them obeyed, than he would prove to be as a king, grappling with politicians and principles.

James was 26 when his brother was restored to the throne and he accompanied him on the return to England. As Lord High Admiral he took a leading role in the naval wars with the Dutch. He had his own mini-court at St James's Palace, which kept him and his wife Anne Hyde, the daughter of his brother's chief minister, permanently in debt while she grew mountainously plump. James was even more devoted to the pursuit of women than his brother, and he also enjoyed hunting and racing at Newmarket.

The Black Box

James, Duke of Monmouth, was Charles II's bastard son by Lucy Walter, born in Rotterdam in 1649 during Charles's exile. He was the obvious Protestant alternative to his uncle James, and to legitimize his claim that he was the rightful heir to the throne he and his backers maintained that Charles had married Lucy Walter. Papers proving the marriage were supposedly contained in a mysterious black box. Monmouth was implicated in the Rye House Plot of 1683. His father's fondness for him saved his bacon, but James II exiled him to Holland. His invasion in 1685, his final desperate throw for the throne, led him to his death. He tried to save his skin by turning Roman Catholic, but it was no use and he was beheaded at the age of 36.

James's problem was that he was irresistibly drawn to the Roman Catholic Church, in which he found an authority that his temperament needed. He himself said that he was persuaded by the divisions among Protestants and 'the necessity of an infallible judge to decide controversies', which meant the Bishop of Rome. Anne, too, was a Catholic by the time she died in 1671. James was still conforming outwardly to the Church of England, but in 1673, as a Catholic, he resigned his office of Lord High Admiral because of the Test Act. Meanwhile, Charles II had insisted on James's daughters Mary and Anne, potential heirs to the throne, being brought up as Protestants. In 1673 James married his second wife, the Italian Mary of Modena, who was 15 to his 40 and only four years older than his daughter Mary. She was a devout Catholic, which deepened Protestant suspicions and one ridiculous rumour made her a daughter of the pope.

In some ways James was a throwback to his grandfather Charles I. On a point of principle he was immovable. In the hysteria aroused by the bogus Popish Plot and efforts in Parliament to exclude him from the succession as a Catholic, he refused to alter his stance. His brother sent him out of England, to Brussels, and in 1680 to Edinburgh to take charge of matters in Scotland. James believed that what was really at issue was not his Catholicism but whether the monarchy would survive or again be replaced by a republic. He returned to London in 1682, when the political pendulum had swung his way, and later attended his brother's deathbed.

James's succession to the throne went surprisingly well at first. He made no bones about attending mass, and communion was dropped from his coronation ceremony in Westminster Abbey, but he gave out that he would protect the Church of England, and the royalist Parliament was generous with money and backed him against an attempt to oust him by his Protestant illegitimate nephew James, Duke of Monmouth who mounted an invasion.

Monmouth landed at Lyme Regis from Holland with three ships and some 80 men. He had badly misjudged the moment and gathered only some 3,000 supporters of the poorer sort (apparently including Daniel Defoe, afterwards the author of *Robinson Crusoe*), who were crushed by royalist troops under John Churchill, the future Duke of Marlborough, at Sedgemoor in Somerset in July. Monmouth paid with his head, and Lord Chief Justice Jeffreys descended from London with sadistic glee to conduct his 'Bloody Assizes', which condemned hundreds of unfortunates to be hanged and quartered, and another 850 to be transported to virtual slavery in the West Indies.

It soon became clear that the king was committed to the revival of Catholicism in Britain. He sent Parliament home and ignored the law in order to put Catholics in important positions in government, the army and the universities. In 1687 he issued a Declaration of Indulgence, aiming at complete toleration for Catholics, Anglicans and Protestant dissenters alike. It was widely assumed to cloak a design for bringing England back to the pope. Anglicans were extremely alarmed and through the Dutch ambassador in London, William of Orange, Protestant husband of James's daughter Mary, started to take quiet soundings of English opinion.

A second Declaration of Indulgence was issued in May 1688 and the Archbishop of Canterbury and six bishops were put on trial for objecting to its being read out in churches. They were acquitted to wild rejoicing in the streets, but the critical moment had come earlier in June, when Mary of Modena gave birth to a son at St James's Palace. Her many previous babies had all died in infancy, and there had been whispers – which her step-daughter Anne believed – that this latest pregnancy was a fake. The baby arrived in a room crowded with witnesses, but a story circulated that he had been smuggled into the queen's bed in a warming pan. The serious point was that there was now a Catholic heir to the throne. A group of highly placed Englishmen, including Bishop Compton of London and the dukes of Devonshire and Shrewsbury, sent an invitation to William of Orange, assuring him of support. The curtain was about to rise on the 'glorious revolution' that would replace James II with William III.

James, Duke of Monmouth, wearing the sash of the Order of the Garter, by Sir Peter Lely. James was Charles II's favourite son and was always treated indulgently by his father, but his Protestant faith made him the candidate for the throne among those Protestant extremists who were fiercely opposed to the succession of James II.

The Glorious Revolution

William of Orange led the only successful invasion of England since the Norman Conquest. A Protestant wind that allowed him to evade the English navy brought him into Torbay in November 1688 with some 500 ships and 21,000 men. Disembarking at Brixham, he told the watching crowd, 'I come to do you goot. I am here for all your goots.' He moved his army slowly towards London through rain and mud, giving time for the landed classes to see which way the wind was blowing.

James had miscalculated upper-class allegiance to Anglicanism and dislike of arbitrary government. Panicky concessions and a promise to call Parliament were not enough to save him. Country magnates deserted him. So did leading army officers, including John Churchill, and so did his daughter Anne. In December Mary of Modena left Whitehall Palace disguised as a washerwoman, with her baby son, and went to Gravesend and took a royal yacht to France. James himself soon followed, but was seized by fishermen in Kent and sent ignominiously back to London. Welcomed by cheering crowds he hoped to reinstate himself, but received a message from William asking him to quit London. Dutch troops escorted him to Rochester and he was allowed to leave for France, where he arrived as a Christmas present for Louis XIV, who installed him and his family at St Germain-en-Laye. From his opponents' point of view, it was far better to let him go.

William of Orange landing at Brixham in Devon, greeted by the local functionaries. He had been preparing the invasion since the spring, waiting for the right 'Protestant wind'.

James's departure meant that he could plausibly be said to have abdicated, leaving the vacant throne to his daughter Mary and her husband William, who were duly installed on it by Parliament in 1689. The next few years saw a succession of acts of parliament that limited the powers of the Crown. The English monarchy was never to be the same again.

William III
1689–1702
& Mary II
1689–1694

BORN	Mary: 30 April 1662 at St James's Palace William: 4 November 1650 at The Hague, Holland
PARENTS	Mary: James II and Anne Hyde William: William II of Orange and Mary Stuart, daughter of Charles I
CROWNED	11 April 1689 at Westminster Abbey, when William was 38 and Mary was 26
CHILDREN	Three, all stillborn
DIED	Mary: 28 December 1694 at Kensington Palace, aged 32. William: 8 March 1702 at Kensington Palace, aged 51

William was short and ugly, and young Mary wept for a day and a half when she was told she had to marry him.

William was James II's nephew as well as his son-in-law. His father died before he was born, he lost his mother when he was ten, and he grew up among family and political power struggles. He was only about 5ft 6in tall, but he emerged as a forceful and determined figure, who was respected but not liked. He was reserved, silent, haughty and abrupt. Advisers tried to persuade him to be more approachable, but audiences with him tended to be brutish and short. Occasionally he would get himself wildly drunk. He had few intimates. London was bad for his asthma and he never really understood the English.

Mary was much more popular than William and an important factor in getting the new regime accepted. The three kings before William had all had foreign Roman Catholic wives, who were objects of suspicion, but Mary was English and Protestant.

Ope reason William of Orange gave for invading England was the need to establish the truth about the new son of James II and Mary of Modena and another was 'to rescue the religion and the nation'. An underlying motive sprang from European power politics. Effectively the Dutch head of state since his early twenties, William had spent years fighting off Louis XIV's Catholic and aggressive France. The spectre of a Catholic England in an Anglo-French alliance, which would bring English seapower to the French side, appalled him. In 1688 he was expecting a French invasion, which allowed him to let James II think that the Dutch military and naval preparations for the invasion of England were actually directed against the French.

He was soon joined in London by his wife, who flatly refused to consider any suggestion of ruling by herself. It was agreed they would be joint sovereigns, with William in command, and the pair were crowned in April. James II's supporters inevitably criticized Mary for betraying her father, but she firmly believed that God had brought her husband and herself to their throne. It was a belief in which her husband encouraged her. There was never any doubt about who was the dominant partner and Mary spent much of her time sewing and gardening, gossiping, playing cards and trying to cut down English drunkenness, swearing and profanation of Sunday, which shocked her. After a difficult start to their married life William and Mary had become fond of each other but after three stillborn babies in the first few years, there were no more pregnancies. Mary grew prim and William was suspected of homosexual inclinations, although he had a mistress called Elizabeth Villiers.

The Orange Triumph

Mary's exiled father settled down in comfort at St Germain and would have stayed there, hunting and praying, if Louis XIV had not told him

Kensington Palace

William of Orange suffered from chronic asthma. London was too smoky and foggy for him and at Whitehall Palace the air from the Thames was too damp. He and Mary liked Hampton Court, but it was inconveniently far away and, before the end of their first year in England, they acquired Nottingham House in Kensington, which was then a separate village outside London. They had it rebuilt in style by Sir Christopher Wren and Nicholas Hawksmoor, and gave it gardens in the formal Dutch manner – they both loved gardens – and built a private road through the park to London, part of which is now Rotten Row. The road was so infested by highwaymen and footpads that it was lighted at night by lamps on posts, an early example of street lighting.

it was dishonourable to loll about making no attempt to recover his kingdom. James duly went to Ireland, but his Irish Catholic supporters wanted him to be their Catholic king, which ensured that the Protestants in Ulster would fight for William of Orange. The issue was decided at the Battle of the Boyne in July 1690, celebrated by Protestant 'Orangemen' in Ireland ever since. William was victorious and James returned to France. In London Mary was hugely relieved that her husband had won and her father had survived. In Scotland, Catholics in the Highlands sympathetic to James were ordered to swear allegiance to William and Mary by the end of 1691. The MacDonald clan delayed in taking the oath, which was the excuse for the massacre in which the Campbells killed MacDonald men, women and children among the grim peaks of Glencoe in 1692. A total of 38 were slaughtered and others perished in the frozen mountains.

A Royal Bedding

William and Mary were married in St James's Palace in 1677 on William's 26th birthday. Humourless and surly, with a hooked nose and black teeth, and much shorter than Mary, he was not a prepossessing bridegroom. The 15-year-old Mary, in the throes of a girlish crush on an older woman, had wept for hours on being told she was to marry him. When the time came to put the newlyweds to bed, William declined to take off his underclothes, which he said he always wore in bed. After some argument about it, Charles II, who had given the bride away, let the matter go and drew the curtains round the bed, saying, 'Now, nephew to your work! Hey! Saint George for England!' At which they were left to it.

In England a series of acts of parliament restricted the Crown's powers. The monarch was not to ignore laws passed by Parliament, which was to be summoned at regular intervals. Future monarchs were to belong to the Church of England and were not to leave the country or engage in foreign wars without Parliament's permission. Judges were not to be dismissed without Parliament's approval. In addition, toleration was extended to Protestant dissenters, though not to Catholics.

Hampton Court was one of William and Mary's favourite residences, and was partly remodelled for them in magnificent Renaissance style by Sir Christopher Wren.

Anne
1702–1714

BORN	Born 6 February 1665 at St James's Palace
PARENTS	James II and Anne Hyde
CROWNED	23 April 1702, aged 37
MARRIED	George (d. 1708), son of Frederick III of Denmark
CHILDREN	Seventeen, of whom only one, William, survived to the age of 12
DIED	1 August 1714 at Kensington Palace, aged 49

Like her mother before her, Anne grew exceptionally stout. Like her sister Mary, she had the advantage of being a strong adherent of the Church of England. Cheerful, kindly and unabashedly English, unlike her Dutch predecessor, she was very popular with her subjects and generous to good causes. She tried to link herself with Elizabeth I, by dressing like her, and she was the last sovereign to 'touch for the king's evil' (in accordance with the superstition that the royal touch could cure scrofula). One of those touched was the infant Samuel Johnson.

Anne's appetite was phenomenal, but she enjoyed riding until her weight made it impossible. Dumpy, plain and red-faced, she suffered from gout and rheumatism as well as innumerable unsuccessful pregnancies. Such was her size that she had to be conveyed by sedan chair, though she did just manage to wobble up the aisle of Westminster Abbey for

her coronation. She had a mind of her own, however, and an obstinate streak, and although the monarchy's powers had been cut back she used her influence to effect. She often attended debates in the House of Lords, incognito.

Anne's mother died when the little girl was six. Her father then married Mary of Modena, which probably contributed to her lifelong bias against Catholics. She grew up to speak fluent French, but she was no intellectual. She spent a few months in Scotland, the last British monarch to go there until George IV, and thought the Scots 'a strange people'. In 1683 she was married to Prince George of Denmark, who was 30 to her 18 and no intellectual either, but he proved a loving and faithful husband. Contemporaries regarded him as an amiable booby, but there is a feeling now that he may have exercised more influence behind the scenes than he was given credit for. A Lutheran, born in Copenhagen, he had been considered for the throne of Poland in 1674, but was not chosen. As Anne's consort he was given various meaningless if honorific titles, but was kept in the background. Someone unkindly remarked that unless he breathed harder, he might be taken for dead and buried by mistake. Though a Fellow of the Royal Society, he was handicapped by an inadequate grasp of English and chronic asthma. However, Prince George was certainly attentive to his husbandly duties. He fathered handfuls of children, with the result that his wife spent at least 13 of their 25 years of married life pregnant. Tragically, few of their 17 babies were born alive and none survived to grow up.

In 1688 Anne and George deserted her father and went over to William of Orange. Anne agreed to William and Mary's joint succession to the throne. However, she fell out with the new regime, partly over John Churchill, now Earl of Marlborough, who was accused of intriguing with the exiled James II. Anne was told to dismiss his wife Sarah from her service, but Sarah was her much-loved friend and counsellor – 'Mrs Freeman' to her 'Mrs Morley' – and she flatly refused. She and Prince George were thrown out of their quarters in Whitehall Palace, and Anne and her sister Mary never spoke to each other again. After Mary's death, relationships with William III were correct, but

Mrs Freeman and Mrs Morley

Sarah Jenyns, or Jennings, started her career in her teens in 1673 as a maid of honour to Mary of Modena. She soon became friends with the Princess Anne, who was five years younger. Strong-minded, assertive and sharp-tongued, at 17 she married John Churchill, a soldier of genius on his way up in the world from a Dorset landed family (his father was a Sir Winston Churchill). He was the only person Sarah seems ever to have deferred to in her entire life, although he would occasionally find himself the butt of her temper. In 1700, in a rage with her husband, she cut off her blonde hair, which he greatly admired, threw the severed locks at him, and stalked off. After his death years afterwards, she found her tresses in his private cabinet, tied up with silk ribbons. From Anne's marriage in 1683, Sarah Churchill was a lady of her bedchamber and her closest confidant, so close that in private Sarah was 'Mrs Freeman' and Anne was 'Mrs Morley', while gossip improbably made them lesbians. When Anne became queen, Sarah dominated the court, while her husband, created Duke of Marlborough in 1702, won the Battle of Blenheim in 1704, one of a string of English victories in the War of Spanish Succession. The Churchills' gigantic Oxfordshire mansion, Blenheim Palace, was built with public money granted by Anne. Anne and Sarah fell out, however, and Anne eventually dismissed her. Marlborough died in 1722, but his formidable duchess lived on, terrorizing everyone within reach until 1744.

cool. In 1700 Anne and George's solitary surviving child William, Duke of Gloucester, who would have been King William IV if he had lived, died at the age of 12, to the despairing grief of both his parents.

Once on the throne, Anne tried to steer a middle course through fierce strife between the Whigs and the Tories. The modern party political system was developing. The Whigs – who included some of the country's greatest landowners and richest financiers and businessmen – approved of limited monarchy and Parliament's new authority. They supported the Hanoverian succession and tended to support intervention in Europe. The Tories, whose maxim was 'Church and King', included many of the country gentry. They had a fondness for tradition, believed in loyal obedience to authority, distrusted the Whigs as a power-hungry faction and were alarmed by concessions to Protestant dissent. Anne's own sympathies leaned to the Tory side, but she did not want her governments to be partisan and she tried to keep a balance.

Abroad, Anne's reign was dominated by the War of the Spanish Succession, which lasted until 1713. John Churchill, Duke of Marlborough, won victory after victory in command of the British and allied armies. In 1704 the British under Admiral Sir George Rooke took Gibraltar in July, and in August Marlborough won his most famous victory at Blenheim. Success in war boosted English national pride and the queen's popularity. At home, in 1707, with Anne's encouragement, the Act of Union at last joined England and Scotland as the single kingdom of Great Britain. The Scottish Parliament merged with the English one and the first British general election followed in 1708. The act was intended to secure the Hanoverian succession after Anne, to which the Scottish Parliament had declined to commit itself until suitably sweetened with commercial advantages for Scotland, principally free trade with England.

Anne always needed a close female friend, but by this time she was tired of being bullied by Sarah Churchill, who was too obsessive a Whig and had become altogether too big for her boots. Anne found a more affectionate and considerate friend in Abigail Masham, Sarah's inconspicuous cousin and a lady of the bedchamber, who was useful in keeping the queen quietly in touch with the Marlboroughs' political opponents. When Sarah found out, she was furious. She and Anne had an embarrassing quarrel at a thanksgiving service in St Paul's in 1708 for another Marlborough victory, when Sarah actually shouted at the queen in public to hold her tongue. The death of her husband later that year, from complications of asthma, aged 55, sent Anne into a paroxysm of grief and she went on desperately kissing George's lifeless body until Sarah managed to persuade her to stop. The 43-year-old queen was lonely and bereft, and it was Abigail to whom she turned for comfort. Anne finally sent Sarah packing in 1711, despite Marlborough's going on his knees to beg her to relent. Anne refused and demanded Sarah's keys of office, which Sarah angrily hurled on the floor, saying that her husband could go on his knees again to retrieve them if he cared to – which he did, and took them to Anne.

By the time of the Treaty of Utrecht – which ended the European war in 1713 and brought Britain more territory in North America and the contract for shipping slaves to the Spanish colonies – Anne could no longer stand up. Her time was plainly running out. In Germany the Hanoverians were waiting anxiously. James II's son James, the 'warming pan' baby', now in his twenties, was in exile on the Continent. Some Tory politicians sent to him asking him to renounce his Catholicism in return for support for his succession to the throne, but he refused to consider it. Anne died after violent convulsions that left her virtually unable to speak. When she was buried in Westminster Abbey, her coffin had to be almost square to accommodate her bulk.

Meanwhile...

1604   James I proclaims smoking as 'harmful to the lungs' in his Counterblast to Tobacco, and imposes a tax on tobacco.

1614   Scottish mathematician John Napier publishes his theory of logarithms, which simplify calculations for navigators.

1616   Inigo Jones begins work on the Queen's House at Greenwich, now acknowledged as being Britain's first classical building.

1621   Francis Bacon, the Lord Chancellor, is fined and imprisoned for corruption, but later pardoned by the king.

1623   The first collected edition of Shakespeare's work – The first folio – is published seven years after the playwright's death.

1628   Physician William Harvey, from Folkestone, demonstrates how the heart makes blood pump around the body.

1603   1614   1644   1666   1679

1635   Covent Garden Piazza in London is completed to the designs of the Surveyor to the Crown, Inigo Jones.

1644   Oliver Cromwell and the Puritans enforce an Act of Parliament banning Christmas Day celebrations.

1661   The English gain control of the port of Bombay, India, as a trading base for textiles and spices.

1664   England seizes the Dutch settlement of New Amsterdam in America, changing its name to New York.

1666   Following the Great Fire, Christopher Wren is appointed to supervise the rebuilding of London.

1673   The Test Act excludes non-Anglicans from public office unless they take communion in the Church of England.

1679	Parliament passes the Act of Habeas Corpus, which forbids imprisonment without trial.
1686	Edmund Halley draws the first meteorological map, showing weather systems.
1687	Isaac Newton sets out his theories of gravity and lays the foundations for modern physics in his *Principia*.
1687	James II issues a Declaration of Liberty of Conscience, which extends toleration to all religions.
1688	Nobles invite James II's Dutch Protestant son-in-law William of Orange to take the throne.
1689	Henry Purcell's *Dido and Aeneas*, the first English opera, is performed by a girls' boarding school.

687   1690   1699   **1705**   1714

1690	The French fleet bombards the fishing village of Teignmouth, Devon.
1698	Off the coast of Cornwall, the first Eddystone Lighthouse is built.
1699	Doctor and anatomist Edward Tyson publishes a report claiming that the chimpanzee is man's closest relative.
1704	Society dandy and social fixer Beau Nash is appointed Master of Ceremonies at fashionable Bath.
1705	Astronomer Edmund Halley calculates that a comet last seen in 1682 will reappear in 1758: it is dubbed Halley's Comet.
1705	Parliament passes the Statute of Anne – Britain's first copyright laws.
1713	Jonathan Swift, clergyman and satirist, is appointed Dean of St Patrick's Cathedral in Dublin.

The Hanoverians
1714–1917

British democracy was difficult for any foreign ruler to adjust to. It had no equivalent on the Continent. Even so, the new German dynasty doused Jacobite hopes for a Stuart restoration and would see Britain grow into the greatest maritime, industrial and imperial power on earth. George I was a tinpot princeling from Hanover with hardly a word of English. Two hundred years later Edward VII was Emperor of India and a fifth of the land surface of the globe was coloured bright red on the map (despite the loss of the 13 American colonies in George III's time). George III's reign lasted an unprecedented 59 years, but Queen Victoria outdid him with 63 years on the throne. Both of them set an example of duty, responsibility and moral decency that many of their subjects valued. At the same time, the industrial revolution made Britain the workshop of the world and Victoria presided over a period of tremendous vitality and achievement in science, engineering, literature and the arts, from Faraday and Darwin to Brunel and Paxton, Dickens and Tennyson, Turner and the Pre-Raphaelites. Meanwhile, through successive reigns the power of the monarchy ebbed away as effective authority passed from kings and their councillors to prime ministers and party politicians.

George I
1714–1727

BORN	28 May 1660 at Osnabrück, Hanover
PARENTS	Ernst August, Duke of Brunswick and Elector of Hanover, and Sophia Stuart
CROWNED	20 October 1714, aged 54
MARRIED	Sophia Dorothea von Celle (d. 1726)
CHILDREN	Two legitimate (George and Sophia Dorothea); three illegitimate daughters by Melusine von der Schulenburg
DIED	11 June 1727 at Osnabrück, aged 67

The Hanoverian succession did not seem as sure a thing at the time as it looks in retrospect. Queen Anne had not let any of the Hanoverians settle in England and they waited in Germany with their fingers crossed for the news of her death. They were in close touch with leading Whig politicians and when the word came, Georg Ludwig made for England to be crowned as George I. A Lutheran and a soldier at heart, he had fought in various campaigns in Europe and had been Elector of Hanover since 1698. He spoke several languages, but his command of English was never more than rudimentary and affairs of state in his new realm were discussed in French or Latin.

Portrait of King George I by Sir Godfrey Kneller, the leading portrait painter in England during the late 17th and early 18th centuries, and court painter to British monarchs from Charles II to George I.

George's wife did not accompany him. Years before, the beautiful Sophia Dorothea had taken a dashing Swedish lover, Count Philip von Königsmarck. He mysteriously disappeared, apparently murdered, and in 1694 George divorced Sophia Dorothea for desertion and kept her locked away in a castle for the rest of her life. The woman he took to England was his mistress, Melusine von der Schulenburg, created Duchess of Kendal, who was so tall and thin that Londoners nicknamed her 'Maypole'. In court circles she was treated as the king's wife (they may perhaps have married privately), and she bore him three illegitimate daughters. Malicious rumour made George and his half-sister Sophia Charlotte von Kielmansegg lovers. She was so stout that together they were nicknamed the 'Elephant and Castle'.

Four-fifths of George's life had already passed when he arrived in London. Resented as a foreigner, he was criticized for neglecting England in favour of Hanover, and he often returned there for months at a time, but he was more competent than his critics admitted and he gave the new dynasty a secure start. Shy and reserved, he loved hunting, was interested in science, backed the early experiments in inoculation against smallpox and was fond of music, especially opera. Handel worked for him in Hanover and England, and the *Water Music* was composed for a royal occasion in 1715.

George's reign was a time of peace and general prosperity. He was perforce a constitutional monarch, which was one reason why he concentrated on foreign affairs, and the government was dominated throughout his reign by Whigs, who he knew were loyal to him. A Jacobite uprising in 1715 was quelled easily enough and the Old Pretender ran back to France with his tail between his legs, but the Tories were damned by association. The king viewed them with deep suspicion and Tories were purged from the civil service, the army and the law. Rising men of ambition took care to be Whigs.

The effective opposition came from George's son, the future George II, who apparently resented the treatment of his mother. Expelled from court in 1717, he set up a rival London household at Leicester House, which was a focus for discontent and attracted an ambitious Whig politician named Robert Walpole, who was currently out of office. The king and his son were reconciled in 1720 and Walpole returned to the government. His position was cemented by his masterly sorting out of the South Sea Bubble crisis of 1721, a financial disaster in which thousands of people were ruined when the South Sea Company collapsed. The king himself lost heavily when the bubble burst, and some of the public figures involved killed themselves or fled abroad.

George died in Germany after a stroke. His mistress Melusine retired to Twickenham, where George was said to visit her in the form of a raven.

The Hanover Connection

The Hanoverian claim to the throne went back to James I. In 1613 at 17 his daughter Elizabeth, the 'winter queen' of Bohemia, was married to Frederick V of the Rhine. She gave him 13 children before his death in 1632. Elizabeth's beauty, vivacious charm and misfortunes inspired romantic sympathy for her in England, where she died in 1662. Her youngest daughter Sophia married the Duke of Brunswick, made Elector of Hanover in 1692, and in the Act of Settlement 1701 she was selected as Queen Anne's successor. Sophia was proud of her Stuart ancestry and looked forward to being queen, but she died a few weeks before Queen Anne, at the age of 84, after incautiously running to get out of the rain. The British throne went to her son Georg Ludwig. Subsequent British monarchs were electors, later kings, of Hanover until 1837 and the death of William IV.

The Jacobite Pretenders

James Francis Edward Stuart, the Chevalier de St George or the Old Pretender (from French *pretendant*, 'claimant'), grew up at St Germain in France and served in the French army, fighting against the British. After Queen Anne's death, uprisings were planned in Scotland and England, and the Earl of Mar raised the Jacobite standard at Braemar in 1715. James, now aged 27, sailed to Scotland in disguise to join Mar, but the military situation was utterly unpromising. He was a singularly uninspiring leader and, as the government moved troops up, his men deserted in droves. He sneaked back to France with Mar and a few others, leaving his supporters to their fate.

James spent most of the rest of his life in Italy as an unwanted guest of the pope. An attempted Jacobite rising in 1719 came to nothing, and another plot was discovered and foiled by the British government in 1722. In 1719 James had married Clementina Sobieska, granddaughter of King John Sobieski of Poland, and they had two sons, Charles Edward born in 1720 and Henry Benedict in 1725. The Old Pretender died in Rome in 1766, aged 77.

Charles Edward Stuart, the Young Chevalier or Young Pretender, grew up in Rome. From his boyhood he was exceptionally self-willed and had the personal magnetism that his father lacked. As a result the Jacobite uprising for which he was the focus would become one of the great romantic episodes of Scottish history. At the age of 24 he landed in the Hebrides in July 1745 with a mere seven men. The Stuart standard was raised the following month at Glenfinnan at the head of Loch Shiel, with support from Camerons and MacDonalds. The Jacobite army, gathering strength, moved on to Perth and then to Edinburgh, where the young prince was first called 'Bonnie' Prince Charlie.

Sweeping aside government forces, the prince invaded England, heading for London and reaching as far south as

The Old Pretender, painted in 1741 by French artist Louis Gabriel Blanchet. The 'warming pan' baby, son of James II, spent almost his entire life in France and Italy. His refusal to give up his Roman Catholic faith left him no realistic chance of regaining the throne.

The Young Pretender, or 'Bonnie' Prince Charlie. He was a far more dashing and romantic figure than his father, but his hopes also came to nothing, fundamentally because most of his potential English and Scottish subjects preferred the devil they knew.

Derby in December before his officers made him turn back. The English did not come out for him and his Scottish and Irish lieutenants were at odds. He retreated to Scotland, to be crushed in April 1746 by English and Scottish troops under the Duke of Cumberland at Culloden, near Inverness. He then spent five months as a hunted fugitive in the Highlands, with many hairbreadth escapes. Often close to starving and incessantly gnawed by midges, he was sheltered by poor Scots despite the tempting price on his head. On Skye, Flora MacDonald disguised him as a servant girl and he got away to France in September.

In 1750 the prince made a secret visit to London. He met leading English Jacobites and was received into the Church of England, but he soon left, discouraged. Living in Italy as the years dragged by and his hopes came to nothing, convinced that everyone had let him down, he grew drunken and prey to violent rages. He fell out with his family and his mistress Clementina Walkinshaw. In 1772 he married Princess Louise of Stolberg, but it went sour and there were no children. His heir when he died at 67 in 1788 was his brother, Henry, who had gone into the Church and was now a cardinal. The so-called Henry IX died in 1807, the last of the direct Stuart male line.

The main consequence of the Jacobite risings was the further weakening of the Highland clans. The wearing of Highland dress and tartans was forbidden, as was the carrying of weapons, and new Highland regiments, such as the Black Watch, were raised to attract clan loyalties to the Hanoverian regime. Increased farming of sheep later drove many Highlanders off the land, and from the 1770s there was considerable emigration to North America, Australia and New Zealand.

George II
1727–1760

BORN	10 November 1683 at Herrenhausen, Hanover
PARENTS	George I and Sophia Dorothea
CROWNED	4 October 1727, aged 43
MARRIED	Caroline of Ansbach (d. 1737), daughter of the Margrave of Brandenburg-Ansbach
CHILDREN	Seven surviving, including two sons, Frederick Louis and William Augustus
DIED	25 October 1760 at Kensington Palace, aged 76

The second George was less unpopular than the first. He and the English had more time to get used to each other: from the age of 17 he had been a likely successor to the British throne, and he actually occupied it for 33 years. He spoke English, though with a heavy German accent, and his personal courage aroused admiration. His reign saw British successes in war and he had the advantage of a perspicacious, delightful and Protestant wife. The fact that she had refused the future Holy Roman Emperor because it would have meant becoming Catholic was made much of in Britain and she was an important factor in making the Hanoverian dynasty acceptable.

The painter Enoch Seeman the Younger enjoyed royal patronage, executing a full-length portrait of George I in his coronation robes. This patronage was sustained through the late 1730s with this portrait of George II, now part of the Royal Collection.

The last British monarch born abroad, George was separated from his mother as a boy, when his father divorced her, and brought up in Hanover largely by his Stuart grandmother. He married Caroline of Ansbach in 1705, when he was 21 and she 22, and was devoted to her, though not physically faithful to her. In his twenties George fought with outstanding courage in battle under the Duke of Marlborough, and when he was 30 he accompanied his father to London to become Prince of Wales. By this time, the hostility between father and son was firmly established and the prince openly supported Robert Walpole in direct opposition to the king. After George I's death, Walpole continued as prime minister – though the term was not yet official – for another 15 years, bolstered by a close alliance with Queen Caroline: as he privately put it, he had the right sow by the ear. The most influential of all Hanoverian queen consorts, she was an enthusiast for gardens and her lasting legacy to London was the creation of Kensington Gardens and the Serpentine.

George had an explosive temper and a tendency to bluster, and the animosity that had existed between him and his own father emerged again in this generation. George and Caroline took against their eldest son, Frederick Louis, early on. They much preferred his younger brother William Augustus, the soldier and 'Butcher' Duke of Cumberland. The more sophisticated Frederick, who was fond of art, botany, gambling, games and women, set up a rival court at Leicester House, this one ironically a focus of opposition to Walpole. Queen Caroline died at the age of 54 in 1737, to the distraught sorrow of her husband. He had faithfully attended her in her last days, sleeping on the floor of her room, and on her death bed he assured her that he would never marry again. For some time afterwards he could not bear the sight of a queen in a pack of cards and they had to be removed before he sat down to play.

There were complaints in England that the War of the Austrian Succession (1740–48), with Britain and Austria on one side and France, Spain and Prussia on the other, was fought for Hanover's sake rather than Britain's. The power struggle on the Continent, sparked by the death of the Austrian emperor, Charles VI, made Hanover vulnerable to invasion by the French. The last British monarch personally to command his troops in battle, George led a combined British, Austrian and Hanoverian force to win the Battle of Dettingen in 1743. Walpole had been forced out in 1742, though the Whig ascendancy continued and William Pitt the Elder was beginning to come to the fore. His friendship with Prince Frederick did not endear him to the king. Fierce hostility between the king and the Prince of Wales raged on unabated until Frederick died at the age of 44 in 1751, reportedly after being struck hard on the chest by a ball when playing cricket. Another story made it a tennis ball, but he more likely died of pneumonia. The unforgiving George said he was glad to be rid of him.

The Final Years

As George's reign came to a close, the British were winning the struggle for empire against the French. Robert Clive's successes in the 1740s and 1750s in India began a British take-over of the subcontinent. The Seven Years War of 1756–63 saw Britain allied with Prussia against France, and the seizure of Quebec from the French in 1759 foreshadowed the British acquisition of Canada. By this time the king was completely deaf and blind in one eye. He died ignominiously of a heart attack while sitting on the lavatory at Kensington Palace, and was buried as he had wished it, alongside Caroline in her tomb. They were the last British monarchs to be interred at Westminster Abbey.

George III
1760–1820

BORN	4 June 1738 at Norfolk House, St James's Square, London
PARENTS	Frederick, Prince of Wales, and Augusta of Saxe-Gotha
CROWNED	22 September 1761, aged 23
MARRIED	Charlotte of Mecklenburg-Strelitz (d. 1818)
CHILDREN	Fifteen, of whom 13 survived: seven sons (including future kings George and William); six daughters
DIED	January 1829 at Windsor Castle, aged 81

The new king had been waiting impatiently for his grandfather to die and get out of his way. He had an ideal of kingship and he wanted to put it into practice. The first of his line born and bred in England, he spoke English as his first language and, although he had fluent German as well, he took no interest in Hanover and never went there in his life. He would concentrate his attention on Britain and the wider empire – to the dismay of politicians who would have preferred him not to.

George William Frederick spent his boyhood mainly at Leicester House in London and at Kew, where Prince Frederick had bought a country retreat. George's mother, Princess Augusta, opened a botanic garden there in 1759, which eventually blossomed into Kew Gardens. George was 12 when he succeeded his father as Prince of Wales. His adoles-

cence was dominated by his widowed mother – who had expected to be queen one day and had no reason to like her father-in-law – and her principal counsellor the Earl of Bute. He was a Stuart (descended from an illegitimate son of Robert II of Scots) and was widely believed to be Augusta's lover. Leicester House remained a focus of criticism of the administration.

Young George paid attentions to an attractive Quaker girl called Hannah Lightfoot, the daughter of a cobbler from Wapping. Rumour said they married and had three children, but it seems unlikely. He was later drawn to the ravishing, 15-year-old Lady Sarah Lennox, but was told his duty required him to marry abroad. The choice fell on a plain German Lutheran princess, Charlotte of Mecklenburg-Strelitz, who was 17 to his 23 at their wedding at St James's Palace. They had been introduced to each other at 3 o'clock that afternoon and were married six hours later. The couple fell devotedly in love and in private called each other Mr and Mrs King. Their son and heir, another George, was born within a year of the wedding. George III never took a mistress and Charlotte spent the first 23 years of her married life busy with childbearing. Their court was quiet, eminently respectable and a focus of Church of England piety. George ate and drank sparingly and disapproved of gambling. Lively spirits found court life dismayingly boring and cynics jeered at the king and queen's frugal, humdrum domesticity, but their subjects found it attractive.

A contemporary described the new king as tall and well built, cheerful and good-natured, with fair hair and blue eyes and an occasional pimple. He disliked Kensington Palace and never lived there, and he was not fond of Hampton Court. St James's Palace lacked privacy and in 1762 he bought Buckingham House, the future Buckingham Palace. George called it the Queen's House and he and Charlotte loved it. Most of their children were born there. They also spent much time at Kew, where George rebuilt the royal palace, and later at Windsor. In his whole long life he never visited Wales, Scotland, Ireland or the north of England.

The Patriot King

George was not of the very first intelligence, but he had no need to be. He was conscientious, hard-working, punctual and an early riser. From his father and also from Bute, whom he hero-worshipped, George had imbibed the ideal of 'the patriot king', who would override party faction and rule actively in the nation's interests. It was to take a long time for reality to penetrate this notion. George wanted to end the long Whig ascendancy of the two previous reigns and he brought Tories into favour, earning himself the hostility of many Whigs, who accused him of wanting to restore tyranny.

The King's Library

George III was one of the greatest book collectors who ever lived, possibly *the* greatest. From early in his reign he began buying books, paid for entirely from his private resources. Agents acted for him at sales in London and abroad, and Dr Johnson was consulted. The king eventually owned 65,000 volumes, as well as pamphlets, manuscripts and maps. The collection includes the Caxton edition of Chaucer's *Canterbury Tales*, a first edition of Milton's *Paradise Lost*, a Gutenberg Bible, Shakespeare folios, and many other rare and virtually priceless treasures. Special rooms were designed to house them in Buckingham House and the library was freely open to scholars. After the king's death, George IV gave the entire superb collection to the British Museum, and the King's Library now occupies its own tower in the British Library.

A succession of administrations in the 1760s saw an end to the Seven Years War, Canada secured for Britain and signs of unrest in the American colonies. In 1770 Captain Cook added a chunk of Australia to the British empire and christened it New South Wales. In that year George at last found in Lord North an efficient prime minister in whom he could feel confidence. Because he was satisfied with North, and no doubt because he was learning from experience, George now interfered in government less. North was criticized all the same for being too much under the king's thumb, but he lasted until 1782, when in the wake of the unsuccessful war against the 13 colonies he fell out with George over the issue of recognizing American independence. The king seriously contemplated abdication. North and Charles James Fox joined forces in power briefly in 1783, but George was relieved when William Pitt the Younger, who was only 24, accepted his invitation to form an administration, which lasted until 1801. Meanwhile, George had demonstrated courage and coolness when in 1780 a demonstration in London led by Lord George Gordon against relaxation of the laws against Catholics set off mob violence that caused some 300 deaths. With the authorities dithering helplessly, the king intervened, called in troops and made sure the rioting was stopped.

The king's constant 'What?', 'What?' was a sign of nervousness, but in 1788 he began to show alarming signs of derangement. Now aged 50, he was seen talking to a tree in Windsor Great Park under the impression that it was the King of Prussia. He also began babbling unstoppably and sometimes obscenely, announced a lustful passion for the Countess of Pembroke, one of the queen's ladies, and accused the queen herself of adultery. Other signs, such as frothing at the mouth and bloodshot eyes, suggest that he may have been suffering from porphyria, a blood disorder that causes poisoning of the nervous system and mental disturbance. However, at the time, the unfortunate king

William Blake, poet and artist, painted in his fifties in 1807. He was an obscure figure in his own time, but his warnings against the 'dark satanic mills' of the industrial revolution have resonated ever since.

was treated with the brutality considered necessary to effect a cure by the 'mad doctors' of the day. He was put in a strait-jacket or a restraining chair and his head was blistered to draw out malignant 'humours' from the brain. The opposition called for his eldest son (the future George IV), to be made regent, but the king recovered, to great popular rejoicing. He went to Weymouth to recuperate and enjoyed sea-bathing and sailing.

From 1789 the French Revolution helped to heighten suspicion towards radicals. The French king and queen went to the guillotine, but there was never the remotest possibility of such a thing happening to George III, which was

Farmer George

The 18th century witnessed dramatic advances in agricultural productivity. New crops were introduced, with new systems of crop rotation and stock-breeding, and exports of surplus grain to the Continent became an important factor in the British economy. An agricultural revolution was in progress, in parallel with the industrial revolution. More of George III's subjects were employed in agriculture than in anything else and the king was so interested in it that he earned the nickname 'Farmer George'. He created a model farm on which he set his sons to work in their boyhood, which they did not enjoy. He liked to hobnob with farmers and pick their brains, and he wrote articles on agriculture under the pen-name of Ralph Robinson.

testimony to his successful handling of his royal role. That the king was still an important figure no one doubted, but exactly what the powers of the sovereign were was uncertain and had to be gradually worked out over years of interaction between the Crown and the politicians. Far from being the would-be tyrant of Whig and American propaganda, George admired the 'glorious revolution' and the British constitution. He did his best to preserve an effective role for the Crown, but the development of party politics and the office of prime minister along with the increasing complexity of public business contributed to a slow decline in the monarchy's political power. It was becoming more of a symbol of the nation and a rallying point for national pride.

William Wordsworth, painted by Benjamin Robert Haydon in 1842. He was a leading figure in the new Romantic movement in literature of George III's time, which also involved Wordsworth's friend Coleridge, as well as Sir Walter Scott. Wordsworth settled in the Lake District in 1799 and was one of the first to hail the romantic beauties of its landscape.

The Sad Last Years

Belying his bucolic image and his nickname of 'Farmer George', the king was a keen patron of the arts, commissioned pictures from Gainsborough, Lawrence and other leading artists, and himself drew and painted well. He took a major role in the founding of the Royal Academy in 1768. He also loved music and played the harpsichord and the flute. He was interested in astronomy and science as well as agricultural developments and gave his court astronomer, William Herschel, financial support. The reign saw the beginnings of the industrial revolution, the discovery of steam power and the mechanization of spinning and weaving. Blake, Scott, Wordsworth and Coleridge led a flowering of literature and there was a curious vogue for Gothic horror novels.

George III genuinely liked his subjects, enjoyed talking to them and would sometimes drop in on them in their houses in a friendly way, unannounced. They liked him in return and his mental troubles aroused their sympathy. The king's popularity rested partly on his image as a devoted family man and loving husband and father but he was a domestic tyrant. Determined to bring his children up the way they should go, he was particularly demanding and hard on his sons, and George, the eldest, especially resented his father's constant preach-

The Battle of Trafalgar in 1805, painted here by Thomas Whitcombe, was a decisive victory in Britain's long struggle against the French, culminating in the Napoleonic Wars. The British under Lord Nelson brought the allied French and Spanish fleets under Admiral Villeneuve to action off Cape Trafalgar on the Spanish coast and routed them. Nelson's death at the height of the battle gave the victory an especially heroic lustre and it ensured that Britannia would rule the waves for the following century.

ing and interference. His and his younger brothers' debts and tangled love lives caused their father much anxiety. George was much easier on his daughters, but he loved them so dearly that he put every possible difficulty in the way of their marrying. Their mother hated the subject to be broached for fear of worsening her husband's mental problems, and they resented being kept in what they called 'the nunnery'. Two of the princesses did not marry until they were in their forties and others had love affairs.

In 1800 George survived an attempt on his life at Drury Lane Theatre when a lunatic, James Hadfield, fired two shots at the king in the royal box and only narrowly missed him. George calmly ordered the entertainment to continue and was so cool about it that he presently went to sleep, or pretended to. Trouble in Ireland led to the Act of Union and the creation of the United Kingdom, but Pitt resigned when the king refused to consent to Catholic emancipation. The king had another bout of his madness and told his doctor that he was praying to God to spare his reason or let him die. He recovered after a month, but Queen Charlotte was now frightened of him and after their many years of happiness together she locked her bedroom door against him.

The royal title of King of France was dropped at long last in 1801. Britain was in the course of a long struggle against the French, and inspiring victories at sea – including Nelson's triumphs at the Nile and Trafalgar – combined with Wellington's successful campaign in Spain and Portugal boosted national pride in king and country. The king, however, found himself aggravated by the marital troubles of the Prince and Princess of Wales, while in 1809 his favourite son, Frederick, Duke of York, was accused of corruptly selling army commissions through his mistress, Mary Anne Clark, and had to resign as commander-in-chief. George's jubilee that year, marking his 50th year on the throne, was celebrated with tremendous popular rejoicing, but after the premature death in 1810 of George's youngest and favourite daughter, Princess Amelia, his malady returned.

George was in his seventies now, and back in the strait-jacket. His son George was Prince Regent from 1811. The king never recovered and spent his last years shut away at Windsor, going blind and increasingly deaf. He would hold conversations with Lord North or other people long dead or inspect imaginary parades. In time he could no longer recognize his own family. After being virtually a widow for her final years, Queen Charlotte died in 1818. George himself died of pneumonia at Windsor.

The King, Ireland and Catholic Emancipation

The French Revolution sharpened both the Irish appetite for independence and English concern about Ireland, which was a fruitful source of soldiers for the British army. In the 1790s Irish Catholics got the vote and were allowed to marry Protestants, but they still could not sit in the Irish parliament. In 1798 there were risings in Ireland against the English, with an attempted French invasion, and 20,000 or more Irish rebels were killed. Something had to be done, and in 1800 the Act of Union created the United Kingdom of Great Britain and Ireland and merged the Irish parliament into the Westminster parliament. George III approved, but not of the related measure of Catholic emancipation, which would have allowed Catholics to sit at Westminster and which Pitt the Younger wanted to bring in. The king regarded it as a breach of his coronation oath to defend the Protestant faith and an attack on the Church of England. The measure did not finally become law until after his time, in 1829.

George III and the American Revolution

A string of 13 British colonies stretched down the American eastern seaboard from Maine to Georgia, with a total population approaching two million. In the eyes of radical Americans George III was the tyrant at the head of the British attempt to crush them and deny them their independence. He has remained a bogeyman to Americans ever since, though his attitude was shared by many other Englishmen of the time and his authority over the British government and parliament was far less than it seemed, or was made to seem, from 4,827km (3,000 miles) away across the Atlantic.

From the British side of the water, the American colonies were simply a market for British exports and the source of products such as tobacco and rice. The colonists' demands for more control over their affairs, which had mounted with their growing wealth and confidence, were greeted in England at first with puzzlement and later with indignation.

The colonies had no members in the House of Commons. In the 1760s, on the principle that there should be 'no taxation without representation', they were resisting London's demands for increased taxes and duties to pay for the cost of defending them. In 1770 Lord North's government abolished all the duties except the one on tea, which provoked the famous Boston Tea Party of 1773. Dressed as American Indians, protesters boarded a British ship in Boston harbour,

Portrait of George Washington as the first president of the United States of America. The successful commander-in-chief in the War of Independence, he took office as president in 1789.

threw its cargo of tea overboard and tarred and feathered a customs official. The British retaliated by closing the port at Boston. The following year a Continental Congress met in Philadelphia. It called for civil disobedience from American citizens and demanded that no legislation be imposed on the American colonists without their consent.

George III's attitude was that the colonists must be brought to heel. It was also the attitude of Lord North's administration and of a majority of members of the House of Commons. Many American colonists, for that matter, were loyalists, but radical American politicians were ominously referring to Britain as 'a foreign power' and talking of 'the attempts of a wicked administration to enslave America'. Benjamin Franklin remarked, 'Every man in England seems to regard himself as a sovereign over America.' In 1774 the king told North that 'blows must decide whether they are to be subject to this country or independent'. Opening Parliament the following year he said that 'the most decisive exertions' were needed.

Fighting broke out between British troops and Americans in New England in 1775. In 1776 the Continental Congress created the Continental Army under George Washington and issued the Declaration of Independence, which, in addition to proclaiming self-government, listed acts of tyranny committed by George III and Parliament. The British were hampered by the difficulties of fighting a war at such a distance. George realized that it was Parliament rather than the Crown that was under attack and did his best to stiffen his government's spine. In 1778 he asked North to contemplate 'the beauty, excellence and perfection of the British constitution as by law established and consider that if any one branch of the empire is allowed to cast off its dependency then the others will infallibly follow the example.'

The war broadened out as the French joined the colonists' side in 1778, Spain in 1779 and the Dutch in 1780. The decisive moment came in 1781 when Washington trapped a British army at Yorktown in Virginia and forced an ignominious surrender. Opinion in Britain had changed from support for the war to a reluctant recognition that the war was lost and that the American demands must be met. The king would still not change his stance and North resigned in 1782 (he returned in a coalition with Fox in 1783). The war was formally ended the following year by a peace treaty in which Britain at last officially recognized American independence and various disputes over territories were settled between the British, French, Spanish and Dutch governments.

The Boston Tea Party of 1773, by an unknown artist. One of the most famous events in American history, it was a response to the British government's insistence on retaining a small duty on tea imported into North America by the East India Company, after other duties and taxes had been withdrawn. It aroused a violent response when protesters calling themselves Sons of Liberty boarded cargo ships in Boston harbour and threw 342 chests of tea overboard.

George IV
1820–1830

BORN	12 August 1762 at St James's Palace
PARENTS	George III and Charlotte of Mecklenburg-Strelitz
CROWNED	19 July 1821, aged 58
MARRIED	(1) Maria Fitzherbert (d. 1837). (2) Caroline of Brunswick-Wolfenbüttel (d. 1821)
CHILDREN	One legitimate daughter, Charlotte Augusta (by Caroline), and an uncertain tally of illegitimate children
DIED	26 June 1830 at Windsor Castle, aged 67

If George III was one of the most popular of British monarchs, his son and successor was one of the least. He was lazy, irresponsible, a fashionable man about town, a superb mimic, a charmer and a spendthrift who lavished money far beyond his means on clothes, horses, buildings, smart parties and a cavalcade of women. When George IV died, *The Times* newspaper commented, 'There was never an individual less regretted by his fellow creatures than this deceased King.'

Painting of George IV as Prince of Wales by John Hoppner, the most celebrated portrait painter in Britain at the time. Hoppner was Sir Joshua Reynolds' successor and dominated the British art scene from 1790–1810. As well as painting the Prince, his subjects also included great heroes such as Nelson and Wellington.

As a small boy the future George IV was packed off to Kew with his next brother Frederick for a thorough education in the classics, modern languages and mathematics, with instruction in music, fencing and boxing. The virtues of hard work, truthfulness and punctuality were beaten viciously into the boys with a whip. 'Prinny' grew up to be a superbly gifted connoisseur and patron of the arts, who added pictures by Rembrandt, Rubens and Stubbs to the royal collection, but in every other way he was very unlike his father and he resented George III's efforts to keep him on track. The Hanoverian pattern of animosity between father and eldest son emerged yet again.

The young Prince of Wales was 16 in 1779 when he was bowled over by an actress, Mary 'Perdita' Robinson, and incautiously began writing to her under the name of Florizel. When his gaze turned elsewhere two years later, she threatened to publish the letters and George III had to buy her off. After other amorous adventures the prince fell in love with Maria Fitzherbert, a curly-haired, full-figured, respectable Roman Catholic widow who declined his advances until he dramatically stabbed himself – not too deeply – to pressure her into marrying him. The wedding took place in 1785 when he was 23 and she was 29. It was entirely illegal and had to be celebrated secretly in the bride's Mayfair drawing room – the Royal Marriages Act of 1772 forbade royal marriages without the permission of the sovereign. Strictly speaking it meant that George lost his right to the throne.

His friendship with Charles James Fox and his clique, who were opposed to the government, helped to alienate him from his father. It also meant that he was not given any responsible position in which to develop his talents. Despite protestations of everlasting love for Mrs Fitzherbert, George took the Countess of Jersey as a mistress and passed his time in dissipation, spending a colossal amount of money on doing up his London residence, Carlton House in Pall Mall, and growing fat enough to be nicknamed Prince of Whales. His glee at the prospect of taking over from his father when the king went off his head damaged the prince's already dubious reputation and harmed his relationship with his mother, who blamed his behaviour for her husband's plight. By 1794 he was in debt to the tune of some £600,000 (more than £38 million now) and the only solution seemed to be to make a marriage that would be legal, produce an heir and attract parliamentary approval, and so get his immense debts paid off. When consulted, the prince shrugged his shoulders and said that one damned German *frau* was as good as another. The choice fell on his cousin Princess Caroline of Brunswick. It was to prove utterly disastrous.

Tactlessly, he sent Lady Jersey to meet the princess on her arrival in England in 1795. Caroline was 26 to George's 33. Coarse, lively minded and unconventional, she swore like a trooper and had a distinct disinclination to wash.

Pavilioned in Splendour

Seaside resorts were a new phenomenon in the 18th century and the Prince Regent made Brighton the most fashionable of its kind. He bought a house there for himself and Mrs Fitzherbert in the 1780s, had it rebuilt and from 1815 employed his favourite architect John Nash to transform it into the fabulous Royal Pavilion, an oriental pleasure dome worthy of Kubla Khan. The prince also steadfastly encouraged Nash in the creation in London of Regent Street and Regent's Park, where handsome town houses and terraces were set in an idyllic country landscape. Completed in 1827 and a delight to Londoners ever since, it was the ancestor of the garden suburb.

When she was introduced to her future husband he took one look at her and called for a glass of brandy. She was no more impressed with him. According to her, he spent their wedding night in St James's Palace helplessly drunk, passed out in the fireplace, before getting into bed with her in the morning. Caroline gave birth to a daughter, Charlotte, nine months later, but complained that George spent most of their honeymoon drunk and ignoring her, while Lady Jersey, of all people, was taken along as her only female companion.

The Throne at Last

There would be no more children. Three days after his daughter's birth George made a will in which he left Caroline one shilling and declared that his true wife was Mrs Fitzherbert, 'the wife of my heart and soul'. George III tried to mediate, but the couple separated and Caroline took a house in Blackheath, where she entertained Pitt the Younger and other leading figures of the day. Gossip said her lovers included Sir Thomas Lawrence, the painter, and Admiral Sir Sydney Smith and that she had at least one illegitimate child. An official investigation in 1806 found no proof of adultery, but reproved her 'levity of conduct'.

George had persuaded Mrs Fitzherbert to return to him by threatening further suicide attempts, but he was soon enjoying the ample charms of the Marchioness of Hertford. He became Prince Regent in 1811 and two years later Caroline left England for travels abroad. Creating scandal everywhere

'A Voluptuary under the horrors of Digestion', 1792. George, Prince of Wales, also known as the 'Prince of Whales', and later Prince Regent and George IV, is mercilessly caricatured picking his teeth with a table fork, having demolished a heavy meal and a lot of wine. The Prince was notoriously dissolute and spendthrift. His room is depicted as littered with empty bottles, pills and unpaid bills. His passion for gambling is indicated by dice, lists of horse races and accounts of his losses at cards.

A VOLUPTUARY under the horrors of Digestion.

Princess Charlotte

Charlotte Augusta would have been queen if she had lived. Her short life was spent in the shadow of her parents' mutual animosity. Blonde, plump and tomboyish, she grew up in her own separate household, under governesses, dining once a week with each parent and unable to feel comfortable with either. George III, her grandfather, was very fond of her. She also became extremely popular with the people at large and was cheered by crowds when she was seen in public, which made her father jealous. Her mother's decision to leave England, which meant that Charlotte could no longer see her, made things easier. In 1816, aged 20, she married Prince Leopold of Saxe-Coburg. She described him privately as 'the perfection of a lover', but she died the following year giving birth to a stillborn son after 50 hours of labour. There was a great outpouring of public grief and Sir Richard Croft, the doctor who had attended her in childbed, committed suicide.

she went, she had a household headed by a handsome young Italian named Bartolomeo Bergami, who doubled as her lover. Her husband paid spies to gather evidence for a divorce. Meanwhile, the wars against France ended at last with the defeat of Napoleon at Waterloo, Regency architecture and canal-building both flourished, Jane Austen's *Pride and Prejudice* was published, Lord Byron's *Childe Harold* made him famous overnight and Mary Shelley wrote *Frankenstein*.

When George III died in 1820 and the prince, now in his late fifties, became king at last, Caroline returned to England hoping to take her place as queen. She was greeted by strong popular sympathy and noisy demonstrations of support. The government tried to get a divorce for the king by act of parliament, which led to what was generally regarded as a trial of Caroline in the House of Lords for adultery, attracting yet more support for her from huge crowds in the streets. Many of the peers found the evidence convincing, but fear that the proceedings might set off a popular uprising led the government to drop the whole thing. The coronation was mainly remarkable for Caroline's attempts to get into Westminster Abbey, whose doors had been locked against her on George's orders. She went from door to door, hammering and shouting in vain to be let in, while being jeered at by the same crowds that had been cheering her to the echo weeks before. Suddenly taken ill, she died within a month, to her husband's profound relief.

Patron of the Arts

George abandoned Carlton House and spent a fortune rebuilding Buckingham Palace and Windsor Castle. He helped to found the National Gallery and visited Ireland and Scotland, the first Hanoverian to do so. He found he was more popular there than in London. On his Scottish trip in 1822, organized by Sir Walter Scott, he wore the tartan, looked favourably on Scottish dancing and malt whisky, and helped to inspire a new romantic view of the Highlands and 'bonnie Scotland'. He also visited Wales and Hanover, but his political incompetence and self-indulgent idleness contributed to the dwindling away of the Crown's powers. In his later years he liked to recall his imaginary adventures with Wellington in the Peninsula and at Waterloo. They included winning one battle by leading a cavalry charge in disguise. The greatest royal patron of art since Charles I spent his last days stuffing himself with huge quantities of food and swilling down cherry brandy and laudanum until he was finally killed by a ruptured blood vessel in his stomach.

William IV
1830–1837

BORN	21 August 1765 at Buckingham Palace
PARENTS	George III and Charlotte of Mecklenburg-Strelitz
CROWNED	8 September 1831, aged 66
MARRIED	Adelaide of Saxe-Meiningen (d. 1849)
CHILDREN	Two daughters who died in infancy; at least 10 illegitimate children by Dorothy Jordan
DIED	20 June 1837 at Windsor Castle, aged 71

William IV was the oldest person ever to accede to the British throne. George III's third son, he had been heir presumptive since the death in 1827 of his elder brother Frederick. Those close to William thought him crotchety, irascible and obstinate. He had a head shaped like a coconut and he had been unkindly nicknamed 'Silly Billy', but he was much more popular with his subjects than his predecessor. He was considered a character – a bluff, patriotic jack tar who spoke his mind, disliked ceremony and fuss, and detested foreigners, especially the French.

His father sent William into the navy at 13. He enjoyed navy life, and numerous women while he was at it, rising up the ranks and becoming a friend of Horatio Nelson. In 1789 he was made Rear Admiral and Duke of Clarence. Two years later William took up with a delightful Irish

actress, Dorothy Jordan, who lived with him for 20 years and bore him at least ten children, who were given the surname of Fitzclarence. She kept her career going in the intervals between childbirth because they needed the money.

In 1811 the two separated, just as William was being made Admiral of the Fleet. Dorothy had taken to drink and was losing her looks and her stage roles, and William needed a rich and suitable wife. Dorothy fled to France to escape her creditors and died there in poverty in 1816. Approaches to various foreign princesses failed until Princess Charlotte's death in 1817 made the succession situation critical (George IV's separation from Caroline made it unlikely that he would produce any more heirs). A bride was at last found for William in Princess Adelaide of Saxe-Meiningen. She was 25 to his 52 when they married in 1818. Their attempts to produce a legitimate heir failed – none of their offspring lived beyond infancy – but they suited each other and she was a kind stepmother to his brood of bastard children.

William had no time for Buckingham Palace and lived at Clarence House in St James's. He liked to walk about unguarded and unattended, and ask stray people in to dinner. He took no interest whatever in art, literature or science and disapproved of lavish spending. He accepted constitutional monarchy, but interfered in politics more than his predecessor had done. Disliking party politics and the increasing power of the House of Commons, he viewed with misgiving the important changes that passed though Parliament in his time, including the reform of the electoral system, the ending of child labour in factories and the abolition of slavery. He was the last British monarch to attempt to replace a prime minister without House of Commons approval.

William liked his niece and heir, the young Princess Victoria, but he detested her mother, the widow of his younger brother Edward, Duke of Kent. The duchess had ostentatiously kept the princess clear of the royal bastards and had snubbed Queen Adelaide, and William was determined to live long enough to ensure she did not become regent. He brought it off and after seven years on the throne he died of pneumonia and cirrhosis of the liver only weeks after Victoria's 18th birthday. His last words to his sorrowing wife at his bedside were 'Bear up! Oh come – bear up, bear up!'

The King and the Reform Bill

Earl Grey became prime minister in 1830. In 1831 the government introduced a bill to reform the electoral system by abolishing rotten boroughs, which were controlled by a tiny number of voters or a powerful patron. The bill also gave the vote to prosperous middle-class men and representation in the House of Commons to the new industrial towns, such as Manchester and Birmingham. The government mustered just enough votes to pass the Reform Bill in the Commons – the second reading was carried by a majority of one – but a new parliament was elected the following month, in which the bill commanded a majority of 136. The Tory peers were adamantly opposed, however, so Grey asked the king to create new peers to get the bill through the House of Lords. William reluctantly agreed, thinking it would need 20 new peerages, but when the government demanded 50, he balked, at which Grey and his cabinet resigned. The king tried to set up a new administration under the Duke of Wellington, but failed and had to surrender to Grey. He wrote to opposition peers asking them to abstain and this with the threat of more peers carried the bill through in 1832. It was a landmark in British political history and it was clear that the Crown and the Lords could no longer prevail over the House of Commons.

Victoria
1837–1901

BORN	24 May 1819 at Kensington Palace
PARENTS	Edward, Duke of Kent (son of George III), and Victoria of Saxe-Coburg-Saalfeld
CROWNED	28 June 1838 at Westminster Abbey, aged 19
MARRIED	Albert of Saxe-Coburg-Gotha (d. 1861)
CHILDREN	Nine: five girls and four boys
DIED	22 January 1901 at Osborne House, Isle of Wight, aged 82

Queen Victoria's 63-year reign was the longest in British history. When she died, most of her subjects could not remember a time when she had not been on the throne. The population of the United Kingdom had almost doubled since her accession, from around 25 million to 45 million, and the everyday world had changed dramatically. Her time coincided with an unprecedented period of scientific invention and innovation, immense social, political and economic change, a huge expansion of British power around the globe and the transformation of the monarchy into the constitutional model that would be recognizable today.

A photographic study of Queen Victoria taken by Bassano in 1883. At 64, Victoria had been reigning monarch for 46 years. The photograph was published in the Illustrated London News.

Queen Victoria's reign saw the coming of the railways, postage stamps, trade unions, electric light, radio signals, X-rays, the motor car, barbed wire, the machine gun, the dum dum bullet, the London underground, Marks and Spencer, and the Salvation Army. Victoria was the first queen to have an anaesthetic when giving birth (chloroform in 1853). She was the first British monarch to be photographed and she made the first ever private telephone call (in 1878 from her house on the Isle of Wight). Margarine and table tennis were invented, along with Christmas cards, factory-made cigarettes, records and record players, gas fires, escalators, man-made fibres, diesel engines, cash registers and carpet sweepers.

George III's granddaughter, Victoria was a mixture of Hanover on her father's side and Saxe-Coburg on her mother's side. After Princess Charlotte died in 1817, George IV's younger brothers bestirred themselves to find wives and give the family a legitimate heir. Edward, Duke of Kent, fourth son of George III, abandoned his French mistress and married Princess Victoria of Saxe-Coburg-Saalfeld, a widow with two children by her first husband. She was 31 to his 50 and the sister of Prince Leopold, Charlotte's widower. She duly gave birth to a daughter, Alexandrina Victoria, the future queen. Edward soon died, in 1820, apparently to general relief, and his daughter would have no memory of him. Unusually for a woman of her class, the widowed duchess suckled the baby herself instead of relying on a wet-nurse. She depended heavily on her brother for money and support and Uncle Leopold was the nearest thing the young Victoria had to a father.

Princess Victoria at the age of nine in 1828, pictured in a charming bonnet and dress against the romantic background of a very English landscape. Much of the future queen's girlhood was actually spent in lonely unhappiness in a run-down set of apartments in Kensington Palace, where she felt unloved. Years later, she would feel remorseful when she read her dead mother's diary and discovered how she had been dearly loved as a child.

Victoria grew up in shabby apartments in Kensington Palace, where her mother's head of household was Sir John Conroy, who believed rightly or wrongly that his wife was a bastard daughter of Victoria's father, the Duke of Kent. Gossip improbably made him the duchess's lover and he hoped to dominate the princess's future court. William IV used to call him King John. Victoria always slept in her mother's bed, and she was kept away from the court and her half-cousins, William's illegitimate children. Her only regular

The Saxe-Coburgs

The minor German princely house of Saxe-Coburg made its way up in the world through strategic marriages. George III's mother was a Saxe-Coburg, but the key figure was Prince Leopold, a handsome soldier and impoverished younger son of the Duke of Saxe-Coburg-Saalfeld, who came to London in 1814 and happened to bump into Princess Charlotte, George IV's teenage daughter. She was attracted, they married and he would have been British prince consort if she had lived. Now comfortably provided for, he stayed in England and in 1818 masterminded the marriage of his older sister Victoria to the Duke of Kent, which produced the future Queen Victoria. Leopold turned down the Greek throne in 1830 and the following year was made King of the Belgians. Meanwhile, in 1826, Leopold's older brother had exchanged Saalfeld for Gotha and become Duke of Saxe-Coburg-Gotha. In 1837 Leopold brought off his pet scheme for his nephew Albert's marriage to Victoria. Albert's older brother Ernst succeeded to the German duchy. On his death in 1893 it went to Albert and Victoria's son Alfred, who was Duke of Saxe-Coburg -Gotha until his death in 1900.

companions were her half-sister Feodore and Conroy's two daughters, whom she disliked. She felt lonely and unloved.

The princess's childhood German accent was corrected by her tutor and she was taken on crowd-pleasing progresses around the country in deliberate emulation of Elizabeth I. The grace and dignity with which at the age of 18 she received the news of her accession to the throne, at Kensington Palace in the middle of the night, made a thoroughly favourable impression and the prime minister, Lord Melbourne, took avuncular charge of her. At the same time, it was clear that Victoria had a mind of her own and she at once put her mother and Conroy firmly in their places, quitted her mother's bed and soon moved herself into Buckingham Palace.

Love and Marriage

Victoria had a particularly attractive voice and, although no intellectual, she spoke German, French and Italian, sketched and painted, loved music and especially opera, and wrote an engaging diary. She was warm-hearted, quick-tempered, vivacious, emotional – sometimes almost to the point of hysteria – uninhibited and obstinate. Though she was only 4ft 11in tall, she would not be ordered about and she made up her own mind about who to marry. There were numerous candidates, but she had met her cousin Prince Albert of Saxe-Coburg-Gotha the year before, when he and his elder brother Ernst visited England at the crafty suggestion of their Uncle Leopold. Albert, like Victoria, had felt unloved as a child. When Albert was five his mother had been sent packing by his womanizing father, and he missed her badly. Now both 17, Albert and Victoria took to each other and she thought him 'extremely good-looking'. After much speculation and manoeuvring, Albert and his brother returned to England in 1839. Victoria decided she was in love with the 'beautiful' Albert and asked him to marry her. Protocol required her to do the asking.

She told her diary: 'He is perfection in every way – in beauty, in everything … Oh, how I adore and love him … .' The wedding was at St James's Palace in 1840. Bride and groom were both 20 and when alone usually spoke to each other in German. They had frequent rows – blazing on her side, coldly reserved on his – but their marriage was a strong and loving one. He was too intellectual, too serious-minded, too German to be really popular in England, but he was a conscientious, hard-working, public-spirited man with a good head on his shoulders, who was always both at and on Victoria's side. He was her consort, not king, but he read the state papers that came across her desk and gave her realistic advice on which she came to rely. He described himself as 'the private secretary of the sovereign and her permanent minister', but there were those who thought he was king in all but name. He improved the running of the royal household and estate, and oversaw the children's upbringing, while much of what became the 'traditional' English Christmas was imported from Germany by Albert.

The queen's affection for Lord Melbourne did not at first extend to Sir Robert Peel, Tory prime minister from 1841, who created the modern Conservative Party, but under Albert's influence she came to admire him. The Whigs turned into liberals and the queen tried not to take sides in party terms, but she found some prominent liberals, including Lord Palmerston and Mr Gladstone, hard to stomach. Like George III, she and Albert believed in a constitutional monarchy that stood above the swings and roundabouts of party politics and acted in the interests of the whole nation. They were helped by the fact that between 1846 and 1859 no party commanded an effective majority in the House of Commons, but from Palmerston's return to power in

Queen Victoria and Prince Albert photographed together in 1854, when they were both in their mid thirties. Victoria was the first British monarch in history to be photographed and this was one of the earliest ever taken. All government business came to Victoria and Albert's desks and Albert, who considered himself her private secretary, was especially conscientious in dealing with it.

Miniature portraits of Prince Albert and Queen Victoria at about the time of their wedding in 1840. The young queen was quite bowled over by Albert's good looks and they enjoyed a very passionate marriage.

1859, with Gladstone as chancellor of the exchequer, the political parties and the growing bureaucracy tightened their grip and the queen was forced to put up with politicians she had no time for. On the other hand, constitutional monarchy and the fact that Britain was the most democratic country in Europe kept the throne safe while revolutions wracked the Continent.

Loss and Mourning

The Victorian Age would bring dramatic improvements in education, public health and the living conditions of the working class. Victoria gave substantial amounts of her own money to charity and firmly believed in the duty of the rich to help the poor, although she thought it should be a matter of private initiative rather than action by the state. She and Albert were particularly interested in foreign affairs and established close links with Continental royal families. When Victoria went to Paris in 1843 she was the first British sovereign to visit the ruler of France since Henry VIII. The Tsar of Russia and the Crown Prince of Germany both visited England the following year.

Prince Albert and the Great Exhibition

The prince consort was the leading creator, against much vexatious opposition, of the Great Exhibition of 1851 in Hyde Park in London for which the Crystal Palace was specially built. Created by Joseph Paxton, the huge structure consisted of 4,500 tons of iron framework holding almost 300,000 panes of glass and, at 19.5m (64ft) high, it enclosed a number of the park's trees along with a great many birds. The problem of how to evict the birds was resolved when the Duke of Wellington suggested introducing sparrowhawks. Prince Albert raised most of the money for the exhibition, which was opened by the queen herself on what she declared was the proudest and happiest day of her life. More than 6 million people visited it to enjoy more than 100,000 exhibits and admire Britain's achievements in industry, technology and design. The exhibition gave a boost to both British commerce and British self-confidence. Prince Albert and the organizing committee made sure that the profits went on the new educational institutions and museums in South Kensington, including the Victoria and Albert Museum, the Natural History Museum and the Imperial College of Science and Technology, as well as the Royal College of Music and the Albert Hall. The prince's statue in the ornate Albert Memorial shows him holding the catalogue of the Great Exhibition.

During the Crimean War in the 1850s, which Victoria had very sensibly opposed, she took care to see many of 'her' soldiers off to war personally. She warmly approved of Florence Nightingale, took an effective interest in the treatment of wounded soldiers and frequently visited them in hospital. It was she who suggested the motto 'For Valour' for the Victoria Cross, the country's supreme decoration for bravery.

Meanwhile, for the first time since George III's day, Victoria and Albert created a respectable, upright, decently behaved royal family that could be admired and emulated. Court life was humdrum and for many courtiers deeply boring. Victoria was well aware of the sexual and financial scandals that had surrounded her father's generation of her family, and was determined to avoid them herself, but Victorian prudishness has been wildly exaggerated. The queen's image suffered badly in the 20th-century reaction against the Victorian Age, but she was not a prude or a hypocrite and probably never said, 'We are not amused.' On the contrary, she had an engaging capacity for amusement. Victoria passionately enjoyed the physical side of her marriage and those nights alone with her husband when, as she wrote, 'the world seemed only to be ourselves'. She hated pregnancy and likened small babies to frogs, but she had six children between 1840 and 1848, and three more between 1850 and 1857. What Victoria disapproved of was not sex, but unfaithfulness and irresponsibility, and especially divorce, which was still a rarity. Divorcees were not welcomed at court and she even frowned on widows remarrying.

In 1861, tragedy struck. Albert and Victoria were worrying about their eldest son, Bertie (the future Edward VII) having an affair with a girl when Albert, already anxious and exhausted by this problem, was caught in pouring rain while inspecting new buildings at Sandhurst. He went down with a chill, which turned into the typhoid fever that killed him. Left widowed at

42, Victoria was shattered. She blamed Bertie for Albert's premature death, believed she would never be able to look at him without a shudder and for years would not let him anywhere near affairs of state. Behaving as if her own life was effectively over, she retreated to Osborne with occasional forays to Windsor and Balmoral. She wore mourning black for the rest of her days and every bed she slept in had a photograph of Albert on his deathbed hanging over it. She shunned London and withdrew from public life, corresponding with her ministers almost entirely by post and often refusing to open Parliament. Her sanity began to be questioned and criticism was sharpened by rumours about her relationship with her favourite domestic servant John Brown. It reached the point where there was even talk of discarding the monarchy altogether.

The queen, now in her fifties, began to recover and reappear in public in the 1870s and a revived sense of purpose was encouraged from 1874 by Benjamin Disraeli, a Conservative and Victoria's favourite prime minister, who knew exactly how to flatter and coax her. In 1876, at her suggestion, he made her Empress of India. She returned fully to what Albert would have considered her duty, ploughing her way conscientiously through mountains of state papers, carrying out her ceremonial functions and insisting on her cabinet ministers informing and consulting her – they were still always officially 'her' ministers. In 1885 she administered a blistering public rebuke to Gladstone over the death of General Gordon at Khartoum.

The Two Jubilees

Admiration for the monarchy mounted steadily for the rest of the reign along with rising prosperity and pride in the empire and British power in the world. Mainly as a result of Prince Albert's influence, the queen had come to stand for the characteristic Victorian virtues of self-reliance, sobriety, common sense, hard work and consideration for others. The values were middle-class rather than aristocratic and Lord Salisbury, her last prime minister, would say that if he knew what the queen thought about anything then he knew what the middle class would think.

A Protestant of the low church variety, the queen disliked the High Church ritualist movement in the Church of England. She also disapproved of cruelty to animals, the infant feminist movement and racial prejudice. One of her Indian servants, Abdul Karim, was almost a successor to John Brown and gave her lessons in Hindi. From 1876 Victoria's youngest son, Leopold, Duke of Albany, was her private secretary, but he suffered from both epilepsy and haemophilia, and died in 1884. Her mainstay became Princess Beatrice, the youngest of her children, who the queen said was like a sunbeam in the house. Beatrice married Prince Henry of Battenberg in 1885 and at Victoria's insistence they both lived with her. Under their influence court life became a little livelier. There were musical evenings, amateur theatricals and command performances at Windsor and Balmoral by famous actors and entertainers.

Victoria resumed travelling abroad and helped to make Biarritz a fashionable resort. Her children's marriages strengthened the British monarchy's links with European royalty. Only one of them married a Briton – her daughter Louise, yoked unhappily to the Duke of Argyll. Four of the others married into the German, Russian and Danish royal families and four more into German princely houses. Victoria's descendants would be kings or queens of Britain, Russia, Germany, Spain, Denmark, Sweden, Norway, Greece, Romania and Yugoslavia.

The golden and diamond jubilees of 1887 and 1897 testified to the queen's popularity as the focus of national pride in Britain and the British empire. When Victoria rode in procession to a thanksgiving service in Westminster

Abbey in 1887, her carriage was followed by 30 of her sons, sons-in-law and grandsons from all over Europe. She also went to see Buffalo Bill's Wild West Show, which she found 'very extraordinary and interesting'. The diamond jubilee of 1897, marking her 60 glorious years on the throne, was deliberately staged as a colossal patriotic celebration of the empire, with magnificent processions and grand military and naval reviews. The podgy little old lady in black in her carriage cheered to the echo by huge crowds all the way to St Paul's burst into helpless tears.

The Queen and John Brown

John Brown was in his early twenties and a ghillie at Balmoral when Victoria and Prince Albert took the estate. He soon made a favourable impression on the queen and always led her pony when she was out riding. In 1858 Albert made him her principal servant in Scotland, which put him in a commanding position among the domestics. After the prince consort's death, Brown became indispensable to Victoria, who valued him for his loyalty, efficiency and commanding, no-nonsense ways. He called her 'wumman' and bossed her about. Gossip inevitably spread, and the queen was even said to have borne a child by him. What the truth of their relationship was no one knows or is ever likely to, but though the widowed queen did not conceal that she needed desperately to be taken care of it is unlikely they were lovers. Brown was 56 when he died in his rooms at Windsor Castle in 1883 and Victoria publicly described him as her 'devoted personal attendant and faithful friend'. She drafted a memoir of him, which suggests that there was nothing between them that needed concealing, but her courtiers persuaded her to drop it.

By late 1900, suffering from rheumatism, insomnia and loss of appetite, the queen was fading away and eventually even her iron constitution failed. She was buried beside her beloved Albert. Among the mementoes placed in her coffin were her wedding veil, Albert's dressing gown, a cast of his hand and a lock of John Brown's hair.

Osborne and Balmoral

Victoria and Albert bought Osborne House on the Isle of Wight as a holiday retreat in 1845 and remodelled the house and grounds on lines dictated by Albert himself. In 1853, the royal children's Swiss Cottage, complete with its own garden, was added to the grounds. Here, in what has been called possibly the world's first Wendy House, the children learnt gardening, domestic skills and the principles of commerce by selling their garden produce to Prince Albert for use in the main house. In 1848 Victoria and Albert leased the Balmoral estate in the Scottish Highlands and Albert supervised the Scots baronial design of Balmoral Castle. Victoria called it 'this dear paradise ... my dearest Albert's own creation'. The visiting Tsar of Russia said Siberia was warmer, and cabinet ministers dreaded staying there, but Victoria and Albert both loved it. Albert went deer-stalking and Victoria adored the scenery, liked tartans, shawls and porridge, and found the Scots refreshingly straightforward and unsycophantic. Her Highland journals, published in 1867 and 1883, sold like hot bannocks and gave the public an unprecedented view of royal domestic and family life. Royal enthusiasm for the Highlands contributed to the romantic image of 'bonnie Scotland', which many Scots always disliked.

Queen Victoria is seen smiling cheerfully in a sepia photograph taken for her golden jubilee in 1887, marking her 50 years on the throne. By this time she was 'the grandmother of Europe' and numerous European royalties attended the celebrations as well as Indian rajahs and the Queen of Hawaii.

Monarchy and Empire

By the end of Victoria's reign the days of personal rule by kings and queens were long past. The development of organized political parties, with the extension of the vote to more and more British citizens after the Reform Act of 1832, made it impossible for the monarch to play one small faction off against another, and the Crown no longer controlled the swelling bureaucracy through which the government interfered

for good or ill with the lives of the country's citizens. Walter Bagehot's classic book, *The English Constitution*, which came out in 1867, defined the monarch's position in a way that has been accepted ever since as 'the right to be consulted, the right to encourage and the right to warn'.

The British Empire. This shows the fullest extent of the Empire, after World War I, when something like one-fifth of the world was coloured red on maps to describe it.

The Empire was very complex, with several different kinds of government – some direct from Britain and some with self-governing status.

At is height it was the largest empire the world had known. Queen Victoria presided over its greatest period, and was very proud to be Empress of India, as well as being genuinely interested in her subjects throughout the world.

Edward VII
1901–1910

BORN	9 November 1841 at Buckingham Palace
PARENTS	Victoria and Albert of Saxe-Coburg-Gotha
CROWNED	9 August 1902, aged 60
MARRIED	Alexandra of Denmark (d. 1925)
CHILDREN	Five who survived infancy: two boys and three girls
DIED	6 May 1910 at Buckingham Palace, aged 68

Edward VII had been Prince of Wales from the age of one month until he was 59. For most of that time he had been dismissed by his parents as lazy and irresponsible, his behaviour alarmingly recalling his licentious Hanoverian great-uncles. But when he finally acceded to the throne he proved to be a far abler monarch than might have been expected – and certainly far better than his mother had always feared. Though he reigned for less than ten years the new king would leave his name to the period, an age of opulent comfort and self-indulgence that fitted him like a glove.

Edward VII was a Hanoverian on his mother's side, a Saxe-Coburg on his father's, he was christened Albert Edward and called 'Bertie' in the family. In the typical Hanoverian pattern he had a fraught

relationship with his parents. His father was constantly held up to him by his mother as a model of ideal manhood, but Bertie was very unlike his father and his parents were profoundly disappointed in him. They considered him light-minded and prone to listlessness, dismayingly given to sliding down the stairs on tea-trays instead of doing his lessons. Bertie learned fluent German and French, though he never managed to spell. He was not stupid, but he was not bookish and he suffered by comparison with his bright older sister Victoria. His parents were seriously worried about his backwardness and referred to him disparagingly as 'poor Bertie'. Not surprisingly perhaps, he stammered, bullied his younger siblings and was given to furious tantrums. At 13, taken on a royal visit to Paris, he told the Emperor Napoleon III, 'I would like to be your son.' All the rest of his life, he was pro-French.

When Bertie was 17, his father described him as 'lively, quick and sharp when his mind is set on anything, which is seldom.' He was given his own household at White Lodge in Richmond Park with three young men as companions, two of whom had won VCs in the Crimea. They were to teach him correct manners, deportment and polite conversation, in which they were successful. Their instructions to keep him away from cards and billiards, and to curb his dandyish tendency, proved less easy to achieve. In 1860 he made a successful visit to Canada and the United States, where his genial charm won plaudits. A year later, aged 19, he was sent for military training in Ireland, and his young fellow officers put him to bed with a girl called Nellie Clifden (who may not have been his first). Word of the affair soon leaked out and caused his parents the strain that Queen Victoria blamed for Prince Albert's death.

Wedding photograph of the Prince of Wales and Princess Alexandra, from the Illustrated London News. *The princess's growing deafness tended to isolate her and in time she and the prince came more and more to lead separate lives.*

An apparently accidental meeting had already been organized for Bertie in Germany with Princess Alexandra, daughter of King Christian IX of Denmark. She was beautiful, elegant and gentle, and rather deaf. They were married in 1863, when she was 19 and he was 22. They both spent money like water, she would bear patiently with his infidelities, and at their London residence, Marlborough House in Pall Mall, they enjoyed entertaining their smart set of friends. Six children were born in seven years from 1864 to 1871. Alexandra loved the children, created a cosy, undemanding family atmosphere and was known at home as 'Motherdear' (not the more formal 'Mama' that was favoured by the aristocracy). There were further scandals, however, including two in which Bertie would have to appear in court: in 1870, when he was subpoenaed to give evidence in a society divorce case, and again 20 years later after an illegal game of baccarat at a house party at Tranby Croft in Yorkshire had given rise to accusations of cheating and an action for slander.

The Ambassador King

In the 1870s Queen Victoria at last allowed Bertie to make some of her public appearances for her. He carried them off well. Following the Canadian trip, his visit to India in 1876 established a tradition of grand royal progresses to the empire and he shot six tigers on his first day of big-game hunting. But he was not allowed to see important state papers until he was in his fifties, and with little of any importance to do he devoted himself to love affairs, gambling, cards, horse-racing, hunting, shooting and eating. Getting through 20 cigarettes a day and a dozen massive cigars, he tucked into five hearty meals a day, including a 12-course dinner, with supper last thing. His swelling girth earned him the nickname Tum Tum and obliged him to leave the bottom button of his waist-coat undone, which was immediately fashionable and has been the correct thing ever since. He took fashion seriously and made the dinner jacket with black tie acceptable evening wear. He won the Derby three times and the Grand National once, owned a succession of racing yachts and took a lively interest in the early motor cars. He played cricket, golf and ice-hockey, had a bowling alley installed at Sandringham and took up bridge. He frequently travelled abroad, staying regularly at Biarritz and Marienbad.

Bertie's childhood had given him a need for approval and affection, which his position, wealth, good looks and charm won for him from women, smart society and financiers. Like many other men he disapproved of giving women the vote but, like his mother, he also disapproved of racial prejudice and his circle included successful Jewish businessmen such as Sir Ernest Cassel,

The King's Women

Edward VII liked women and they liked him. He is thought to have had at least 13 mistresses. The media made little of his affairs, and high society and the mistresses themselves were generally discreet.

The best-known of his early lights of love as Prince of Wales was the beautiful 'Jersey Lily', the actress Lillie Langtry, whose portrait by Millais in 1878 drew crowds to the Royal Academy. In 1889 he met his 'Darling Daisy wife', the excitable Countess of Warwick, who developed socialist tendencies. She was replaced from the late 1890s by the witty, worldly, sweet-tempered, voluptuous Mrs George Keppel. Her daughter Sonia was widely believed to be the prince's (and would be the grandmother of Camilla Parker-Bowles). The king was at Biarritz with Alice Keppel when he had the heart attack that precipitated his death. With characteristic generosity Queen Alexandra invited her to Sandringham to take her final leave of him.

Nathaniel Rothschild and the Sassoons. Cassel's handling of his finances from 1890 made him much richer than Queen Victoria.

Becoming king at last in 1901, Bertie significantly chose to be Edward VII, not Albert I. He had all the royal palaces refurbished, destroyed all remaining traces of John Brown and created the prestigious Order of Merit to honour exceptional distinction. He chose the members himself. He continued his mother's interest in appointments, chivvied ministers when he thought they needed it and promoted military and naval reform. He disliked the Liberal government's assaults on the incomes and privileges of the landed classes, but intervened to help their measures through the House of Lords. He understood how the world worked and his wide-ranging family connections, shrewdness and charm made him an effective ambassador for his country abroad. Always pro-French, in 1904 he encouraged the entente cordiale with France, which the British government favoured (and which would take an appalling toll of British lives in World War I). Lord Esher, said: 'He stands for our country, our empire and all our people, in the eyes of Europe and of the world.'

The royal court, very unlike Queen Victoria's, was a centre of smart society and fashion. Despite or often because of his self-indulgent life, Edward VII was very popular. He looked kingly and he had dignity and courteous manners. He obviously liked being king and his enjoyment was infectious. Queen Alexandra was popular, too, for her unpretentious kindliness and devotion to good causes. Despite her growing deafness and lameness, she worked hard for the Red Cross, hospitals and the sick and built up the tradition of royal work for charity.

By 1909 the king was suffering badly from bronchitis and after a heart attack at Biarritz the following year he was brought home to Sandringham to die. Nine European sovereigns followed his coffin on his last journey, and so did his favourite terrier, Caesar.

The Royal Family and Sandringham

In 1861, not long before his death, Prince Albert arranged to buy the Sandringham House estate in Norfolk as a country home for his eldest son in the vain hope of weaning him from the raffish pleasures of London society. The future Edward VII took to Sandringham and after his marriage to Princess Alexandra in 1863 it became the house they both liked best. They replaced it in the following decade with a larger, opulently comfortable 270-room residence. Their eldest son died there in 1892. The prince bred racehorses there successfully and held lavish hunting and shooting parties, for which his gamekeepers provided 30,000 partridges and pheasants every season. The future King George V and his family had a small house on the estate, but Queen Alexandra kept the main house until her death in 1925. Sandringham became the royal family's much-loved winter retreat and helped to give the monarchy a country gentleman image. Both George V and George VI died there.

Sandringham House in 1994. It was the home that Edward VII liked best of the royal residences and Queen Alexandra, who also loved it, would live there throughout her long widowhood.

Meanwhile...

1717   The Freemasons' Society opens a headquarters in Covent Garden, London.

1719   Journalist Daniel Defoe publishes *Robinson Crusoe*, a landmark in the development of the novel.

1725   Guy's Hospital, founded by bookseller and philanthropist Thomas Guy, opens in London.

1726   *Gulliver's Travels*, the satire by Jonathan Swift, is a huge publishing success.

1728   First performance of John Gay's *The Beggar's Opera*, at Lincoln's Inn Fields Theatre.

1729   Charles Wesley founds a religious society known as the Methodists at Lincoln College, Oxford.

1717   1734   1742   1769   1801

1734   Jethro Tull publishes a series of essays on his improvements to farming technology, including the seed drill.

1742   Handel's great oratorio *Messiah*, composed in a matter of weeks in London, is first performed in Dublin.

1769   Richard Arkwright invents the water-powered loom and opens the first water-powered mill at Cromford in 1771.

1779   Ironmaster Abraham Darby builds the world's first iron bridge near Coalbrookdale in Shropshire.

1801   The first national census reveals that the population of Britain and Ireland is just under 16 million.

1825   Locomotion No. 1, built by George Stephenson, pulls the world's first passenger train, from Stockton to Darlington.

1826	James Sharp invents the first practical domestic stove, installed in his Northampton home.
1829	Some 1,000 men, mostly ex-soldiers, form the first police force, established by the Home Secretary, Sir Robert Peel.
1831	Michael Faraday demonstrates the production of electric current by magnetism.
1833	Slavery is abolished throughout the British Empire, after a long campaign by Quakers and politician William Wilberforce.
1834	Labourers at Tolpuddle in Dorset are arrested and transported to Australia for setting up a trade union.
1836	Charles Darwin returns from a five-year voyage researching natural history in South America and the Pacific.

1825   1833   1867   1891   1908

1862	The world's first underground railway is opened in London, running from Paddington to Farringdon.
1867	Karl Marx publishes the first volume of *Das Kapital*, analysing the workings of industrial capitalism.
1891	Free schooling is made available to all children, 11 years after it became compulsory for all children to attend school.
1905	In Dublin, Arthur Griffith founds the nationalist party Sinn Féin in the cause of political freedom for Ireland.
1906	Eleven suffragettes, including Emmeline Pankhurst, are jailed for demonstrating for women's rights at the House of Commons.
1908	The first old-age pensions are made available to those over 70 with incomes of less than ten shillings a week.

The Windsors
1910–Present

The British royal family changed its official style to House of Windsor in 1917 to avoid any backlash from anti-German feeling in the country during World War I. It was one of many changes and challenges that the monarchy had to survive, including the two world wars, the end of the British Empire and its replacement by the Commonwealth, the onward march of socialism, the coming of the mass media, the gradual melting away of old class distinctions and deference, and the replacement of Britain by the United States as the world's strongest power. George V overcame his shyness to become a popular and effective monarch, but Edward VIII seemed to have no serious interest in politics and George VI, who had never expected the throne, lacked the self-confidence to use his political influence in the way earlier monarchs had done. He repaired some of the damage caused by his brother's abdication and he and his family were a rallying point during World War II, but constitutional monarchy now came to mean carrying out a traditional ceremonial role, involvement in charitable good works and acting as a symbol of the nation rather than wielding political influence.

George V
1910–1936

BORN	3 June 1865 at Marlborough House, London
PARENTS	Edward VII and Alexandra of Denmark
CROWNED	22 June 1911, aged 46
MARRIED	Mary of Teck (d. 1953)
CHILDREN	Six
DIED	20 January 1936 at Sandringham House, Norfolk, aged 70

George V brought to the monarchy a renewed air of solid responsibility, married faithfulness, straightforwardness and attention to duty. Like William IV before him, he had been trained in the navy and all his adult life he had a bluff, no-nonsense nautical air about him, which many of his subjects came to admire. He was a man of simple tastes, and unlike his father he disliked fashionable society, had little command of foreign languages and took only a limited interest in 'abroad'. He was meticulous about details of etiquette and so obsessed with punctuality that he kept all the Sandringham clocks half an hour fast.

George was not originally expected to be king. The heir apparent was his brother Prince Albert Victor, Duke of Clarence, known in the family as Eddy, who was a year older. Prince Eddy has had a

thoroughly bad press. Described as mentally backward, idle and dissipated, he has even been a candidate for Jack the Ripper, the murderer of prostitutes in London's East End in the 1880s. Late in 1891 it was announced that Eddy was to marry Princess Mary of Teck, but he died of double pneumonia the following January at Sandringham, aged 28, before the wedding could take place. He was buried in St George's Chapel at Windsor in an astonishingly elaborate art nouveau tomb designed by the English sculptor Alfred Gilbert (1854–1934). A story grew up that to prevent Eddy's succession to the throne the family had faked his death and shut him away at Glamis Castle until his actual death years afterwards in 1933. His reputation remained under a cloud until a biography by Andrew Cook, published in 2005, attempted to rehabilitate him.

Mary of Teck came from an impoverished German princely family, but she had been born in Kensington Palace in the same room as Queen Victoria and brought up in England. The question of what to do with the 24-year-old princess now Eddy was dead was solved by simply betrothing her to the 26-year-old George instead. Remarkably, it worked. They suited each other and the succession was secured by the birth of their first son within a year of their marriage and their second the following year. Though she complained of his undemonstrativeness, they remained together for more than 40 years in what turned out to be one of the longest-lasting royal marriages on record. In 1901, as the newly created Prince and Princess of Wales, George and Mary set off on a royal tour of the empire in which they visited Australia, New Zealand, South Africa and Canada, covered 72,500km (45,000 miles), reviewed 60,000 troops, laid 21 foundation stones and shook hands at official receptions with 25,000 people.

George and Mary's country residence was York Cottage on the Sandringham estate, where he enjoyed the life of a country gentleman. He was a first-class shot, loved hunting and fishing, played golf and enjoyed yachting and horse-racing. In 1913, after he had become king, a suffragette threw herself to her death under his runner in the Derby. He spent hours every week with his stamp collection, which he built into one of the largest and most valuable in the world. His wife, who was far more interested in and knowledgeable about art, had an acquisitive eye for antiques, fans, lace and Wedgwood china. She worked hard for charities – partly as a deliberate strategy to counter socialism and potential working-class discontent with the monarchy – but she developed a regal air and her stiffness and formality attracted criticism of her as 'a royal robot'.

Making a Go of It

Edward VII had trained George for his future role, but the younger man lacked his father's commanding charm. To begin with he found

Imperial Zenith

At George V's insistence, he and Queen Mary went to Delhi in 1911 to be crowned Emperor and Empress of India. A spacious city of tents was erected and 90,000 rats were eliminated for the occasion. The royals were lodged in carpeted and silk-lined splendour and George wore his new imperial crown – it was heavy and hurt his head – before a glittering gathering of rajahs and maharajahs, high-ranking officials and military men. Watched by an audience of more than 100,000 people, it was the ceremonial zenith of the old empire and in his diary the king called it 'the most beautiful and wonderful sight I ever saw'. He relaxed by going off to Nepal in a party with 600 elephants and 14,000 beaters, and shooting 21 tigers.

A photograph of King George V and Queen Mary, taken early in the reign in 1914, when they were both in their late forties. They married in 1893 and their children were born between 1894 and 1905. The youngest, John, suffered from epilepsy and was kept out of public view at Sandringham until his premature death at the age of 13.

being king difficult – he was so shy that he shook with nerves when opening Parliament – but he stuck gamely to it, as he would all his life. Immediately on succeeding to the crown in 1910 he was faced with a crisis over the Liberal government's determination to limit the powers of the House of Lords. He did not like it, but he behaved constitutionally and did so again in a crisis over home rule for Ireland in 1912.

In 1914 Europe was plunged into the catastrophe of World War I. George, now 49, busied himself with morale-boosting visits to the troops at the front, which included thousands from the empire, and to hospitals, factories and shipyards at home, while Queen Mary plunged into wartime charity work. However, the royal family was embarrassed by its German ancestry and relationships – George and the Emperor of Germany, 'Kaiser Bill', were both grandsons of Queen Victoria. The war gave the king himself a lasting distaste for Germans and in 1917, on government advice, he decided to adopt the style of House of Windsor. For fear of stimulating revolutionary attitudes in Britain, he refused to let his cousin Tsar Nicholas II and his family take refuge in England from the Russian Revolution. Nicholas and his wife and their five children were murdered in 1918, but George apparently never regretted his decision.

As with his predecessors, the fact that George V was a constitutional monarch did not stop him exercising political influence. He chose Stanley Baldwin in preference to Lord Curzon as prime minister in 1923. In 1924 he got on far better with the country's first Labour government under Ramsay MacDonald than was expected. During the national strike of 1926 he encouraged the Baldwin cabinet to conciliate the trade unions and he strongly supported the formation of the national government in 1931 under MacDonald (who later called him 'a gracious and kingly friend'). Meanwhile the British Empire's nature was changing. Canada, Australia, New Zealand and South Africa had become virtually self-governing and in 1931 the Statute of Westminster gave the dominions complete legislative independence from the United Kingdom. It was a step on the road to the Commonwealth.

At Christmas, in 1932, the king made a radio broadcast to his people. It was drafted by Rudyard Kipling. 'I speak now from my home and from my heart to you all, to men and women so cut off by the snows, the desert or the sea, that only voices out of the air can reach them.' It was the first time any monarch had been able to speak directly to the masses in this way. It went down extremely well and cemented the king's popularity. When his silver jubilee was celebrated in 1935, he was astonished at the crowds that cheered him everywhere he went. 'I had no idea they felt like that about me,' he said to Queen Mary at one point. 'I'm beginning to think they really like me for myself.'

The king's health had been deteriorating for some years – he had a weak chest and was a heavy smoker – and by the beginning of 1936 he clearly had little time left. Whether he actually said, 'Bugger Bognor!' when urged to go there for his health is doubtful, but it became his most frequently quoted utterance. His hand shook so badly that he could no longer write his diary and his doctor, Lord Dawson of Penn, issued a bulletin from Sandringham: 'The king's life is moving peacefully to its close'. He gave the dying man drugs to ease the pain and also apparently to hasten the end so that he news of the death would appear in the quality morning press rather than the evening papers. The king died that same night.

Ireland Divided

The Liberal government passed home rule for Ireland through the House of Commons in 1912, but met determined opposition from Protestants in Ulster, with support from the Conservative party and many British army officers. The king warned his prime minister, H. H. Asquith, not to use the army against Ulster, tried to persuade the Conservatives to be reasonable and organized a conference of all parties at Buckingham Palace in 1914. No agreement was reached, the Easter Rising of 1916 in Dublin was suppressed by force, and after a period of guerrilla warfare and coercion an Act of Parliament in 1920 proposed to divide Ireland, with separate parliaments in Dublin and Belfast. The king opened the Ulster parliament in person. He apparently told the newspaper magnate Lord Northcliffe that he could not go on having his people in the south of Ireland being killed, and he helped to persuade the south to accept dominion status in 1921 as the Irish Free State. George was now officially the ruler of the United Kingdom of Great Britain and Northern Ireland.

The future George V (right) was photographed when yachting at Cowes in 1909 with the Tsar of Russia, Nicholas II. The family resemblance is striking. George has been much criticized for refusing to give the tsar and his family asylum in England after the revolution in Russia.

Edward VIII
1936

BORN	23 June 1894 at White Lodge, Richmond, Surrey
PARENTS	George V and Mary of Teck
CROWNED	Uncrowned
MARRIED	Wallis Warfield Simpson (d. 1986)
CHILDREN	None
DIED	28 May 1972 in Paris, aged 77

Edward was a Prince Charming who enjoyed fashionable society and pursued married women who were generally older than himself. He disdained convention, disliked the pomp and ceremony of royalty, which he thought antediluvian, dressed casually, puffed incessantly on cigarettes and loved nightclubs and dancing. He also resented his father's attempts to discipline him. Edward started life with a superfluity of Christian names – Edward Albert Christian George Andrew Patrick David – which included the names of his future realm's four patron saints. He was known in the family as David and he was no saint.

When the future Edward VIII was born, Queen Victoria commented that it was unprecedented in the history of the British monarchy for the sovereign and three direct heirs – her son, her grandson and her baby great-grandson – to be alive at the same time.

Unfortunately, the old Hanoverian pattern of hostility between father and eldest son appeared once more in George V's relationship with his successor. George and Queen Mary were not unloving parents, but they were reserved and undemonstrative and did not easily show affection. They had little understanding of children and were more indulgent with other people's offspring than with their own. Edward felt thoroughly unloved and he later described his childhood as 'wretched'.

As small children, Edward and his next brother Bertie (the future George VI) were placed in the charge of a nursemaid who neglected Bertie and doted on Edward. When she took Edward down to his parents in the drawing room, she would surreptitiously pinch him to make him cry, so that she would be told to take him back to the nursery where she could have him to herself. At the age of 12 he was sent to the Royal Naval College, where he was bullied and which he hated, and at 18 he went to Magdalen College, Oxford, where he was happy and well-liked – intellectually he did not shine, but he learnt to play the banjo.

During World War I the prince had a commission in the Grenadier Guards. He pressed hard to serve at the front, pointing out that he had brothers to take his place if needed. He appealed personally to Lord Kitchener, but to no effect and he was kept well out of harm's way and felt humiliated. In London he fell in love with a married woman, Freda Dudley Ward, who became his substitute mother and principal mistress. His strait-laced father and mother were not pleased and he tried to keep his private life to himself, including an affair with an American socialite, Thelma, Lady Furness.

The young prince's easy manners and modern ways were assets in a programme of visits abroad, which were an imperial equivalent of Elizabeth I's royal progresses. Between 1919 and 1925 he went to almost every corner of the British Empire, and also to the United States, which he took to and which

The former king photographed with the love of his life after he had given up his throne to marry her. Her attitude to him has never been clear. It seems that she might have been content to be his mistress, but he could not be satisfied with that.

took to him. At home he showed little interest in his state papers, but enjoyed hunting, point-to-point racing, golf and playing the bagpipes. When the great Depression struck in the 1930s, he expressed sympathy for the unemployed. On a visit to South Wales, he famously said that 'something must be done', but it was an empty sentiment.

In 1930 the prince bought a country house in Surrey – Fort Belvedere near Virginia Water – where he kept informal court. There he met Wallis Simpson and was enslaved, summarily dropping Freda Dudley Ward in 1934. When she phoned him, she was told he had given orders not to put her through, and she never heard from him again. The prince was 42 when he became king and by then he was determined to marry Wallis. She tried to break the affair off, but he won her over and she started divorce proceedings against Ernest Simpson. Edward discussed the situation with the prime minister, Stanley Baldwin, who eventually told him that marriage to a twice-divorced woman with two husbands living could not be reconciled with his position as head of the Church of England. The king said he must marry Wallis Simpson or abdicate.

The story broke in the British press in December 1936. The government, the Church of England and the dominions were adamantly opposed to the marriage, and although there was much sympathy for the king he did not try to rally support. Wallis Simpson again offered to renounce the king, but he would not allow it and signed the abdication papers at Fort Belvedere later in December in the presence of his younger brothers. Next evening, after a farewell dinner with his family – which included his brother Bertie, who was now George VI – he made a poignant broadcast to the nation, explaining that he could not carry on without the help and support of the woman he loved. That night he left for Portsmouth and took a warship across the Channel to exile in France. He had occupied the throne for less than a year.

The rest was anti-climax. The ex-king, now His Royal Highness the Duke of Windsor, married Wallis at a French château in June 1937, but she was not allowed the style of royal highness and he bitterly resented the fact afterwards. The duke and duchess visited Nazi Germany, where the regime had his restoration to the throne in mind if Germany won the war that was looming in Europe, but it does not seem likely that he had any idea of it. When war came and the Germans invaded France in 1940, the duke and duchess had to leave in a hurry for Madrid. A German plot to kidnap the duke was foiled and he was pushed into a siding as the wartime Governor of the Bahamas. Afterwards the Windsors lived mainly in Paris, until his death of cancer. The duchess lived on alone for 14 more years, sinking into senility before she died at the age of 79.

The Femme Fatale

The woman for whom Edward VIII renounced his throne was improbably said to have lured him with arts of love she learned in a Chinese brothel. More prosaically, she was born Bessie Wallis Warfield in 1896 to an old Pennsylvania family that had fallen on hard times. An impoverished upbringing left her with an acquisitive streak. In 1916, aged 20, she married an American airman called Earl Winfield Spencer. He was a drunk and they divorced in 1927. A year later she married Ernest Simpson, an American businessman in London with connections in smart society, and in 1931 she met the Prince of Wales. He was fascinated by the witty Wallis, who treated him with far less than the accustomed deference, and they became lovers on a Mediterranean cruise in 1934. She would apparently have been content to be his reigning mistress, but he insisted on marriage and the crown was lost.

The Monarchy and the Media

From today's perspective, the most remarkable feature of the abdication crisis of 1936 was the British media's silence about the king's love affair with Mrs Simpson. By 1934 newspapers in the United States and Europe were full of it, but there was a conspiracy of silence in the British press, apparently fundamentally based on patriotic reluctance to throw mud at the institution of monarchy.

The development of popular newspapers, film, radio and later television gave the monarchy an unprecedented opportunity to make a favourable impression on the country, the empire and the world. In 1924 George V's speech at the opening of the British Empire Exhibition at Wembley reached a radio audience estimated at 10 million people. In 1932 he made the historic Christmas broadcast that became a regular part of the nation's festivities. The text was 251 words long and took just two-and-a-half minutes to deliver and the king was shaking with nerves, but the impact was remarkable. When Edward VIII abdicated in 1936, he announced the fact to the nation in person on the radio. George VI made certain that his coronation the following year was broadcast to the nation, the empire and the world by the BBC. Press photographs of the king and his family in a happy domestic setting were effective public relations for the monarchy, as were photographs of the king and queen in wartime.

The BBC's regular television service, launched in 1936, resumed after the war. Sales of TV sets soared in the 1950s, helped by the broadcast of Elizabeth II's coronation in 1953, which reached millions of viewers all over the world and was excellent propaganda for the monarchy. The world was changing, however, and the weapon of publicity would prove to be double-edged. The media's reluctance to throw mud vanished and the royal family would find some of the postwar coverage thoroughly uncomfortable.

Elizabeth II's coronation procession passing through Trafalgar Square in 1953. The ceremony in Westminster Abbey was beamed all over the world on television and attracted a huge audience, but publicity, which had always been one of the monarchy's weapons, would soon prove to have its disadvantages.

George VI
1936–1952

BORN	14 December 1895 at York Cottage on the Sandringham estate
PARENTS	George V and Mary of Teck
CROWNED	12 May 1937, aged 41
MARRIED	Elizabeth Bowes-Lyon (d. 2002), daughter of the Earl of Strathmore
CHILDREN	Two: Elizabeth and Margaret Rose
DIED	6 February 1952 at Sandringham, aged 56

George VI was horrified by the prospect of being king. 'This is terrible!' he told his cousin Lord Louis Mountbatten, 'I never wanted this to happen.' He was shy, painfully self-conscious and afflicted with a bad stammer that made public appearances a nightmare. On the other hand, he had inherited the courage and sense of duty of his father, George V. 'I am new to the job,' he wrote to the prime minister, Stanley Baldwin, 'but I hope that time will be allowed to me to make amends for what has happened.' He also had the advantage of having exactly the right wife and the two of them would win the respect and affection of the majority of their subjects.

Queen Victoria was still alive when the future king was born on the anniversary of the Prince Consort's death, which upset her. Inevitably christened Albert, he was known as 'Bertie' in the family.

He shared the nursery at York Cottage on the Sandringham estate with his elder brother David (the future Edward VIII), who outshone him. As a child, he was bad at his lessons, often ill and given to rages and floods of tears. When it was realized that he was left-handed, he was forced to write with his right, which may have caused or exacerbated the stammer that started when he was seven.

In 1908 he was sent to the Royal Naval College, where he came 68th out of a class of 68, but he was intended for a career in the navy and though he suffered from sea-sickness he came to enjoy it. At the age of 20 in 1916 he saw action at the Battle of Jutland, where his presence was an excellent advertisement for the royal family. He then went into the Royal Naval Air Service and became the first family member to qualify as a pilot. In 1920 he was created Duke of York.

Bertie was now falling in love with Lady Elizabeth Bowes-Lyon, a descendant of both Robert II of Scots and Owain Glyn Dwr. She had been born and brought up in England. Charming, attractive, vivacious and forceful, she had lost a dearly loved brother in World War I and had served as a nurse. She feared that as a member of the royal family she would lose her freedom to act and speak as she chose, and Bertie had to propose to her three times before he was accepted. They were married in 1923, when he was 27 and she was 22, and George V was so taken with her that he even forgave her unpunctuality. They lived at Royal Lodge in Windsor Great Park and also took a house in Piccadilly. They involved themselves diligently in charitable work, his particular interest being the Duke of York's Boys' Camps, which brought working-class boys and public schoolboys together in an attempt to break down class barriers. He was a good enough tennis player to be in the Wimbledon doubles in 1926 and he was an excellent shot, though he found that golf was bad for his temper.

Until almost the last minute, the duke and duchess had no idea of the seriousness of the crisis that was building up over Edward VIII and Mrs

Simpson. They resented the fact that they had not been consulted and the Duchess of York was horrified at the strain the situation put on her husband. She probably had much to do with the frostiness with which the ex-king and his wife were later treated, which was also a sensible exercise in limiting the damage to the monarchy.

A Royal Partnership

The coronation went ahead as planned for Edward VIII, but with a different protagonist. Bertie decided to be crowned as George VI, which he hoped would suggest continuity between his father's reign and his own and help to lessen the damage caused by the abdication crisis. A loving wife and family

Curing the Stammer

Lionel Logue was an Australian speech therapist and Christian Scientist who had treated shell-shocked World War I soldiers suffering from speech disorders. He was particularly successful with stammering, using muscle relaxation exercises, correct breathing techniques and advising the sufferer to speak more slowly. He also emphasized the need to bolster the patient's self-confidence. Logue moved to London in 1924, established himself in Harley Street and built up a successful practice. Far and away his most famous patient was the future George VI, who went to him for treatment in 1926. He prescribed gargling, intoning vowels while standing at an open window, and practising saying difficult words and tongue-twisters. Logue coached the new king for his coronation service and his broadcast that evening, and continued to prepare him for speaking engagements and broadcasts until his death.

George VI and Queen Elizabeth enjoying a friendly visit with the locals in a bombed area of the East End of London during World War II. Their adamant refusal to leave London, the fact that Buckingham Palace itself was bombed and their constant visits to blitzed towns helped to boost both the reputation of the monarchy and national morale.

helped to give the new king greater security and self-confidence. His daughters, Elizabeth and Margaret Rose (she hated the Rose), had been born in 1926 and 1930. Professional speech therapy after 1926 helped to bring the royal stammer under control and there was a highly effective state visit to Canada in 1939, followed by a useful visit to the United States and President Roosevelt, who had suggested it as a way of fostering Anglo-American co-operation. The

Chamberlain government had planned to move the court, the government and Parliament out of London if war came, to be safe from bombing, but the king and queen would have none of it. As Queen Elizabeth put it: 'The children won't leave without me; I won't leave without the king; and the king will never leave.'

George VI and Queen Elizabeth stayed in London all through the Blitz. They were seen constantly moving through the blasted streets, sympathizing with the victims and boosting morale. They ate Spam off their gold plates in Buckingham Palace and when it was bombed in 1940 the queen characteristi-

A Prime Minister for War

The prospect of a second war brought back all too vividly the horrors of the first and George VI, who shared the contemporary determination to avoid it at almost any price, backed the efforts of Neville Chamberlain as prime minister and Lord Halifax as foreign secretary to appease Nazi Germany. At one point he suggested writing personally to Adolf Hitler as one ex-serviceman to another, but the government demurred. When Chamberlain lost the confidence of the House of Commons, the king along with most Conservative opinion regarded Halifax as the right successor and distrusted Winston Churchill. Chamberlain, Halifax and Churchill met to settle the issue and Halifax said he could not act as prime minister from the House of Lords: whether he said this because he really believed it or because it let him out of a job he did not feel up to is not clear. Churchill remained silent and the premiership was his. George VI made no attempt to intervene and soon came to admire Churchill enormously.

cally said she was glad of it because she could now look the East End in the face. They also made innumerable visits to armaments factories, shipyards and bombed towns, and they won affectionate respect. On the king's initiative, the George Cross and the George Medal were instituted in 1940 for acts of conspicuous bravery by civilians. The George Cross was conferred on the island of Malta in 1942 on the king's initiative. He also took an active part in the presentation of a sword of honour to Stalingrad. He calculated that during the war he had personally conferred more than 44,000 decorations and orders.

Winston Churchill and the king had lunch together every Tuesday, with no advisers or secretaries present, which besides keeping the king informed made sure that the court did not interfere with the conduct of the war. In 1943 George VI visited troops in North Africa and in 1944 he and Churchill both wanted to accompany the D-Day landings in person and had to be dissuaded. When the war at last ended, Buckingham Palace was the natural and appropriate centre of rejoicing, with applauding crowds calling the king and queen back to the balcony over and over again.

After the war the king refrained from interfering, as his predecessors might have tried to do, with the Labour government's wholesale changes: the development of the welfare state, the creation of the National Health Service and the nationalization of industries. Indian independence took away the king's title of emperor, and the British Empire became the British Commonwealth of Nations, with the monarch as the symbolic head, which George VI saw as an admirable development.

Sadly, the king's health steadily worsened. He had always smoked heavily and he developed lung cancer, though he was not told. In January 1952 he saw his daughter Elizabeth and his-son-in-law Philip off from Heathrow Airport on a Commonwealth tour and returned to Sandringham. On 5 February he spent a happy day shooting with friends and was found dead in bed the next morning by his valet.

The king's body lay in state in Westminster Hall and three queens in mourning black attended his obsequies: his mother Queen Mary, his widow, Queen Elizabeth the Queen Mother, as she was now to be called, and his daughter and successor Queen Elizabeth II. The funeral tributes included one from Winston Churchill in the shape of a George Cross, with the inscription 'For Gallantry'.

The royal family on the balcony at Buckingham Palace, acknowledging the cheers of an enthusiastic crowd after the coronation in 1937. From left to right, Queen Elizabeth, Princess Elizabeth, Queen Mary, Princess Margaret and George VI.

Elizabeth II
1952–Present

BORN	21 April 1926 at 17 Bruton Street, London
PARENTS	George VI and Elizabeth Bowes-Lyon
CROWNED	2 June 1953, aged 27
MARRIED	Philip of Greece
CHILDREN	Four

The second Elizabeth had been heir to the throne since her father's accession in 1936, when she was ten, and she had been carefully trained for her role. On the news of her father's death in 1952, when she was 27, the new queen immediately flew back from Kenya. She was crowned in Westminster Abbey the following year in a ceremony thought to have been watched on television by more than half the adult population of the country. The popular media would prove to be sometimes an ally and sometimes an intrusive enemy in the course of a reign that has now lasted more than 50 years, one of the longest in the monarchy's history.

Christened Elizabeth Alexandra Mary, Elizabeth grew up in a happy family atmosphere and was a great favourite with George V. She was his 'sweet little Lilibet' and he was her 'Grandpa England'. At the age of seven a photograph of her holding a Welsh corgi in her arms appeared

in the press. Corgis have been associated with her ever since. Aged 13 in 1939, on a visit to Dartmouth Naval College, the princess met the 18-year-old Philip of Greece, her third cousin, son of Prince Andrew of Greece. Of Danish descent, Philip was the grandson of King George of the Hellenes and on his mother's side a great-great-great grandson of Queen Victoria. He had been to Gordonstoun, an English public school with a reputation for toughness, and then went into the navy and had a good war.

Elizabeth and Philip were married in Westminster Abbey in 1947 and he was created Duke of Edinburgh that day. Her corgi Susan rode with the newlyweds in their carriage back to Buckingham Palace. Philip had taken British citizenship and the name Mountbatten (he was Lord Louis Mountbatten's nephew) in preference to what would otherwise have been a mouthful of a surname with all the wrong associations – Schleswig-Holstein-Sonderburg-Glücksburg. Prince Charles, the future Prince of Wales, was born at Buckingham Palace the following year and three more children followed: Anne, Princess Royal, born in 1950, Andrew, Duke of York, born in 1960 and Edward, Earl of Wessex, born in 1964.

The coronation in 1953 set off much media talk about a new Elizabethan age, but in fact the country slid into what began to seem an irreversible decline in power, wealth and national pride, which inevitably affected the monarchy. The empire was going or gone. India and Pakistan had become independent republics in 1947 and Elizabeth II was not an empress but Head of the Commonwealth. The adjective British had been dropped from the title in 1948. Everyone tried to pretend that the Commonwealth was a continuation of the empire by other means, but in reality it was its opposite. As the historian David Cannadine summed it up: the empire was about power, the Commonwealth was about sentiment.

Princess Elizabeth and Lieutenant Philip Mountbatten at Buckingham Palace in 1947, after their engagement had been announced. The flood of intrusive publicity that followed brought home to her how much her privacy was going to be invaded by the media.

The Queen took her Commonwealth role seriously, made successful visits to former dominions and colonies, and opened meetings of the Commonwealth heads of state, but Britain no longer counted for as much in the world, and so neither did the British monarchy. Most of the Commonwealth states were republics and though the Queen remained sovereign of Canada, Australia and New Zealand, there were doubts about how long that would last. Prince Charles hoped to be Governor-General of Australia, but was told that too many Australians would not welcome it. British politicians later began to concentrate on taking Britain into the European Union and the monarchy lost its imperial glamour.

The Queen and Prince Philip loyally carried out their royal duties at home, opening institutions, planting commemorative trees, visiting hospitals, waving nicely at people from cars and carriages, and presiding with dignity at ceremonial functions. Philip became known and liked for outspokenness and dropping occasional bricks. Diligent attempts were made to modernize the monarchy, but it was easier said than done and the fundamental problem of being more accessible while preserving dignity and a certain air of mystery was not solved. The Queen herself was mainly felt to do a good job. She was extremely well informed and her prime ministers needed to have done their homework, but she did not reveal her own political views and, as far as was known, did not attempt to influence her governments in any unconstitutional way.

Criticism focused on the institution of monarchy itself and the behaviour of some of the younger royals. Princess Margaret's marriage ended in divorce in 1978 and the media found her a good subject for gossip. The wedding of Prince Charles and Lady Diana in 1981 amid a blaze of worldwide attention was excellent publicity for the monarchy, but in time it became all too evident that the marriage had gone wrong, to the accompaniment of rival biographies, media briefings and deliberately damaging leaks. The couple separated in 1992 to intrusive and hypocritical coverage in the tabloids of a kind that was good for sales, but that would not have been dreamed of back in the 1950s. Princess Anne's marriage ended in 1992 and so did Prince Andrew's, and there was a serious fire at Windsor Castle. It turned out that the building was not insured, so the repairs would be at the cost of the taxpayers. There was an uproar and the Queen agreed to pay income tax for the first time. In her 1992 Christmas address she described the year as her *annus horribilis*.

Princess Diana's tragic death in 1997 stirred up more criticism of the Queen and the royal family for allegedly not paying her the proper respect, but the Queen Mother's death in 2002 showed that there was still a deep reservoir of affectionate loyalty to the Crown. So did the celebrations of Elizabeth II's golden jubilee in 2002, though even then, the authorities did them on the cheap. The Department of the Environment forked out a miserable £175,000 for banners in Trafalgar Square and the Mall in London, and the City of London's official expenditure was £150. National pride was still deprecated

The Fairytale Princess

Diana Spencer was born on the Sandringham estate in 1961 into a family with close royal connections. Her parents, Earl and Countess Spencer, divorced when she was seven. After attending a finishing school in Switzerland, she lived in London and worked as a teacher at a kindergarten. She and Prince Charles first met in 1977 and from 1980, when one of the tabloids proclaimed that the prince was in love, Diana was to be besieged by armies of photographers and reporters for the rest of her life. The couple were married in St Paul's Cathedral in 1981, when he was 32 and she was 20. With hindsight, she was far too young, but her looks, graceful bearing, affection for children and aristocratic habit of treating everyone the same won her affection bordering on adulation. The royal pair lived at Kensington Palace and their two sons, Prince William and Prince Harry, were born in 1982 and 1984, but their interests were very different and the princess suffered from bulimia and nervous afflictions. The media took a nosy, remorseless interest in everything about her, including her real or alleged love affairs, and the marriage finally ended in divorce in 1996. Princess Diana's death in a car crash in Paris in 1997, at the age of 36, set off an astonishing, hysterical explosion of public grief.

The Queen Mother

Queen Elizabeth was 51 when her husband died and always believed that the strain of his unexpected accession had contributed to his early death. It came close to breaking her, but there was granite beneath the charm and she gradually recovered, lived at Clarence House, near St James's Palace, and resumed an active royal role that lasted for another 50 years and turned her into a national institution as 'Queen Mum'. Her genuine interest in everyone she met and her love of fun and horse-racing won people's hearts, while her extravagance and fondness for a glass of gin did no harm to her popularity. On her hundredth birthday she appeared on the balcony at Buckingham Palace with 26 other members of the royal family, to the applause of a huge crowd, and when she died at Windsor in 2002 at the age of 101 she was the longest-lived member of the royal family there had ever been. Thousands of people queued for miles to file past her coffin lying in state in Westminster Hall.

at official levels, and there was talk of the Queen possibly abdicating in favour of Prince Charles or even Prince William and the monarchy's future began to seem uncomfortably insecure.

On the other hand, the monarchy has weathered storms many times before in its long history, including some much fiercer ones, and as the early years of the 21st century rolled by, it seemed clear that the substantial majority of the British public – majority opinion in the media, for that matter – preferred monarchy to the alternative of a republic, presumably with some retired politician or other as a dubious and unconvincing figurehead. More than a million people flocked into central London for the golden jubilee celebrations. No other figure in the country could have matched that simply to honour 50 years in office. Asked what the royal family would do if the monarchy were to be abolished and replaced by a republic, the Queen's stock answer has always been, 'We'll go quietly.' It hardly looks as if there will be any need for a graceful exit yet.

Elizabeth II smiling at flag-waving children celebrating her golden jubilee at Wells in Somerset in 2002. The jubilee was a personal triumph for the queen who was 13 years short of breaking Queen Victoria's record for the longest reign.

Meanwhile...

1912   The SS *Titanic* hits an iceberg and sinks on its maiden voyage, despite its supposedly unsinkable design.

1914   After the heir to the Austro-Hungarian empire is murdered, Germany advances on France. Britain declares war.

1919   Just after World War I a flu epidemic, now known to be a form of bird flu, rages around the world.

1924   Britons tune into wireless sets to hear the king's voice for the first time.

1925   John Logie Baird invents the television.

1926   The TUC calls the first General Strike, backing miners' calls to protest against pay cuts.

1928   Alexander Fleming discovers penicillin.

1912   1919   **1939**   1944   1946

1932   Ramblers mount a mass trespass in the Peak District to campaign for public access to the moors.

1936   The Jarrow Crusade sets out to march to London: 200 unemployed take a petition to the government.

1936   100,000 demonstrate against fascist supporters of Sir Oswald Moseley marching in London's East End.

1939   The start of war is followed by a mass evacuation of children from major cities to private homes in the country.

1944   The huge seaborne invasion of Normandy heralds D-Day and the start of the Allied assault against Nazi Germany.

1945   Clement Attlee's Labour party wins a landslide victory against Winston Churchill.

1946	New towns are planned to take overspill from London and elsewhere.
1948	The National Health Service, National Assistance and National Insurance form the basis of Labour's Welfare State.
1951	On blitzed sites on London's South Bank, the Festival of Britain brings colour and fun to the austere postwar era.
1955	Laws restricting the use of coal and establishing smokeless zones spell the end of London's notorious fogs.
1958	Around 3,000 march to the atomic weapons research base at Aldermaston calling for an end to nuclear arms race.
1959	The M1 opens a year after the first motorway (the Preston bypass).
1962	Benjamin Britten's *War Requiem* is performed at Coventry's new cathedral next to its bombed predecessor.

951   1955   1959   1978   2003

1963	The popularity of The Beatles symbolizes a radical change in youth and popular culture.
1978	In Manchester the world's first test-tube baby is delivered – a milestone in the treatment of infertility.
1979	Britain elects its first woman Prime Minister, Margaret Thatcher.
1984	Protesting over pit closures, the miners' strike begins a year-long struggle between the government and Britain's coal miners.
2003	The government announces 30,000 British troops being sent to the Persian Gulf in preparation for war with Iraq.

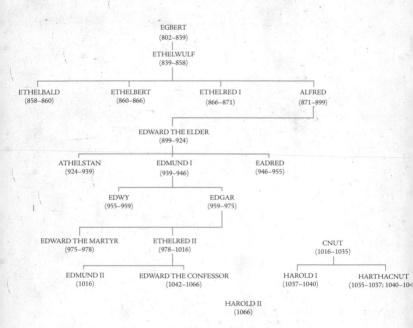

EGBERT
(802–839)

ETHELWULF
(839–858)

ETHELBALD (858–860) | ETHELBERT (860–866) | ETHELRED I (866–871) | ALFRED (871–899)

EDWARD THE ELDER
(899–924)

ATHELSTAN (924–939) | EDMUND I (939–946) | EADRED (946–955)

EDWY (955–959) | EDGAR (959–975)

EDWARD THE MARTYR (975–978) | ETHELRED II (978–1016) | CNUT (1016–1035)

EDMUND II (1016) | EDWARD THE CONFESSOR (1042–1066) | HAROLD I (1037–1040) | HARTHACNUT (1035–1037; 1040–104

HAROLD II
(1066)

Genealogy: Norman

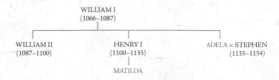

WILLIAM I
(1066–1087)

WILLIAM II (1087–1100) | HENRY I (1100–1135) | ADELA = STEPHEN (1135–1154)

MATILDA

Genealogy: Plantagenet

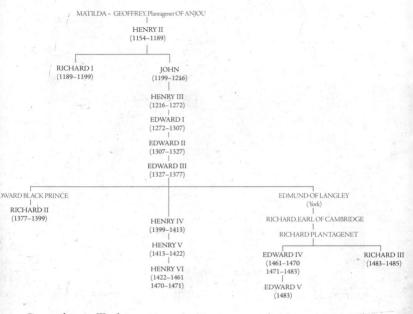

MATILDA = GEOFFREY, Plantagenet OF ANJOU

HENRY II
(1154–1189)

RICHARD I
(1189–1199)

JOHN
(1199–1216)

HENRY III
(1216–1272)

EDWARD I
(1272–1307)

EDWARD II
(1307–1327)

EDWARD III
(1327–1377)

EDWARD BLACK PRINCE

RICHARD II
(1377–1399)

HENRY IV
(1399–1413)

HENRY V
(1413–1422)

HENRY VI
(1422–1461
1470–1471)

EDMUND OF LANGLEY
(York)

RICHARD, EARL OF CAMBRIDGE

RICHARD PLANTAGENET

EDWARD IV
(1461–1470
1471–1483)

RICHARD III
(1483–1485)

EDWARD V
(1483)

Genealogy: Tudor

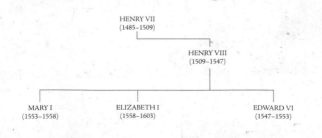

HENRY VII
(1485–1509)

HENRY VIII
(1509–1547)

MARY I
(1553–1558)

ELIZABETH I
(1558–1603)

EDWARD VI
(1547–1553)

Genealogy: Stuart

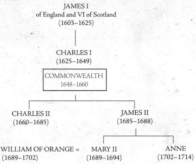

JAMES I
of England and VI of Scotland
(1603–1625)

CHARLES I
(1625–1649)

COMMONWEALTH
1648–1660

CHARLES II
(1660–1685)

JAMES II
(1685–1688)

WILLIAM OF ORANGE =
(1689–1702)

MARY II
(1689–1694)

ANNE
(1702–1714)

Genealogy: Hanover & Saxe-Coburg

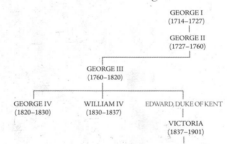

GEORGE I
(1714–1727)

GEORGE II
(1727–1760)

GEORGE III
(1760–1820)

GEORGE IV
(1820–1830)

WILLIAM IV
(1830–1837)

EDWARD, DUKE OF KENT

VICTORIA
(1837–1901)

EDWARD VII
(1901–1910)

Genealogy: Windsor

GEORGE V
(1910–1936)

EDWARD VIII
(1936)

GEORGE VI
(1936–1952)

ELIZABETH II
(1952–PRESENT)

CHARLES

WILLIAM

Index

Note: page numbers in *italics* refer to picture captions.

Picture Credits

II, Private Collection, The Stapleton Collection/The Bridgeman Art Library; 185 Hugh Despenser, Bibliothèque nationale de France, Paris/The Bridgeman Art Library; 187 Edward I Parliament, Private Collection/The Bridgeman Art Library; 188 Simon de Montfort, The Bridgeman Art Library; 191 Edward III, Angelo Hornak/CORBIS; 193 Windsor Castle, Historical Picture Archive/CORBIS; 197 Edward III, The British Library/Heritage-Images; 201 Richard II, Westminster Abbey, London, UK/The Bridgeman Art Library; 206 St George's Chapel, Pawel Libera/Alamy; 209 Henry IV, Private Collection, © Philip Mould, Historical Portraits Ltd, London, UK/The Bridgeman Art Library; 213 Henry V, National Gallery, London, UK/The Bridgeman Art Library; 215 Battle of Agincourt, Lambeth Palace Library, London, UK/The Bridgeman Art Library; 219 Henry V marriage, British Library, London, UK/The Bridgeman Art Library; 221 Henry VI, Eton College, Windsor, UK/The Bridgeman Art Library; 223 Joan of Arc, Musee Dobree, Nantes, France/The Bridgeman Art Library; 225 Battle of Barnet, Centrale Bibliotheek van de Universiteit, Ghent, Belgium/The Bridgeman Art Library; 229 Edward IV, Ann Ronan Picture Library/Heritage-Images; 233 Richard III,

Society of Antiquaries, London, UK/The Bridgeman Art Library; 240 Linlithgow Palace, Bruce Percy/Alamy; 243 James I, Scottish National Portrait Gallery, Edinburgh, Scotland/The Bridgeman Art Library; 245 Robert II seal, The British Library/Heritage-Images; 247 James and Margaret, National Library of Scotland/Licensor www.scran.ac.uk; 251 Mary and James, Falkland Palace, Falkland, Fife, Scotland/The Bridgeman Art Library; 255 Wolf of Badenoch, Crown Copyright reproduced courtesy of Historic Scotland; 257 Mary QOS, Victoria & Albert Museum, London, UK/The Bridgeman Art Library; 261 Mary Death Mask, P. Tomkins/VisitScotland/Scottish Viewpoint; 262 Hampton Court, Chris Taylor/Cordaiy Photo Library Ltd./CORBIS; 265 Henry VII, Phillips, The International Fine Art Auctioneers, UK, © Bonhams, London, UK/The Bridgeman Art Library; 269 Henry VIII, Gustavo Tomsich/CORBIS; 274 & 275 Family of Henry VIII, The Royal Collection © 2006, Her Majesty Queen Elizabeth II;277 Edward VI, Private Collection, © Richard Philp, London/The Bridgeman Art Library; 281 Mary I, National Portrait Gallery, London, UK/The Bridgeman Art Library; 286 Martyrs, Mary Evans Picture Library; 289 Elizabeth I, National Portrait Gallery.

London, UK/The Bridgeman Art Library; 292 Robert Dudley, Yale Center for British Art, Paul Mellon Collection, USA/The Bridgeman Art Library; 297 Ermine Portrait, By courtesy of the Marquess of Salisbury; 298 Kenilworth Castle, David Lyons; 302 Blenheim Palace, Ancient Art & Architecture Collection; 305 James I, Art Media/Heritage-Images; 309 Flag, National Library of Scotland/Licensor www.scran.ac.uk; 311 Gunpowder plotters, The Art Archive; 313 Charles I, Arte & Immagini srl/CORBIS; 318 Charles I, Art Media/Heritage-Images; 321 Cromwell, Birmingham Museums and Art Gallery/The Bridgeman Art Library; 323 Charles II, Private Collection, © Philip Mould, Historical Portraits Ltd, London, UK/The Bridgeman Art Library; 329 Observatory, Bettmann/CORBIS; 331 Nell Gwynne, Royal Hospital Chelsea, London, UK/The Bridgeman Art Library; 333 James II, Bolton Museum and Art Gallery, Lancashire, UK/The Bridgeman Art Library; 337 Duke Monmouth, Private Collection, © Philip Mould, Historical Portraits Ltd, London, UK/The Bridgeman Art Library; 339 William III, Bettmann/CORBIS; 341 Mary II, Scottish National Portrait Gallery, Edinburgh, Scotland/The Bridgeman Art Library; 341 William III, The Holburne Museum of Art, Bath, UK/The Bridgeman Art

Library; 344 & 345 Hampton Court, Rupert Horrox/CORBIS; 347 Queen Anne, Private Collection, © Philip Mould, Historical Portraits Ltd, London, UK/The Bridgeman Art Library; 355 Pavillion, JTB Photo/Alamy; 357 George I, The Crown Estate/The Bridgeman Art Library; 361 Prince Edward Stuart, National Portrait Gallery, London; 362 Bonnie Prince Charlie, Scottish National Portrait Gallery, Edinburgh, Scotland/The Bridgeman Art Library; 365 George II, The Crown Estate/The Bridgeman Art Library; 369 George III, Private Collection/© Philip Mould, Historical Portraits Ltd, London, UK/The Bridgeman Art Library; 373 William Blake, Art Media, National Portrait Gallery, London/Heritage-Images; 375 William Wordsworth, National Portrait Gallery, London, UK/The Bridgeman Art Library; 377 Battle of Trafalgar, Private Collection, © Christie's Images/The Bridgeman Art Library;

381 George Washington, The British Library/Heritage-Images; 383 Boston Tea Party, Private Collection/The Bridgeman Art Library; 385 George IV, Wallace Collection, London, UK/The Bridgeman Art Library; 389 Gillray cartoon, The British Museum/Heritage-Images; 393 William IV, National Portrait Gallery, London; 397 Queen Victoria, The Illustrated London News; 399 Princess Victoria, Private Collection, © Christopher Wood Gallery, London, UK/The Bridgeman Art Library; 403 Victoria and Albert, Hulton-Deutsch Collection/CORBIS; 404 Prince Albert, Ashmolean Museum, University of Oxford, UK/The Bridgeman Art Library; 404 Queen Victoria, Ashmolean Museum, University of Oxford, UK/The Bridgeman Art Library; 411 Queen Victoria, Private Collection, The Stapleton Collection/The Bridgeman Art Library; 417 Edward VII, Getty Images; 419 Edward and Alexandra, The

Illustrated London News; 423 Sandringham, Tim Graham/CORBIS; 427 Windsor Castle, Pawel Libera/Alamy; 429 George V, Private Collection, © Philip Mould, Historical Portraits Ltd, London, UK/The Bridgeman Art Library; 432 George and Mary, Private Collection/The Bridgeman Art Library; 435 George V and Tsar, Bettmann/CORBIS; 437 Edward VIII, Getty Images; 439 Duke Duchess Windsor, Bettmann/CORBIS; 443 QEII Coronation, © popperfoto.com; 445 George VI, Hulton-Deutsch Collection/CORBIS; 448 Queen Mother, Hulton-Deutsch Collection/CORBIS; 451 Coronation, Hulton-Deutsch Collection/CORBIS; 453 QEII Coronation PA/Empics; 455 Elizabeth and Philip, Hulton-Deutsch Collection/CORBIS; 459 Queen Elizabeth II, Tim Graham/Corbis.

Acknowledgments

The authors and publishers are grateful to the following people for their involvement in the production of this book: Marilynne Lanng of Bookwork Creative Associates for project management and editorial work on the original publication, Tehmina Boman for picture research, Tim and Anne Locke for additional writing in the original edition, Neil Bromley for the page borders, Ethan Danielson of EdanArt for the maps and David Lyons for many of the castle photographs. The publishers would also like to thank Ame Verso for her editorial work on this edition, and Lisa Footitt for the index.